# Rough Enough

## Richard H. Clow's Letters and Diary from the Civil and Indian Wars 1865-1875

American Book Classics™
An imprint of American Book Publishing
14510 Big Basin Way #155
Saratoga Village, Ca 95070
www.americanbookpublishing.com
Printed in the United States of America on acid-free paper.

**Rough Enough**

Designed by Andriy Yankovskyy, design@americanbookpublishing.com

*Publisher's Note: This publication is designed to provide accurate and authoritative information in regard to the subject matter covered. It is sold or distributed with the understanding that the publisher and author is not engaged in rendering legal, accounting, or other professional service. If legal advice or other expert assistance is required, the services of a competent professional person in a consultation capacity should be sought.*

**Library of Congress Cataloging-in-Publication Data**

Clow, Richard H., 1847-1926.
Rough enough : Richard H. Clow's letters and diary from the Civil and Indian Wars 1865-1875 / with comments and notes by Richard H. McBee Jr.
pages cm
Includes bibliographical references and index.
ISBN-13: 978-1-58982-713-4 (alk. paper)
ISBN-10: 1-58982-713-9 (alk. paper)
1. Clow, Richard H.. 1847-1926--Correspondence. 2. Clow, Richard H.. 1847-1926--Diaries. 3. United States. Army. Massachusetts Infantry Regiment, 56th (1863-1865) 4. United States--History–Civil War, 1861-1865--Personal narratives. 5. Virginia--History–Civil War, 1861-1865--Personal narratives. 6. Massachusetts--History–Civil War, 1861-1865--Personal narratives. 7. United States. Army. Infantry Regiment, 13th (1861-1957) 8. Indians of North America--Wars--1866-1895--Personal narratives. I. McBee, Richard H., Jr., editor of compilation. II. Title.
E513.55 6th C56 2012
973.7'8092--dc23
2012042202

*Special Sales*
These books are available at special discounts for bulk purchases. Special editions, including personalized covers, excerpts of existing books, and corporate imprints, can be created in large quantities for special needs. For more information, e-mail info@americanbookpublishing.com.

# Rough Enough

## Richard H. Clow's Letters and Diary from the Civil and Indian Wars 1865-1875

With comments and notes by
**Richard H. McBee Jr.**

# Dedication

*Rough Enough* is dedicated to the thousands of unsung Civil War Soldiers on both sides of the battlefield whose lives were changed forever by this "most costly" of American Wars. Richard Clow was one of those extraordinary men.

Richard Headley Clow in Civil War Uniform—1865

# Preface

Richard Clow was a handsome young man who avidly wrote letters to his older sister, Agnes,while serving as a teenage soldier during the Civil War. Later in life, while serving on the frontier, he regularly corresponded with another of his sisters, Bertha.

Clow's writing gives us a picture of something more than just warfare and its horrors. It shows us how a carefree young man matures as he encounters the awful conditions of war. It illustrates a portion of the life of a tough yet sensitive young man who could still long for an occasional magazine to read or think about going hunting for moose while on the battle front of Petersburg.

From his writing we sense that he had an eye for the inherent beauties of nature and his surroundings. We are privy to his thoughts as he enjoys the small pleasures of life and takes advantage of them to help maintain a positive attitude while enduring the harsh conditions of war and life on the frontier.

The following fourteen letters and short diary, which are transcribed within the text of the three book sections, paint a portrait of an adventurous seventeen-year-old. He starts off as a boy who enlists and goes off to war almost as if it were a lark. Then with each letter home we see how his personality is molded by each new military experience and the stark realities of war. We also catch a glimpse of the events that mature him into a hardened full-fledged infantry soldier. By the end of the story, we see a grown man with a wife, living on his farm in Dakota Territory. It is an image that is significantly different from the young naïve boy who signed up itching to go off and fight a war.

The reader will note that I have retained Richard Clow's spelling and punctuation errors in the transcribed texts of those letters. This allows the reader to connect with Richard as he views and experiences each new situation. In places where his errors may affect understanding, I have made corrections or clarifications, placing these inside a parenthesis [ ]. In some cases I have written a [sic] to affirm that this is the correct way that Richard spelled the word. It is quite obvious that Richard could write well, but had a spelling problem that extended even to the repeated misspelling his own sister Agnes's name.

# Table of Contents


Section 1: The Civil War Period 1864-1865 ..................................................15
    Chapter 1—Raring to Go! ......................................................................15
    Chapter 2—Introduction to Military Life: Camp Meigs ......................21
    Chapter 3—Reenlistment and the Holding Company..........................27
    Chapter 4—Arrival and Initiation into Battle ....................................35
    Chapter 5—A Close Call with the Angel of Death ..............................41
    Chapter 6—The Final Assault Begins ..................................................49
    Chapter 7—The Assault of Petersburg on April 2, 1865 ....................57
    Chapter 8—The Grand Review and Brothers Reunited ......................65

Section 2: The Indian Wars ............................................................................77
    Chapter 9—The Road to Reenlistment................................................77
    Chapter 10—The Route to Montana and the Forts ............................83
    Chapter 11—Fort Ellis Protecting the Bozeman Settlers ....................91
    Chapter 12—Camp Cooke the Rats' Nest ..........................................97
    Chapter 13—Fort Buford ..................................................................103
    Chapter 14—Sitting Bull Near Fort Buford ......................................111
    Chapter 15—A Letter from Indian Country ....................................121
    Chapter 16—Winter and Spring Come to Buford ............................129
    Chapter 17—Leaving the Army at Ft. Buford ..................................139

Section 3: After the Wars, The Diary ............................................................145
    Chapter 18—Leaving Fort Buford ....................................................147
    Chapter 19—Life in Little Sioux; The Tragedy of Winter ................157
    Chapter 20—Settling Accounts, A Love Poem and Moving On .......165
    Chapter 21—The Road to Deadwood, Plans for Mining ..................173

Chapter 22—Days of Work and Spanish Songs in the Gold Fields ..179
Chapter 23—The Miner Sings and Falls in Love ................................193
Chapter 24—Farming, Married Life, and On to Oregon ...................201
Chapter 25—Rough Enough................................................................205

Epilogue—The Day After Cora, November 5, 1881 ..............................211
Chronological Timeline for Richard Headley Clow's Life ......................215
Appendix 1: Richard Clow's Diary................................................................219
Appendix 2.........................................................................................................233
Appendix 3.........................................................................................................235
Photos and Figures for *Rough Enough* ......................................................237
Index...................................................................................................................265
Bibliography......................................................................................................277
Acknowledgments............................................................................................283

**Illustrations:**

Map: Civil War Boston ....................................................................................... v
Map: Richard Clow's Travels on the Frontier ...........................................74

# *Civil War Boston*
## FORTS & TRAINING CAMPS

**Cyrus Alger Cannon Foundry**

*By 1850, this was the largest foundry in the country.*

**Castle Island**

*Recruit Training Camp, Federal Troop Prison, Cannon Testing Site*

**Governor's Island**

*Training, Harbor Defense*

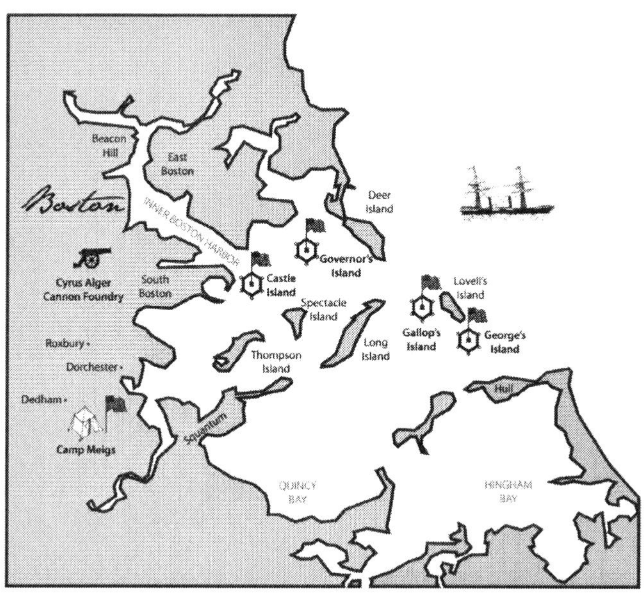


**Camp Meigs**

*Training Camp 54th & 56th Mass. Infantries*

**Gallop's Island**

*Training Camp, Holding Camp for Embarking Soldiers, Discharge Station*

**George's Island**

Fort Warren

*Training Camp, Confederate Prison*

# Section 1: The Civil War Period 1864—1865

# Chapter 1—Raring to Go!

As a seventeen-and-a-half-year-old in mid-summer 1864, Richard Clow was as eager as any of his friends to enlist in the War of the Rebellion and fight the breakaway rebels of the South. The war had been raging for over three years and there were signs that it would end in the future. The latest battles were on everyone's tongues daily as they walked home from school over the broad hills beyond Boston's Charles River to the farm where he lived with his older sister, Agnes Cruikshank (fig. 6) and her husband Alex.

Ma had been dead for a number of years by this time and Pa had gone off to the "West," first to Ohio and finally Wisconsin, in search of a farm and life more suited to his pioneer ways than the bustling city of Boston. Richard's older sister Agnes nearly fifteen years his senior, had been his caretaker since the age of six, when the children of the family boarded a boat in Canada and immigrated to the United States in 1853.

Richard's brother-in-law, Alex, was a well-to-do farmer outside of Boston. He valued education and made sure that Richard was well-schooled at the secondary level so that he would be appropriately prepared to enter a business when he left home. Thus, Richard had become an avid reader and as such devoured the magazines and papers purchased by his older brother-in-law. These pamphlets fed the young man's fascination with the War of Rebellion with their glorious stories of war heroes and Union victories on the battlefront.

*Harper's* magazine was a family favorite and in 1864 it ran a series of dramatic articles on the War of 1812. Each new periodical contained glowing descriptions and artistic renditions of the furious battles and the men who had led America to victory against the British. These stories, coupled with other romantic articles such as that of April 1864 entitled, "Journey to the Source of the Nile," gave Richard ample material to dream about the glories of war and travel in exotic faraway places. He loved to discuss his imaginings both with the family and his friends.

The family also subscribed to *Frank Leslie's Illustrated Newspaper*, which documented current affairs and actions in the Civil War battles. The printed engravings often showed patriotic scenes of victory. These pictures were intended to evoke an emotional response in their audience rather than depict the actual realities of the war. Thus in one issue, daring officers might be seen leading frontal attacks from horseback; while in another issue, armored boats flying 'Old Glory' could be seen to be firing upon rebel forts. The images always showed the Union flag waving supremely while the flag of the Confederacy was crushed into the earth.

When these magazines came out in July of 1864 with sketched pictures and descriptions of the massive tunnel explosion set off by the Union troops outside Petersburg, a surge of patriotic duty must have been felt by scores of young men. If only they could have been there for that battle, perhaps the outcome might have been different. Instead of becoming a shattering defeat for the Union, the outcome might have been more akin to the glowing victories of General Sherman in the Deep South. It could have spelled victory for the Union effort in the war.

With the knowledge that the war might soon be over, these young men would have sensed an urgency to be a part of the glorious final battles. As always, both then and now, the urge to go to war is fired up by young minds concentrating on imagined glories. The publications rarely picture the harsh realities, the death, mud, sweat, fears, smells, and bodies of the front lines. These can be casually ignored.

The latest news from the front lines would have generated discussions about the valiant action during the victories or a second-guessing of the generals who experienced defeats. Each boy would tell what he would be able to do for the nation if only his parents would let him go into battle.

With this in mind, we can understand that Richard and his friends had very likely been pressuring their families to allow them to enlist as the school year ended that spring.

Richard, of course, would not turn eighteen until May of 1865. It must have concerned him greatly that he might miss the end of the war and his one chance to be in heroic battle. He must have considered enlisting. What boy growing up during a time of war has not had thoughts either in favor of or against being in the military? He may have even considered lying about his age and enlisting under a false name. Rumors of the other boys who were joining up must have circulated through the community of young men much in the same manner as they circulated a hundred years later in the author's class of 1962 during the Vietnam War.

The late teens are a stage in male life associated with the belief in one's own indestructibility coupled with immature judgment skills. Peer relationships are more important than parental instruction when it comes to defining which decisions young men will make. Thus, the boys in Richard's social circle would have fed off each of others' enthusiasm like fish swirling around fresh chum thrown into the Charles River.

All these teenage characteristics would have come together in Richard's peer group. The group would have magnified and glorified the war propaganda, all the while being completely ignorant of the realities. Thus, daily lessons at school would have only served to whet their appetites and desires to escape the boring present and gaily march off to war. Their goal would likely have been to join the Massachusetts Volunteers, which began actively seeking enlistments during the summer of 1864. A new regiment was to be formed in August of that year training not far from Boston.

Richard would have known that his brother-in-law's farm needed him for the fall harvesting work. But, as always when one compared the known to the unknown, the drudgery of the daily farm chores paled considerably by comparison to charging over the next hill into battle. The call to action must have been almost unbearable.

Richard and his friends were not familiar with the drudgery of military life as they contemplated enlistment. They couldn't know of the hours of waiting, the cleaning of weapons and the necessities of following orders, the restrictions on freedom of movement, and the general isolation from normal civilian life. They were immersed in the latest news. They could visualize the valiant charge of the Union soldiers into the flaming guns following the gigantic underground explosion at Petersburg. They would have felt anger in discovering that those brave men had been cut down at the very moment when victory was in their grasp. They would have felt that sudden bursting surge of anger as their subconscious told them the charge would not have failed had they only been there to help. They would have truly believed that Petersburg, the last real bastion of Confederate defenses for Richmond, would have fallen due to their efforts.

The abortive assault on Petersburg in July 1864 showed just how fickle the winds of war can be for its participants. A brilliant idea followed by extensive tunneling (done by Pennsylvania coal miners) had put a shaft under the Confederate battlements of Petersburg. When packed with massive amounts of explosive, the subsequent detonation blew the Confederate defenses to bits with remarkable success.

At that point, the Union troops should have easily raced to victory through the breach and overwhelmed the rebel defenders with little resistance. Unfortunately, inept leadership sent the assault troops directly across the depths of the crater formed by the blast. Instead of racing around the sides of the giant hole, the assault troops ran into the crater and became bogged down trying to climb the steep sloped sides.

In the wasted minutes, the blast-dazed Confederate troops were able to rally. As they peered through the ruins of their defensive barriers, they found that they only needed to direct fire downwards into the pit. In a short time, hordes of hapless Union soldiers, trapped within the steep confines, were slaughtered. The result was a complete disaster with the needless loss of some 4,000 of General Grant's Union troops.

As a result of this failed assault, the Northern advantage at Petersburg stalled. The fighting returned to artillery and trench warfare for another eight months.

In addition to the defeat at Petersburg, there would also have been the rumors of a resurgence of strength in the rebel cause. Some of the latest news would have included the recent rapid advances of the Confederate Army in the Shenandoah Valley to threaten the outskirts of Washington, D.C.

As a result of these defeats, more recruits were urgently needed on the front lines. The targets for recruiters, as always, were the patriotic young men like Richard Clow, eager to get into the foray and garner glory before it all ended.

Richard would have heard his brother-in-law Alex's opinions concerning the Confederate victories that summer in the Shenandoah Valley. Led by a Confederate infantry officer, Jubal Early, and accompanied by cavalry, the move against Washington had sent a shiver of fear through the North. It showed that even as the South seemed to be staggering towards inevitable defeat, an unforeseen quirk of fate could change the outcome of the war. Even the President and the Capitol were not completely safe.

Richard would also have heard the political news. He would have known how the latest defeats of the Union Army might also affect the re-election of President "Abe" Lincoln. The strength of the opposition candidate, General McClellan, seemed to be growing with each rebel victory. He was proposing a peace presidency. There were even discussions by 'true patriots' as to whether the general's opposition to the war should be grounds for his removal from the military since he no longer supported his commander-in-chief.

When Jubal Early's men were finally driven back into the lower Shenandoah Valley in late July of 1864, a surge of positive energy would have once again buoyed the nation and Richard's family. The long slog of the war at last seemed to be coming to an end.

It was probably somewhere about this time that Richard would have heard that the Fletcher boy, whom he mentions in one of his letters, had gone missing from home. The consensus at that time was that the young man had enlisted under a false name.

As Richard continued to cajole his sister and her husband into allowing him to enlist, they must have seen the writing on the wall. Either they must give in gracefully and allow Richard to enlist, or they risked his enlisting despite their objections in a manner that might cause them to lose track of him forever. The Fletcher boy's decision must have weighed heavily on them.

Richard's argument was that surely the war would be over by the following May when he turned eighteen. If he enlisted immediately, he would at least be a part of the final glorious victory. Being a part of that victory would be an experience that men who participated in it would talk about for the rest of their lives. Richard had been captured by the propaganda of war. He knew that he had to be a part of that final victory.

His sister Agnes and her husband were already approaching their thirties and had children of their own. They could possibly see beyond the false glory of the rousing headlines and news articles to the horrors of losing a dose family member. Their age and experience would perhaps have also allowed them to better understand the hatred that would divide the nation long after any battlefield strife was over. In their hearts they would have wanted Richard to stay and work on the farm and gain a bit more maturity before he went off to war.

Yet, being adults, they could also understand the flames of youth and recognize how those passions were dragging at Richard. They could see that he was being drawn toward the flames of glory like an unwary moth drawn towards a glowing lamp of death. They knew they could not ultimately stop his enlistment, but perhaps they could help him make a decision that would allow them to sleep more easily with his going to war.

It is probable that upon hearing of the disappearance of the Fletcher boy and in the growing belief that the end of the Civil War was near at hand, that Alexander Cruikshank gave his permission for Richard to sign up for a short enlistment of one hundred days. Although it would seem like an eternity for the family, they most likely believed that going into the service for this short period of time would serve to take some of the enthusiastic military wind out of Richard's sails. Following this short period of service, he would return as a more mature young man and could then proceed with his career and life, knowing that he had been given his chance at being a part of military history.

As we shall see, this initial enlistment would reveal a whole new world for Richard Clow. It would bring him new experiences, some of which would be much tougher than anything he could ever have imagined at the time he put his signature on the enlistment document. In the end it would be, to paraphrase his own words, "Rough Enough," before he reached that eighteenth birthday.

# Chapter 2—Introduction to Military Life: Camp Meigs

*Readville Sept. 8th [64]*
*Dear Agness [sic]*

*I now sit down and write to you again as I did not receive an answer to my first one.*

*I want you to send me a box with the following things in it. I will see that it is paid for when it gets here.*

*Have you got a small bed tick that you do not use? If you have you must send it to me for we have taken up winter quarters here and I have nothing to sleep on / but the hard boards of my bunk. The other boys have them and the captain says he will see that they are not lost if we move. If you have got one send an old quilt that will do well enough. My shoes must come as my boots are wearing out. I do not know of anything else unless you put in some grub.*

*Tell Andrew if he don't write he may be turned tother [sic] end up when I get back. I am very well and having a good time. I will be home in two weeks on a furlow [sic]. Send that box as soon as possible as I would not ask for it if I did not need it. You must write to me as I have only got one letter since I have been here and that was from George.*

*Send me a vest too and my canteen in my trunk as we are not furnished with them.*

*R. H. Clow*
*Company G 3rd regt. Camp Meigs, Readville, Mass.*

Richard's enlistment in the 22nd Massachusetts Volunteer Infantry for training introduced him into a new way of life. Although it was close to home, life at Camp Meigs was completely unfamiliar to Richard. He was now in the company of older and rougher men, many of whom could not read or write and who had no concern for educated thoughts. The totally regimented life of drills, meals, always having to take commands, to be dressed in uniform, and being constantly under the scrutiny of officers and sergeants must have been a rude awakening to his carefree farm upbringing.

In addition, Camp Meigs had only a limited supply of equipment for the new troops. As a consequence, the recruits either provided some of their own equipment or purchased these items. Richard was fortunate enough to have a family that could provide him with some of these amenities.

It was exactly this type of hardship and shock of the first weeks of training that Richard's family was counting on to change his mind about a longer enlistment period. If he could be made to see the error of his decision, then he would be home by Christmas. His one hundred days of combat training would have left his ego satiated and his body none the worse for wear. They wouldn't have to worry about him taking off and enlisting while underage or by using a false name.

An illustration of how this kind of false enlistment was done is seen in examining another young man's enlistment. Luther "Yellowstone" Kelly documented his methodology for enlisting after his parents had refused to allow him into the military at the very end of the war. In his memoirs he states that, having failed to look the first recruiter straight in the eye and swear that he was eighteen years of age, he sought out a second recruiter. This time, having run through the scenario once already, he succeeded in convincing the man, and so enlisted at the age of seventeen in early 1865. Because he was tall, he apparently appeared old enough to not have to use the ruse of writing the number 'eighteen' on the soles of his shoes in order to truthfully say, "I am over eighteen."[1]

Recruiters in those days were more interested in meeting their quotas than in verifying ages or names. Such a task was nearly impossible in a

---

[1] Quaife, M. M., ed., *Yellowstone Kelly* (Lincoln University of Nebraska Press, 1973), 3.

pre-birth certificate era. Thus it was not an abnormal fear for a family to want to prevent a son from disappearing into the insatiable maw of the god of war.

In this first letter, the only surviving one from Richard's first enlistment of 100 days, we get a gist of what a youngster might have been exposed to in the barracks. He would have a bunk with minimal bedding, probably a single blanket and certainly no mattress. Military uniforms at that time were made of cotton, which was fine for August weather. Unfortunately, this same material was not sufficiently warm for the cooler temperatures of fall and the impending winter, hence his request for a vest.

Richard would have had to supply his own shoes or boots and a canteen, as well as any additional clothing or blankets for winter warmth. The purchase of these was charged against his meager salary. The military food would have also been a shock to his digestive tract and it appears that his letter is suggesting a 'care package' in addition to the other items requested.

Richard was not assigned to a combat unit at the end of his training with the 22nd Massachusetts Volunteer Infantry. He thus remained in the Boston area until his discharge in late November of 1864. He is designated as a "Private," "unassigned," in the records of that unit, according to the National Park System of Civil War Soldiers and Sailors.

The unassigned units of the 22nd Massachusetts Infantry (Militia) were organized in order to protect the State of Massachusetts late in the Civil War. Richard's letter indicates that in September he was assigned to Company G of the 3rd Regiment of that unit. The period of duty for these 100 day soldiers began on August 18, 1864 and ended November 2, 1864. The duty station to which they were assigned was Camp Meigs for the duration of their enlistment.[2] Many of the men in this unit actually had longer enlistment obligations, and upon completion of training were assigned to units in the field. Thus, having been marginally prepared for war by drilling and doing some shooting with a musket, Richard was mustered out and arrived back home by Thanksgiving.

He notes in his letter that his unit was under the command of a Captain J. W. Marble. The "George" referred to in this letter is very likely

---

[2] National Park Sevice, *Civil War Soldiers and Sailors,* 2012, http://www.nps.gov/civilwar.

one of Richard's older brothers, George Wyman Clow, who was seven years his senior. The "Andrew" would be one of his sister Agnes's children.

While Richard was completing his first enlistment, the depressed spirits of the nation continued to fall. During the month of September, Grant's troops made several abortive assaults on key fortified railheads in the vicinity of Petersburg. These attacks were against well-entrenched Confederate defenders and over 7,000 more Union soldiers were cut down. The repeated defeats and large losses by the military lowered President Lincoln's popularity to the point that it appeared he would lose his bid for re-election in November 1864. His opponent, the peace platform candidate and former General, George B. McClellan, continued to gain strength with each of Grant's staggering losses of men.

If McClellan had won the election in November, it is likely that a truce would have been called by the new President. This would have resulted in a divided nation with dramatically different consequences for our nation than we see today. The South only had to bring the war to a successful 'draw' in order to come out ahead and achieve secession. The North needed to win by actually defeating the South in order to bring it back into the Union.

Grant's realization that he actually needed to win was one of the things that sparked new orders to General Sherman as he marched his men toward Atlanta. He also gave the same orders to General Sheridan as he took control of the Shenandoah Valley. Those orders, to destroy the crops in the fields, were a drastic change from the way the war had dealt with the civilian population of the South up to this point. By destroying the very food that the Confederacy needed to last through the winter, he was assuring that both the military and civilian populations of the South would suffer starvation. Prescribed starvation of the population had become a weapon of the war.

Fortunately, by Election Day in November, the morale of the North had rebounded following resounding victories by both Generals Sherman and Sheridan. Lincoln won re-election with over seventy percent of the electoral vote, thus allowing the mighty task of defeating the Confederacy to continue.

At the end of his one-hundred-day enlistment, Richard mustered out of the 22nd Massachusetts Infantry and went home to his family. The joy of being reunited with family, and having the Thanksgiving and Christmas holidays as well, must have been a wonderful thing for Richard. He would have also been reunited with his friends and girlfriend, Reina, at this time. It would certainly have been an occasion to celebrate.

Following the Christmas festivities he apparently went off to visit his brother, George, in Charleston, which at that time was a separate town from Boston, on a peninsula just to the north. This visit is described in a later letter dated February 12, 1865.

During that same period of time, Richard also went to the Chelsea section of Boston for a ball and had an occasion to go to the theater and eat oysters. All of these items point to the relative wealth of the family as compared to the commoners of Boston area with whom he had been serving in the military.

With all of this wonderful 'life' to come home to and enjoy, it's hard to understand why Richard would choose to reenlist and sign up for a three-year stint of duty. Perhaps he was attempting to escape some of the social pressures of his higher status in society, or he may have been straight-out rebelling against his father's authority as is suggested in his next letter.

# Chapter 3—Reenlistment and the Holding Company



*Galloupes [sic] Island Feb 5ᵗʰ [65]*
*Dear Sister*

*I am a soldier once more. I told Reina to write and tell you that I was in the engineer corps but it was before I had enlisted and I changed my mind. I am in the 56ᵗʰ Regt. Or to be sent to it. They tell me it was badly cut up and is now in front of Petersburgh [sic] so I expect to have some fun at last. You had better write as soon as you get this because I am liable to be sent away anytime.*

*The bounty we were to receive was $125 cash and $425 next Tuesday/ $200 next payment and our $16 per month or if not, we could have $1220 and take it by instalments [sic] making it so that if we were discharged before our time was up we would loose a good part of it, so I thought I would make sure of it. I am in for three years but you do not mind telling Father unless he asks you.*

*I want you to send me a parcel containing those two towels my razor and any other very small things that you think I will want. I only send this amount because I had to buy a great many more things for three years than I do for three months. (send by express)*

*I send my best wishes to Alex and the children, yourself also.*

*Direct to No. 9 Barracks*
*Galloupes [sic] Island*
*Boston Harbour [sic]*

As Union victories increased during the last four months of 1864, the country re-elected President Lincoln for a second term and public support of the war rose. With the New Year, the continued support of the war effort strengthened the resolve to completely win the war and make the United States whole once more.

His enthusiasm for the war seems to have prompted Richard to seek re-enlistment in the military near the end of January 1865. His first letter home gives us a glimpse of his level of immaturity and his family's disapproval of that decision. Richard evidently didn't wish to face the family directly with his plans, which indicates quite a bit of sibling and parental opposition to his re-enlistment. To prevent his having to meet with them, he used his girlfriend, Reina, as an intermediary to notify everyone. One wonders what she thought of this apparently bold young man who was "tough" enough to go off to war but afraid to tell his closest family of the decision.

Richard's lack of maturity comes through in his written statements which would appear to be in explanation of why he made a decision to choose the infantry over the engineer corps. It would appear to be the combination of cash, guts, and glory that attracted him to the 56[th] Massachusetts Infantry. Perhaps he met up with a highly charismatic and decorated recruiter from the infantry whose personality and charm simply overpowered what little common sense he might have had.

Richard appears to be fairly well estranged from his father. Fearing his wrath, he seems to be avoiding being told that he is making a terrible mistake. By telling his sister Agnes not to tell father unless he happens to ask, we see his fear that his father will negate the enlistment agreement that Richard has entered into. When we stop to realize that "father" (fig. 9) is over five hundred miles away, it is obvious that his is a strong authority figure whom Richard still has trepidations about disobeying.

Richard's youthful immaturity and ignorance about war and death comes through strongly with the statement of "I expect to have some fun at last." As we shall see, he didn't really know what he was letting himself in for.

One can imagine a recruiter dangling money in front of Richard as he quotes, "$125 cash, $425 next Tuesday and $200 next payment." Here is a bright-eyed young man who has no idea of the line he is being spun. A quick analysis of the amounts listed, relative to the sixteen dollars a month pay for a private should have told him that something was fishy. The total bounty sum of seven hundred and fifty dollars is almost four years of pay at that rate.

Richard ultimately begins to figure out his misunderstanding a few weeks later, but of course by then his name is already signed and he is awaiting transport to the front lines.

Once again, we see that recruits are required to purchase or bring a good portion of their own uniform and fighting materials. A very positive note is that Richard has figured out how to send some money home rather than blowing it all or having it stolen.

The "Galloupes Island" that Richard puts as his address is actually Gallop's Island in Boston Harbor. During the Civil War, it was used as an interim station to hold approximately three thousand troops at any one time. These were men who had enlisted and were waiting to be shipped off as soon as transport was available.

An island was a very good place to hold the masses of newly enlisted soldiers. It prevented them from taking any cash they had from their enlistment bonuses and deserting. "Bounty jumping," as it was called, was problematic for the military. It was punishable by death as it was considered desertion during wartime.

As the wait for transport drags on into a week, Richard's next letter reveals that the glowing excitement of re-enlistment is fading. He realizes that he is in a place where gangs of ruffians tend to rule within the transient men. As with his first enlistment, his initial bubbling enthusiasm is being replaced by a more sober and dearer understanding of the situation around him. He immediately sees that anyone stupid enough to not have money sent home through the paymaster risks having it stolen. At least he still seems to be receiving "care packages."

*Galloupes [sic] Island Feb 11[th] 65*
*Dear Sister*

*I received your letter and parcel and was glad to get it because it is rather lonely here and anything from home is very welcome.*

*We have a hard set of boys here, there is not a day but there is [sic] several fights in this barrack. Bounties are taken away from poor foolish countrymen by a lot of New York ruffs but nobody knows who does it.*

*I went to the State house but could find nothing about young Fletcher. There is no such name on the books at all. He must have enlisted under another name. You know* *they do so very often. I left your letter with Reina, she said she would send it to you. I send this money being part of $20 wich [sic] I received of my one hundred 80 more coming, you will keep a look-out for some money. I do not know wether [sic] it will go by express or by mail, by mail I think the paymaster is to send it. I gave into his charge. I have to take a book for a part of it, but I will send home all I can anyway. I have no chance for promotion until I get to my Regt. It doesn't make much difference here because we have no guns and have no beat to stand. I shall have no trouble in getting ahead when I go south. You must answer this as soon as you get it for I expect to go in the next transport. I am going to tell Father today about my enlisting. You know I will tell him a big thing all about how I will be a Colonel and everything ah ah ah ho. Well I am getting foolish now so that's enough for this time. With love to Alex and little ones, yourself also.*

*R. H. Clow*
*Barracks No 9*

Richard is fortunate to still have some contact with the outside world through the mysterious girlfriend Reina. She seems to still be in contact with him, or perhaps he gets to go into Boston on occasion to meet her. She is apparently mailing his letters to his sister. One can only suppose that this was a first love who is now going to become the girl he left behind. Reina's name doesn't appear in any of the family genealogies and she is not mentioned in later letters. We must presume that somewhere along the way they eventually broke up, probably after he returned from the service.

In this letter, note especially what seems to happen to young recruits who take their pay in-hand rather than having the paymaster mail it home. Richard probably learned this lesson during his first enlistment and training at Fort Meigs, hopefully from a friendly sergeant rather than the hard way through theft.

A century later the warnings from sergeants about not flashing money and sleeping with ones wallet still ring true. The author dearly remembers his own drill instructions in the late 1960's to this effect. Certain human behaviors do not seem to change.

The point about enlistment under a false identity comes up again with Richard apparently trying to locate some record of the lad named Fletcher at the state house and failing to do so.

This does not appear to have been a relative, but rather an acquaintance. A young man who, as mentioned earlier, had disappeared and his family had hopes that Richard might run across him while at the Gallop's Island embarkation terminal or by searching through military enlistment records.

In the latter parts of the letter, we once again see Richard's optimism come back when he talks about sending money home, informing his father of his enlistment and getting ahead in the ranks. He very obviously moved through much of this transient stay with a minimum of conflict and looked forward to reaching his final regiment.

Although it seems that his departure in imminent, it is still another four days before Richard's next letter tells us that he knows the name of his transport ship, the De Molay. (Richard's incorrect spelling of the name as D'Malay was fortunately phonetic enough to allow me to trace the ship). This next letter also gives us further details of the conditions on Gallop's Island and the temperatures of that winter which appear to have been far colder than the present.

*Galloups [sic] Island Feb 15 [65]*
*Dear Sister*

*I have received your letter and it came just in time for I leave in the transport in one hour for the south. You need not feel alarmed about my bounty for I am looking out to make all I can. If they will cheat me what will they do to some of these ignorant paddys [sic] who don't know enough to last them out of doors.*

*I am feeling all right and want to get where it rains bullets. It is the worst place here I ever got into. It rains all the time. The other night it was 20 below zero and a man froze to death on his post. They bury three or four every day here from sickness.*

*I suppose I will be sick on board the D'malay [sic] the transport, for we will be thre [sic] or four days going.*

*I forgot to bid Mrs. Gibson goodby [sic], or I did not forget to, but I thought I might come back and they would make fun of me. You keep a lookout for some money there. I could not explain it about the bounty. Anyway you will not receive much more just now.*

*R. H. Clow*

Richard's picture of life on Gallop's Island gives us a glimpse of the grim side of that particular barracks situation. In addition to the undisciplined masses of men apparently left pretty much to their own devices, there seems to have been extremely cold winter weather. That alone must have made keeping warm a real ordeal for men who had nothing but their cotton military uniform and no winter clothing or extra blankets from home.

The winter weather on the eastern seaboard can be atrocious in February. At one point Richard notes that it rains all the time. This must have been during a warm front which was then replaced by an arctic front of terrific cold. That would explain how one of the guards could actually freeze to death while on duty and Richard's note indicating that it was twenty below on that night.

A check of Boston weather history through the National Oceanic and Atmospheric Administration website indicates that the coldest recorded weather temperature ever, occurred on February 9, 1934, when the temperature dropped to -18 degrees. Thus although Richard's thermometer may not have been official, the winter of 1865 was definitely too cold to be posting a man on guard duty in an army issue cotton uniform.

In later years after the Civil War, Gallop's Island became the site of the Boston Harbor Pest House. This became the observation and quarantine site for holding immigrants or seamen coming into Boston showing symptoms that might indicate infection with bubonic plague or other feared diseases. The island was used for this purpose through the beginning of the 20th century. One case is documented by the *New York Times*, January 5, 1900, entitled "Plague Suspect in Boston."

From Richard's description, it becomes apparent that signing on for an enlistment bounty was not the same as actually collecting that bounty. He notes again how he failed to completely understand both the amount of money involved, and the manner of payment of this inducement for a second enlistment.

The system for receiving the enlistment bonus seems to have changed in the middle of the Civil War for very good reasons. In earlier years a large sum was given almost immediately to the enlistee, not in installments. Thus the lump sum system became a loophole for criminals who would enlist for a bounty only to then desert. They would then change their name and re-enlist repeatedly in this manner to amass considerable sums of money.

Captain Crane, the Provost Marshal of Vermont, describes the April 1864 firing squad execution of two such men who were listed as "Bounty Jumpers." They apparently had been making a very comfortable living, using this scheme repeatedly, until they were finally caught. [3]

The installment system also recognized the fact that the war and the need for massive numbers of men to fuel the armies would not go on forever. With the end of the war, there would not be a need for so many soldiers and the plan was to muster many of the men out of service before they completed their full enlistment. Thus, this latter method ensured that men would only receive what they were due and the government would not be left trying to chase down men after the war to try collecting any over-payments for time not served.

The steamer De Molay on which Richard traveled to the South, had been used as a troop transport for a number of years prior to 1865. It is described as a ship that was "commodious, new, an excellent transport."[4] These are words which differ profoundly from the observations made by Richard Clow in one of his letters home, as we shall see.

1863 may have been one of the first uses of that particular steam ship as a troop transport. At that time, she transported the 54[th] Colored Regiment of Infantry to the South. She is mentioned in several letters home during June of that year, written by the young commanding officer of the 54[th], Robert Gould Shaw.[5] His letters were written while on shipboard, an activity which would have been completely impossible for an enlisted man, given the conditions described by Richard Clow two years later under completely different circumstances.

---

[3] Bonekemper, III, Edward H., *How Robert E. Lee Lost the Civil War* (Fredericksburg: Sergeant Kirkland's Press, 1998), 23.

[4] Emilio, *History of the fifty-fourth*, 33; William C. Davis, *Stand in the Day of Battle*, vol. 2 of *The Imperiled Union, 1861—1865*, (Garden City: 1893) 50, in Adams Virginia M., ed., *On the Altar of Freedom* (Cambridge: University of Massachusetts Press, 1995), 25(2).

[5] Shaw, Robert Gould, *Letters to his Family and Other Papers: Robert Gould Shaw 1837:1863* (MSAm1910) (Houghton Library: Harvard University, 2012) http://oasis.lib.harvard.edu/ oasis/deliver/~hou00649.

The De Molay is again referred to in the "Marine Intelligence" report of the *New York Times* for August 20, 1863, as a troop carrier. Later the ship's name appears in the records of the New York State Division of Military Naval Affairs showing that in May of 1864 she transported the 115[th] NY and the 76[th] Pennsylvania Regiments to Fort Monroe at the mouth of the James River near Petersburg, Virginia.[6]

Thus, by the time Richard travelled south from Boston, the De Molay had already had a goodly number of men crammed into her hold. Consequently, the clean and new quarters of 1863 were considerably worse for wear.

That trip to the South must have left the enlisted men of Richard's unit totally exhausted. In his next letter, which is written from Fort Alexander Hayes on the front lines just outside of Petersburg, the description is one which could aptly be applied to the conditions aboard a "slaver" ship.

---

[6] "Marine Intelligence," *New York Times*, August 20, 1863.

# Chapter 4—Arrival and Initiation into Battle

The boat trip from Boston southward along the coast to the James River in Virginia took approximately five days. Thus, as Richard departed Boston on the 15th or 16th of February, he would have arrived in Virginia on approximately the 20th or 21st of that month. It would therefore appear that this letter was written only two or three days after his arrival in the South. Richard's immediate transfer from his point of arrival, which would have been City Point, to Fort Alexander Hayes, gives some indication of the immediate need for men on this front.

Everything in this letter is described with that optimism and resilience that Richard seemed to carry with him despite the hardships that he endured during the ship's passage. It's the viewpoint of a young lad who, after being in the cold, wet, stinking hull of a ship for five days, is finally warm, dry, clean, and with his new unit.

*Fort Hayes Feb 23 65*
*Dear Sister*

*I have got to the regiment at last and am as happy as I can be, but probably I wont[sic] say that for we expect a fight every hour. Last night we had orders to sleep with our harness on guns by our side and with rounds of ammunition. To day the rebels are coming into our lines in large squads. They always do before a fight. We are in winter quarters in the big houses, four men in each.*

## Rough Enough

*I direct from Fort Hayes. It is an earthwork with three guns, six pound rifle guns. We can see the city of Petersburg quite plane. It is just through a small belt of wood. It sounds so funny here to me, the pickets at night – on both sides, fire every ten minutes. The whole line of pits, six men in a pit, and the pits a few rods apart. So it sets up a continual rattle. A stranger would think it an awful battle. Well they do kill a few once in a while as they point right at them. It looks so funny to see the ditches full of dead Johneys [sic] as they call them.*

*I wish Alex had come with me to see the country and gone back again. Coming up the James it was very warm and nice. On both sides were splendid plantations and the remains of splendid mansions where the gunboats shot them to pieces. The country is heavily wooded and full of rabbits and quails. The rivers are full of ducks. I saw more than five million of them.*

*I shall have a non-commission in a short time. They think a goodeal [sic] of me here. I am in the second brigade, second division, $9^{th}$ corps, $56^{th}$ regt. M.I.N., Company G, Colonel Jarvis and Captain Mc Cardeal.*

*I had rather a hard time on board the boat. They put 350 of us in the after hold. It was dark as pitch almost and only one small hole to get out by. There was just room for us all to stand up in it and when it came to lie down in it we were five tier deep and if you wanted to get out from the back of the crud you would have to crawl over all the rest of them and they would put a knife into you. A great many were served this way. I came through all right though.*

*I wrote and told Father I was about to start and I suppose he feels a little uneasy, so I wish you would ease his mind about that critter of his. I will write too. Will you tell Fred Brown to let the folks in Chelsea know where I am, as I said I would let George know too.*

*I am at home now with my regt. It seems to me as if I knew all these boys before and they almost shook hands with me when I came. Two others came to this company, one is a young boy who had a brother here and was coming to be with him and when he got here he found he had been taken prisoner by the Rebs [sic].*

*I saw the Congress and the Cumberland in the James. The Cumberland looks quite new. Her masts are all that you can see. She sets straight up, but the Congress is a rack [sic] of rubbish and grass.*

*I wish you could see Fort Munro. It is all slope of the best kind with big guns. I saw the big gun you have heard about. It sets on the sand and is rusted badly. There is a great fleet on the James at the fort.*

*If you can enclose 2 dollars I will be much obliged.*

*Dick Clow*

The description of the boat trip from Boston down along the Atlantic coast and into the James River estuary comes through as one of nightmarish proportion. The cramped hold with standing-room only in the darkness was a recipe for mass seasickness within the first few hours out of port. Those conditions, coupled with the closely-quartered bunk area where the sick men lay in ranks five deep, created a landlubber's version of Hell.

The retching men must have very quickly turned the innards of the ship into a claustrophobic cesspool. Tempers would have flared. The fact that men all carried knives would have certainly led to fights with nasty consequences.

It appears that the only escape was to go on deck and try to stay there for as long as possible. With the weather that Richard describes in Boston just before the ship's departure, even being on deck would not have meant an easy passage. Being out in the elements of an Atlantic winter would have had its own hazards and was probably only a brief respite from the fetid conditions below decks. For those four or five days, the travel to the south must have been at the level very nearly like those described for slave ships. The "crud" that Richard mentions must have literally covered both the entire floor of the hold and the men occupying that dimly lit prison after several days at sea. What a joy it must have been to emerge from the cold of Boston's winter into the calm waters of the James River estuary and the warmth of a Virginia spring.

The final hours of the voyage, with the troops on deck in the spring weather, must have seemed almost like a sight-seeing tour. The De Molay, moving slowly up river, passed through the Union ships blockading this vital passageway that penetrated deeply into the Confederate heartland. The hulks of the two Union ships, the *Congress* and the *Cumberland* clearly visible, were grim reminders of the success of the Confederacy's armored warship offensive less than a year previous.

One can almost hear honks and quacks of the vast flocks of ducks and geese overwintering in the estuaries of the James. We can sense Richard's excitement at seeing these and wishing that his brother-in-law Alex were there as well. The scenes of the wrecked plantation mansions and farms must have given rise to thoughts of envy in some of the farm boys. One could not help but compare the richness of Virginia with their cold austere Massachusetts homes.

The joy at reaching City Point and disembarking from the steamer must have been almost palpable. Imagine a cheer springing from the throats of three hundred men who have just been given the presumed first order of the day: to strip down and wash off four days' worth of ship's crud in the waters of the James River. Based on Richard's description of the passage, it was probably here that any number of knife wounds were cleaned out, cauterized, and dressed while the few men already suffering from the first stages of severe infection were carted off to an uncertain ending in the masses of hospital tents situated near City Point.

Richard's initial assignment with the 56th Massachusetts Volunteer Infantry appears to have been at Fort Alexander Hayes in some sort of a forward picket unit assisting the firing of artillery into Petersburg. Maps of the Eastern Front of Petersburg show that Fort Hayes was a small fort located approximately one-and-a-half miles to the south of the much larger Union Fort Sedgwick. It faced the extremely strong defensive Confederate Fort Mahone (fig. 4). A small roadside sign and a few brush covered mounds of earth are the only remaining physical signs of this fort today.

The second paragraph of Richard's letter begins with the phrase, "I direct from Fort Hays." This wording is misleading to the reader in that it gives some sense of commanding others and responsibility for the action. I suspect that Richard, despite his superior education to most other enlisted men, was taking orders much like any of the other privates. A more plausible way of saying it would be that he was directing his musket fire from a picket point (fig. 2) towards the enemy, while the supporting artillery units directed rifled cannon fire into the fortifications surrounding Petersburg.

The mention of the rifled guns is a point that is important to note about the latter part of the Civil War. Both the Union and Confederacy gradually moved away from arming their men with smooth bore muskets. The muskets in use by this time would more properly have been called rifled muskets since they were still a muzzle loading weapon like the original muskets, but had rifling inside the barrel to give the molded bullets a spin, giving them greater accuracy and distance than round balls. Richard's musket was very likely a Springfield Model 1861, as this was the most common muzzle loader used by the troops throughout the war.

In addition, Richard mentions the three rifled guns at Fort Hayes which had taken the place of cannons along the Petersburg front. Again, as with the muzzle loading rifle, these more powerful weapons had supplanted the older cannons because of their accuracy, distance, and the many types of explosive shells that they could fire at the enemy.

The sights and smells of the battlefield would have taken some getting used to for these young men. Richard's note about the ditches full of "dead Johneys" must have been an initial shock to his system. In addition to just the numbers of dead bodies, the stench of the unrecovered decaying bodies in the no-man's land between Petersburg and the surrounding Union trenches would have become overpowering with the warmth of spring.

The National Archives and other photographic sites document decaying bodies lying in the ditches around Petersburg and near actual flowing streams. It is little wonder that outbreaks of waterborne diseases such as typhoid were common in the troops. It should be noted here that during its time in service, the 56[th] Massachusetts Volunteer Infantry lost 52 of its men to disease and accidents alone. This is a pretty large percentage of the total unit's war casualties of 209. The remaining casualties included the combat loss of 105 men, 48 men who died as prisoners of war, and 4 missing in action.[7]

Two officers, a "Col. Jarvis and a Capt. McCardeal," are mentioned in Richard's letter. Col. Jarvis is most likely Lt. Col. Horatio D. Jarves, again note the spelling error by Richard. Col. Jarves had been wounded in 1864 at the battle of Spotsylvania.[8] The Captain's name is misspelled by Richard and should be McArdle. Captain James McArdle was in Company E of the 56[th] Massachusetts Voluntary Infantry during most of the war, but mustered out in Company G. This would indicate that he was reassigned during the latter part of the conflict.[9] It is possible that the Captain was in

---

[7] Osborn, Francis A., "Record of Massachusetts Regiments," *The Union Army, vol.1* (Madison: Federal Publishing Company, 1908), 201, http://www.archive.org/stream/unionarmyhistory01madi#page/200/mode/2up.

[8] The Adjutant General, *Massachusetts Soldiers, Sailors and Marines in the Civil War, vol. 4* (Norwood, MA: Norwood Press, 1932), 762, http://www.archives.org.

[9] Ibid. 788.

charge of both companies for a time, thus acting more like a Brevet or field grade Major than a Captain. Both of these officers served with the 56th Massachusetts Volunteer Infantry Regiment through to the end of the conflict.

Prior to Richard's arrival at the front, the 56th Infantry had been stationed at Fort Hays since 1864. In March 1865, shortly after Richard's arrival, the Regiment moved to nearby Fort Stedman, which was also along the Eastern Front of Petersburg. It appears from accounts of the regiment that they were also previously at Fort Monroe, which was near the entrance into Chesapeake Bay and which Richard saw while voyaging south and misspelled as Munro in his letter. [10]

Richard's general gregarious nature comes through again near the end of the letter in describing how he is greeted by the old-timers in the unit. He apparently still feels he is a notch above many of the other "boys," and as such is confident of rising through the ranks. His optimism and apparently cheerful nature appears to have made him a likeable character to everyone he met.

Richard has finally mustered up the courage to tell his father where he is, indicating that he knows he can't be recalled from the front lines. This note also shows that he has a growing awareness that there are a lot of people out in the world who might like to know where he is in case there is a major battle and he is killed. The reality of the war is starting to sink in as he goes on his daily postings to the picket posts to pull a very real duty of trying to pick off opposing soldiers as well as keeping an eye out for attacks and deserters.

---

[10] Osborn, Francis A., "Record of Massachusetts Regiments," *The Union Army, vol.1* (Madison: Federal Publishing Company, 1908), 201, http://www.archive.org/stream/unionarmyhistory01madi#page/201-202/mode/2up.

# Chapter 5—A Close Call with the Angel of Death

The reader will almost immediately note that this particular letter has an impossible date on it as far as Richard's battlefield experience is concerned. On February 12th Richard was still on Gallop's Island in Boston Harbor awaiting transport to Petersburg. From the description of the battlefield and the location, it was probably written about March 12, 1865. It has therefore been placed next in the sequence of events that Richard describes. Note that he now seems to have gotten the Captain's name sorted out for proper spelling. This would also place it in a mental framework for our soldier to have been at the front long enough to become accustomed to the routine and death. He makes a near fatal mistake, forgetting that it isn't a game, when he gets sloppy about keeping his head down after shooting.

*Fort Hayes Feb 12th [65]*
*Dear Sister*

*I received your letter, and was glad to get it. I cannot write very well now for I spraned [sic] my thumb and forefinger a few days ago and they have not got well yet but it don't amount to anything.*

*I wish you had some of our beautiful sunny days in the north. The green grass is beginning to peep up around here and it is nice, I tell you. I am just as happy as I want* to be. I wrote to Father some time ago and have not received an answer yet. Did you write to him or not?

Well we expect a battle in a short time and I don't care how soon it comes. You know there are troops in the rear of Petersburgh [sic] and plenty of them in front and on all sides and it is a rather weak place compared to the others and we expect they will make a break here if they do anywhere. They will be starved out. I believe Sherman is headed this way, but I don't know much about it because I never see a paper.

I wish you would send me a lot of papers, some Harpers Weekly, an Independence, and a Press or two from Miss Adams's.

I was on picket the other night and how the balls did sing around the pit was a caution. One struck the pit just a few inches above my head and fell down in some water. I fired 75 rounds of ammunition that night and it was then they fired at the flash of my gun.

The Captain's name is McArdle. He is a rough looking but nice man and I think he and I will be chumbs [sic] after a while. This is the roughist [sic] regt. In the field, that is rough in a fight. The rebels hate the sight of the men. They can easily tell them because we wear very large black hats like the one Matie [sic] wears at home. I have one and it makes me look first rate. We go into the woods here and kick about solid shot and shell and skulls as many as we take a notion to.

All the rebels that come into our lines are dressed in gray clothes all torn to pieces and they look very care worn and discouraged. They have to run a great risk to get to our lines. They have to come away from there[sic] own picket-line to our whare[sic] the see is firing from both sides, and if they are seen by there[sic] own men they would be shot-at once. When we were on picket the other day we cut down a small tree to burn and there was 4 lbs of lead in it where they had shot in the battle before. You can stand at our pits and look at the rebel side and about all you can see is high embankments and the noses of big guns looking at you. The old soldiers of this regt. dread this campaign. The worst of any they have had or will have.

Do not forget to tell me all the news when you write.

When I was in Charleston, I went to the Navy yard to see Henry Mott. And where do you think he was, that nice young fellow? He had run away with a girl who wasent [sic] much.

Dosent [sic] George and Lexie live nice and cosey [sic]. I went to see George and stayed with him two days and two nights. We went to the theatre and had some oysters. I also went to a ball in Chelsea and had a good time in general.

You must write som [sic]. This ticket is one I had in my pocket when I left.

From Dick

*That was all the bounty you need expect just now. I will send my monthly pay. There are two hundred more coming when my time is up. I got the bounties all mixed up in my head so I did not know when I wrote.*

Richard seems to have been an avid reader, always in search of the latest news. I am sure any second-hand reading material got passed around and might be weeks old by the time it reached his hands. The fact that he was aware of three different news publications indicates his level of education and upbringing. His access to reading material may also be why he appears to have developed some sort of relationship with his Captain.

Interestingly, the "Miss Adams" papers referred to by Richard were not produced by a single publisher. They refer to a large number of one-page informal press sheets and picture brochures that had become popular on the streets in many cities due to the invention and marketing of a small manually-inked press. The press was manufactured by the Adams Press Company beginning in the early 1860s. Their marketing phrase, "Every Man His Own Printer," had given a whole new meaning to the printed word.[11] It allowed local individually published works to be hawked on the streets for pennies, thus getting gossip and commentary to the average person on the street. Richard's family was obviously interested in that side of life as well.

A part of Richard's interest may have been based on his desire to know what was happening with other troop movements around the country. These papers might have given him information pertaining to his older brother, John Sherwin Clow, the "Sher" in later letters (fig. 5). "Sher" had been fighting alongside General Sherman's men for the previous five months as a member of the 4th Minnesota Regiment. He had enlisted in Minnesota about the same time that Richard took his first short enlistment in the August of 1864.

An indication that Richard was following Sherman's movements comes from his statement that he believes Sherman's forces are "headed

---

[11] *Civil War Field Printing: Portable Printing Presses: Small Exhibitions* (Washington: Smithsonian, National Museum of American History, Kenneth E. Behring Center)1, http://americanhistory.si.edu/exhibitions/.

this way." This statement is correct to some degree in that Sherman's troops, including the 4[th] Minnesota, had indeed advanced into North Carolina by early March of 1865 when this letter was probably sent. That is not to say that they were on the border of Virginia or would be in the vicinity of Petersburg for the final battle of that city. It apparently was news that Richard was trying to follow closely in hopes of encountering his older brother.

At the time of Richard's previous letter dated February 23, Sherman's troops would have certainly been well into the Carolina campaign. They had left the burning city of Columbia, South Carolina on the 18[th] of that month. By the time of this current letter, Sherman's troops were pushing through North Carolina at a rapid pace. They were pressing the beleaguered Confederate troops with battles every four to five days. This kind of advance would surely have made the news and convinced Richard that it would only be a matter time before that army would be on the very outskirts of Petersburg itself.

Meanwhile, at Petersburg, the state of the Confederate troops is evident from Richard's comments about the ragged and worn appearance of the deserters. The Confederate railway supply lines extending from Lynchburg to the West of Petersburg were under extreme pressure. Food, ammunition, and clothing were beginning to run short in the city with consequent effects on the defenders' state of mind. It is not surprising that any attack by the Confederates was preceded by a rush of new deserters. The men only had to look over their defensive walls to know that they were nearly surrounded and had been this way for over a year. As supplies ran out many were giving up hope of even surviving the war as a prisoner.

Even though the Confederate forces were weakening, a soldier could never forget that being on the front lines was dangerous duty. The men were still exposed to a continual rain of enemy fire while on sentry or picket duty. Constant vigilance and awareness that one was a target were the only assurances a soldier had of not being shot.

The picket or sentry posts were generally dug by hand and built up into earthen mounds overlain with earth-packed wicker-like baskets and layers of small four-inch poles. The sticks helped prevent the dirt walls of the bunkers from washing away during the heavy spring rains. Additionally, the wooden overlay helped absorb enemy bullets, preventing them from ricocheting into the sentry bunker. The distance to the enemy picket lines was often under a hundred yards, which meant that pickets were in danger of being shot at any moment when they exposed a part of their body above the earthen wall.

On the night in particular that Richard writes about, the buzzing of the lead bees overhead should have been warning of the danger and need for cover. The actual smack of a bullet and its dropping out of the mud just above his head must have been a true wake-up call from Heaven. It was a blunt reminder that on the other side of the line stood defenders who were just as accurate with their firearms as any Union soldier. To become blasé about the fact that an enemy was watching every one of his muzzle flashes very nearly cost Richard his life.

In all probability, he had become used to the continuous sounds and whizzing of bullets at the front and was becoming a bit too cocky about his invulnerability. By his own statement, he had shot off some seventy five rounds that night across the very short distance that lay between the opposing army trenches.

The scenario of an opposing rifleman carefully watching Richard's muzzle flashes and marking lines of fire to his target is not hard to imagine. After a while, the sniper would have had a pretty good idea of exactly where his opposition was setting up to shoot. Each muzzle flare would allow him to get a slightly better idea of the position of the man whose head lay behind and above the flash. After a while it would become only a matter of waiting for the opportune moment to fire.

The sniper would be lying in his bunker with his finger on the trigger, already sighted in on the spot from which he expected Richard's muzzle flash. As the flame of Richard's rifle sent another shot into the darkness, the sniper would squeeze off his shot. It was only Richard's guardian angel and luck that prevented the sharpshooter's bullet from being that crucial six inches lower. One well-placed bullet was all that was needed from a Southern sharpshooter to end the life of a careless young Union soldier.

Pictures of the country side during Civil War-era Virginia show many open fields separated by wooded land and streams lined with willow and underbrush. During fierce battles, much of this underbrush fell as a casualty of the torrent of lead. In many areas around Petersburg, after the building of fortifications, woodcutting for fires, and constant shelling, the countryside became completely denuded of living cover. It is not surprising that the few remaining trees were found to be pumped full of lead by the men who were out of patrol.

As usual, we still get some of Richard's boyishness shining through in his comments about the cool rakish hats worn by this, the toughest of units. We also see his bravado for dealing with death in his statements about kicking shot shells and skulls around the woods while on patrol.

Corpses were a common sight on the battlefield in areas of no-man's land. With no protection from the elements or wild animals, they were soon reduced to nothing but skin, hair and a few gnawed bones. After six months to a year's time, the bones would be completely devoid of flesh while the surrounding rotted bits of a cotton uniform were all that remained to identify the dead man with either side of the conflict.

Richard was well aware of the feelings of fear voiced by the older veterans who had been through a lot of campaigns. Many of these men had by this time seen several years of bloody battles. They had seen their friends die and in the process of enduring repeated conflicts, had lost any bravado about dying for a cause being a valiant act. They had already seen the randomness with which bullets chose which men were to die. Many had already begun to wonder why they were alive while the others around them had died.

In addition, these old soldiers also realized that the tempo of war was beginning to draw to a close. In many cases their greatest fear was that they might be the last man to fall in battle. They were tired of war and ready to go home to loved ones and family. As such, they were less willing than the youngsters to face the impossible odds of charging on foot into the mouths of the big guns. They had learned how to recognize a dangerous situation and knew when to retreat.

Near the end of the letter, Richard shows a bit of nostalgia of the good life he had before he left Boston. His Christmas holidays prior to his second enlistment must have been a ball. He obviously had a great time in Boston's neighboring Charleston and Chelsea prior to shipping out. It is interesting that the girl, Reina, is no longer mentioned in this note listing his brother George and George's wife, Lexie. My research has shed no light on the name Henry Mott, whom he obviously had befriended.

This longing for the good old days at home is not an uncommon thought for soldiers at war. They tend to glamorize what they have left behind as well as forgetting some of the reasons why they left home in the first place. Additionally, they begin to realize how trivial some of their previous life was and are able to focus more clearly on the good things they left behind.

# Chapter 6—The Final Assault Begins

While Richard was involved with settling into the war front on an individual basis and learning the ins and outs of picket duties, battles, and patrols, the war as a whole was progressing rapidly toward its end.

During the month of March, General Grant was gradually increasing the vice-grip of Union pressure surrounding Petersburg and General Lee's Confederate Army. Grant's strategy in all this was blatantly clear: he intended to surround Petersburg, cut the supply lines into the city, and neutralize Lee's defense of the crucial supply lines to Richmond, the capitol of the Confederacy.

With this in mind, the month of March had been one in which the Confederate forces were gradually losing ground. Grant had not yet broken through the Rebel lines, but he had pushed them back almost two miles. As Union forces moved their trenches forward to consolidate the taken ground, General Lee could see that the end was approaching. Once the supply lines to the city were cut, the Confederate troops would be starved out. When they departed, Richmond and the South would fall.

During the same time, to the north on another front, General Sheridan's Union cavalry and infantry had finally defeated Jubal Early's army. Washington was no longer in any danger from further Confederate offenses. This victory on March 3rd allowed Sheridan to move his men southward where they were placed under Grant's command near Petersburg. The arrival of Sheridan's highly mobile cavalry brought the pressure of the war to a boiling point at Petersburg.

Sheridan's troops immediately began by probing the western Confederate defenses, the key to holding the railway heads to Richmond.

This action forced General Lee to make a crucial decision about the defense of Petersburg. He went on the offense against Grant's troops lining the eastern edge of the city. The Union troops below Fort Mahone were to bear a large portion of this thrust.

In attacking the troops to the east of Petersburg Lee hoped to force Grant into shifting a large portion of his troops back to that side of the city. This troop movement would take pressure off the fragile defenses guarding Lee's retreat route and the rail lines to the west. With this in mind, Lee staged a frontal assault on what he considered to be the weakest point of the eastern Union lines, Fort Stedman. He began the attack from Fort Mahone on March 25th, 1865.

Once again we see how the finger of fate can make a seemingly strong bold plan fall apart. On the very day that Lee launched his attack on Fort Stedman Richard's unit, the 56th Massachusetts Infantry moved out of Fort Hayes and reinforced the troops at Fort Stedman.

Thus, as the Confederate troops attempted to punch a hole through the Union lines at Fort Stedman they were met by a much stronger backing force than had been anticipated. The Rebel army was turned back towards Petersburg. This thrust was Lee's final attempt to break out of the city.

A few days later, on March 31st, Sheridan's Union cavalry and infantry again launched an attack on the western Confederate line of defense. In this movement, they pushed towards the south and west and then turned back on April 1st to confront Pickett's Confederate cavalry and infantry.

The Battle of Five Forks brought a key Union victory for the armies of Generals Sheridan and Warren. This triumph immediately put Lee's escape route from Petersburg in jeopardy. It also drew entrenched Confederate forces from the eastern side of Petersburg to the front lines on the west of the city, weakening Fort Mahone. Thus it laid the final groundwork for General Grant's frontal assault on Fort Mahone where it faced Fort Stedman.

Richard is a participant and witness to some of these preliminary skirmishes, the bombardments, and the final mass infantry charges that bring about the fall of Petersburg during the battle that began on April 1st and ended April 2, 1865.

*Richard H. McBee Jr.*

*Fort Hayes April 1ˢᵗ 65*
*Dear Sister*

*I received your last letter and I suppose you think I am slow about answering, but it is no use to write too often. You know I don't like to write very well anyway.*

*I was not in that fight, but was on picket that morning and our pits are quite near whare [sic] it happened so I had a good view of the whole of it. I heard the first of it and saw the whole of it. It was a splendid thing. The roar of the cannon was very tarific [sic]; it was louder than any thunder storm.*

*When it commenced, it was quite dark and to se the shells burst — you could see them from the time they left the guns and when they would burst, fifteen or twenty at a time, you can imagine how it sounded.*

*We could hear each charge they made. The rebs [sic] would run with a kind of yelp like so many hounds and our boys would rush on cheer and shout which could be heard for many miles around. The musketry was splendid, the regular volleys like the sound of a drum only more of a rattle to it. The old veterans said they never heard or saw heavier cannonading or more shells in the air at a time.*

*Well this was in the morning from 4 o'clock to 8 and a little after. In the afternoon of the same day we heard a hard fight going on, on our left — the cannonading was heavy.*

*While I write this there is fighting on our left and a report — that Sherman is whipped and the railroad retaken. We have orders to sleep with our equipments on and ready to move at a moments notice.*

*We have turned out several nights already. One night we had orders to cap our pieces. We were outside the picket line and we had to lie down in the mud to let the bullets pass over us.*

*I am writing this in the evening and tonight I expect to make a charge on the rebels forts. If they do, Lord help the men, for they will be mowed down in swaths.*

*I have a good chance to be promoted for the old vets run like anything and I never shall leave the colors.*

*The other night the men all sneaked off but three of us, and when we went back to camp they were there waiting. These men were our company. There were about 3000 all told out on that scrape.*

*I am trying to write by the firelight and can't.*

*You need not be very careful about — those papers, after you read them will do. You must not wait for me to write.*

51

*Rough Enough*

*I hope you are all well. Tell Alex I send my best wishes. He had ought to have seen the battlefield. The streams and brooks ran red and the clotted blood was inch deep in some places.*

*How are the children? Do they still inquire for me? Will you write to Father for me and tell him you receive letters from me regular. I wrote to him once to him since I enlisted and he did not answer it. I received a letter from Bertha and one from Jessie.*

*That is all this time.*

*Richard Clow*

The above letter was written by firelight on the evening of April 1, 1865. As Richard wrote this, we can imagine his awe at the firepower and sounds of a battle that was enormous compared to what he or any of the other men had been involved in previous to this time. We can also understand some of his fear as he watches with the knowledge that he will soon be in what may be not only the greatest, but also the final battle of his life.

We can pick out some of this fatalistic undertone in his statements about the men being mowed down, his bravado that he won't leave the colors, and his anger directed at the old veterans who always run away leaving others stranded. Additionally there are: the rapid-fire questions and statements about family, mention of receiving letters from his two other sisters, and the request for others to write to his father about what is happening.

A side note of Richard's indicates that at least once he was left sitting out in enemy territory almost by himself as he followed the colors. It would appear that the main force either had been called to retreat or had simply fled en masse—something that was not uncommon and definitely problematic for the officers leading a charge.

Apparently during a previous engagement with considerable enemy contact, Richard and those near him had been forced them to lie down while the main force received some kind of order to fall back. This may have been during the Union counterattack against Lee's breakout attempt, which occurred on the 25th of March.

How Richard, a few other men, and the man carrying the colors could have failed to hear the retreat of the other three thousand men is hard to imagine. One possibility might be that they had outdistanced the main mass of soldiers in a dash forward as the Rebels retreated back towards

52

the fortifications of Fort Mahone. At some point, the Union officers may have called a retreat in order to prevent their units from running into heavy return fire from those fortifications.

It could also have been that these few men were pinned down and remained in a concealed position which put them out of touch with the main body of the army. In either of these scenarios, one can imagine their own hasty but cautious retreat once they discovered that they were the only remaining birds out on the snipe hunt.

Forts Stedman and Monroe were the fortified sections to the east and south of Petersburg under the command of General Parke's IX Corps Army. Across the swale which separated the higher ground of these Union forts lay Fort Mahone some six hundred yards away. Named for a celebrated Southern commander, Fort Mahone was bristling with guns, defensive bunkers, and trenches. In front of this main fortress lay the picket lines with their own bunkers for defense.

In order to take the town, the Union attackers knew they would have to pass across a two-hundred-yard strip of no-man's land between the opposing forts and then break through the sharpened barriers of *abatis* and *cheveaux de frises*, placed in front of the reinforced trenches and twisting passageways that led into the heart of Fort Mahone proper. From the time they left their own picket lines until they could find shelter near the Confederate bunkers, the attackers would be exposed to withering gunfire poured out by the defenders. Once inside the basic defenses, they would still have to face the guns directed along each line of approach through the maze of trenches.

It was such knowledge that made each man aware that he was advancing into what would become a human slaughterhouse.

In fact, this is exactly what happened as the Union troops were thrown back repeatedly by the dogged Confederate defenses during the first assault on the night of April 1st. Ultimately, the IX Corps was pulled off the hill by General Parke when, as Richard notes, "the streams and brooks ran red."

The fierce fighting to the "left" that Richard could hear was located towards the western edge of Petersburg and the railheads where the Confederate troops were strongly entrenched. This lifeline was attacked by Sheridan's men in the Battle of Five Forks on the 1st of April as well.

A very peculiar statement occurs in the midst of Richard's description of the battle. He writes, *'While I write this there is fighting on our left and a report – that Sherman is whipped and the railroad retaken."*

I suspect that in the chaos of men, yells, and explosions, Richard simply mixed up the two general's names and wrote Sherman where he intended to write Sheridan. The presence of General Sherman in the area of Petersburg at this time was impossible, as he was occupied in the Carolina Campaign several hundred miles to the south. Richard was hearing the shouts and yells of Sheridan's men or others who were attempting to break the Rebel lines to the west and therefore to the left of where he was seated and writing.

The other point in this statement, that of being "whipped and the railroad retaken," was probably based on a rumor passed through the troops as the battle raged back and forth. It is very likely that Sheridan and General Warren's first assault on the well-entrenched Confederate lines was not a total success and that they were indeed pushed back by Pickett's men. In the end the Union did prevail. This was, of course, something that Richard could not know until much later, as he was soon to find himself fully occupied as a member of the next wave of the assault on Petersburg.

Richard's description of the man-to-man communication within the Confederate infantry as they charge into battle gives us an appreciation for what the Southern "rebel yell" must have sounded like. From a distance it would initially have sounded like a pack of hounds yipping and baying in the chase. It told each man that his comrades were by his side as they moved forward en-masse. The tempo and energy of this 'baying on the hunt' would gradually build, as the men got closer to the enemy, finally reaching a crescendo as the blue and gray forces clashed together. At this final moment, each man would be yelling out his own individual fighting scream in hopes of paralyzing his opponent and being able to win in what was truly a life-and-death struggle.

It is important to note that by April 1, 1865, General Lee had finally admitted to himself that the Petersburg stronghold could not be held indefinitely. He understood the ramifications of the loss of Petersburg and the crucial railhead supply lines. He knew it would open the pathway for Union advances directly on Richmond and the secessionist government headquarters of Jefferson Davis.

When Lee notified Davis that Richmond should be abandoned, he knew his men could no longer thwart the power of Grant's superior forces. He immediately began making preparations for the withdrawal of his men from Petersburg. It would do the cause no good for him to become trapped by the blue tide.

At this point, in Richmond Jefferson Davis gathered his people together, set fire to the town, destroyed the bridges, and fled to the south. In many respects, the damage done by this "friendly fire" to the city of Richmond was far greater than anything the Union did either to Atlanta or Savannah when they conquered those two cities.

With the leaders of the Confederacy in retreat and General Lee making plans to evacuate his own troops, the way was made a slight bit easier for the second Union assault wave on Petersburg beginning at four in the morning on April 2, 1865.

# Chapter 7—The Assault of Petersburg on April 2, 1865

The assaults during the night and early morning of the 1st and 2nd of April brought about the fall of Petersburg. Richard was in the second wave of the assault which began approximately at four in the morning; this was again a human wave from the IX Army Corps under the command of General Parke.

During the second assault, the Union troops were again pinned down and driven back as had happened the previous day. Later in the day, the resistance from the defenders finally began to show signs of weakening and the attackers surged forward into the town. Unknown to the attackers, this weakening was partly due to the fact that General Lee had begun his withdrawal from Petersburg. This weakness ultimately allowed the Union troops to gain a foothold within the walls of Fort Mahone, take the battlements, and enter the city.

Richard's statement of being one of the first inside the town has to be taken at face-value. On this day, he obviously saw more than enough action for any seventeen-year-old.

The fact that this next letter is written a week after the initial taking of Petersburg gives some idea of the intensity of the military action during the next seven days. For nearly a week, the troops of the IX Corps, including the 56th Massachusetts Infantry raced on foot across the State of Virginia in pursuit of the fleeing General Lee. There simply was no time to stop. For the geographically minded reader, it should be noted that there is no county called Gloway in the state of Virginia. We have to accept that Richard didn't know where he really was and probably asked someone else where they were and this was the answer. It is much dearer to follow the trail of skirmishes and running battles that lead us to the outskirts of Appomattox with the rest of the 56th Massachusetts Infantry and IX Corps.

*Gloway County April 9th 1865*
*Dear sister*

*I am alive yet and in good health. We have been marching for some days and I have not had a chance to write. I can only say a few words now while the Regt. is in a large field waiting for orders.*
*I am quite well and just as leave fight as eat. Write and tell Father so I never heard from him since I enlisted. I expect to be home soon for we have done our part.*
*I was one of the first in the rebel fort April 2nd. It was rough enough.*
*Write to me soon,*

*Dick*

The day after Petersburg fell, April 3rd, the troops of the IX Corps actually paraded in the deserted streets of the town with their band playing. What a day that must have been for those men, both young and old, who had survived the seemingly impossible assault! Perhaps as many tears were shed here following the taking of Petersburg as were shed a few short days later at Appomattox with Lee's actual surrender.

Although there was a moment of respite and celebration for the men of the 56th Massachusetts after the fall of Fort Mahone, that gay time only lasted a few short hours. General Parke's troops were then called upon to proceed westward as part of the force to prevent Lee and his army from escaping to the south. The IX Corps's route took them to the southwest of Petersburg along the railroad tracks leading to the west where they intersect the main tracks that go north to Richmond.

Lee was in the process of making a mad dash to the west in hopes of reaching a depot and ration trains. His troops were in dire need of food and supplies. After that, he hoped to swing southwards and escape into the Carolinas.

There was no time for the men of the IX Corps to dally along the way. Their mission first took them some forty miles to the railhead of Black and Whites and then another thirty miles onwards to Farmville. During those three days of hard marching there was scant time for Richard and the other men to eat their corn meal mush and catch a few winks of sleep, let alone write letters home.

At Farmville the IX Corps moved in behind Sheridan's cavalry and infantry to force Lee's troops away from a supply of rations. Lee's men were then harried northward across the Appomattox River where they once again were able to turn and run to the west.

It was not until April 9th that Richard and the men of the Union Army slowed down as they converged on the small town of Appomattox. It is from this last day before Lee's surrender that we get a sense of how things had suddenly changed. His sentences are short and almost like a man trying to catch his breath after a long run. The last comment of his previous short letter, "It was rough enough," sums up a lot of action. Now with this new note to his sister we are privy to what some of that "rough" situation was as Richard and others of his unit entered Petersburg on April 2, 1865.

With all the action, there had been no real time for an after-battle letdown and contemplation of all that he has been through in one short week, including the loss of a friend. This letter goes off to the mail only a few short hours prior to the announcement of the surrender of General Lee in Appomattox.

Also with this next letter that we see that Richard has now had some time to think about his experience in battle and to reflect on his friend's death. The letter has somewhat of a somber tone to it.

*April 15/65*
*Dear Sister*

*I received your letter last night and was very glad to get it. I wrote to you about a week ago, it was just a few lines, just what you say you are wanting, but I suppose it was lost.*

*I am well and having a good time at foraging as the army has never been here before. The boys know how to relish good things as we have been cut very short of rations for some time. We expect to go into the same city to do prow [sic] duty now the fighting is played out. If we do, we will have good times. We have been guarding 11 hundred rebels who were captured about 18 miles from here.*

*I did not receive those papers you sent me, for about one half the papers never reach the army.*

*I lost my best chumb [sic] in the battle of the 2nd of April. He was hit in the left side of the neck and the ball lodged in the right lung. He was a sergent [sic]. Kierstard was his name. Many a brave man fell there, but the only hope was to press forward amid the shower of lead and iron.*

*I am writing this letter under difficulties. It is raining very hard and I have nothing but a shelter tent and I have a very rough board to write on. I am out of materials for writing. Won't you send me some stamps next time?*

*I do not expect to see Sher now. I had a notion I would see him, but I have given it up as we expect to fall back now.*

*That is all this time, so with love to all I remain your.*

*Dick*
*P.S. Tell Alick [sic] I will be back on the old farm again some day, I hope.*

Following Lee's surrender, the IX Corps moved towards Alexandria and apparently passed through some areas not completely wasted by the other armies during the war. As a consequence, foraging was good. Richard and others who loved to hunt would have had merry times supplementing their low rations. The state of affairs with Union soldiers having low rations was due to General Grant's magnanimously giving a large portion of Union Army rations to the defeated Confederates as they were sent home.

Further information about Richard's involvement in the April 2nd assault on Petersburg comes with the revelation of the death of his close war buddy in that battle. There was very little chance for Richard to stop and comfort his friend in death. Stopping would very likely have brought about his own demise by making himself a motionless target for a confederate bullet or by being bayoneted by the man behind him. As he states, there was nothing to do but forge ahead into the hail of bullets.

Richard's note on Sergeant Keirstard refers to Isaac N. Kierstead, note the spelling, who had enlisted in 1864 from his hometown of Boston. He was severely wounded during the assault on Petersburg and died on April

5, 1865.[12] In Kierstead's case he was probably easily identifiable by his rank. He may also have had his name pinned inside his clothing for identification in case of death.

Lesser ranking soldiers who fell on the field of battle may not have been so lucky with the identification of their remains. The metal dog-tag system for military identification was not introduced into the U.S. military until 1906. It had been suggested during the Civil War, but summarily turned down. Thus it became the responsibility of soldiers to carry their own identification when going into battle. References mention that soldiers often wrote their names on pieces of paper and pinned them to their uniforms in hopes of being identified if killed. Others carried items engraved with their name in hopes of being identified. With thousands of dead during a single battle, it is easy to see how this form of identification might be fairly chancy.

At this point in time, Richard mentions that he missed meeting up with his older brother on the battlefield. This is an incorrect supposition on his part and may have been due to his confusion about which generals had joined forces with Grant. It was General Sheridan's troops that joined Grant's campaign after cleaning out the Rebel opposition in the Shenandoah Valley of northern Virginia. Richard's brother, John Sherwin Clow, was still with General Sherman whose troops were fighting to the south in the Carolinas. They would soon be moving northward towards Washington with the end of fighting.

The approximate location of Sherman's troops on April 15, 1865, at the time Richard wrote this letter, was in Raleigh, North Carolina. Sherman's men, along with the 4th Minnesota Infantry Regiment and Richard's brother, were hounding General Johnston's Confederate troops through the countryside. Johnston eventually surrendered to Sherman on the 26th of April. After that point in time, Sherman's troops marched north into Virginia passing through Richmond to reach Washington in time to take part in the Grand Review of May 24. Thus, a meeting between the two brothers on April 15th was impossible.

An interesting point about Richard's letter is the fact that it was written the day after the shooting of President Lincoln. In all likelihood,

---

[12] The Adjutant General, *Massachusetts Soldiers, Sailors and Marines in the Civil War, vol. 4* (Norwood, MA: Norwood Press, 1932), 762, http:// www.archives.org.

the letter was written shortly after Lincoln died that morning, yet there is nothing mentioned by Richard about this monumental occurrence.

At first it seems a bit curious to those of us living in a world of almost instantaneous news transmission that Richard would not have heard of this momentous earth-shaking event. In fact, since the actual death of President Lincoln occurred on the morning of the April 15, 1865, it was not until the afternoon newspapers came out that the information began to be widely dispersed to the public. By then Richard's letter had gone in the post, thus missing the inclusion of a second world-shaking event in his letters, again perhaps by a matter of a few hours.

Overall, the tone of this particular letter is one of sadness. It starts off with a bit of Richard's upbeat description about foraging which he obviously enjoys, and the anticipation of doing guard duty in a town. After that, it quickly descends into those areas that are preoccupying his mind the most: not receiving any newspapers, the loss of his best friend, sitting in a miserable tent in the rain, the lack of any writing materials, and the disappointment of not seeing his brother.

This letter again brings up the problem of melancholy and depression that arises in soldiers after the battle and adrenaline have worn off. It is now almost two weeks after the beginning of the assault on Petersburg, followed by the week of running battle across the Virginia countryside and the euphoria of hearing of Lee's surrender and the end of the war. It reiterates the plight of combat soldiers everywhere who have suffered through battle trauma and then find themselves still sitting in the pouring rain with time to think and ponder the meaning of all that has occurred. As a tiny droplet in the wave of history, the individual soldier often has trouble understanding the worth of their lone contribution to the ongoing tide of world events. A celebration of victory is needed.

That celebration of victory, the congratulations for doing a good job from the government, and the party spirit to go along with it did eventually come, but first came a winding down of the war effort. There were Confederate prisoners to guard and then release to return to their homes and farms which may have been burned or destroyed as collateral damage of the war. There were thousands of men to demobilize and pay off prior to their end of contract with the military.

During this interim period, the 56th Massachusetts Volunteer Infantry camped outside Alexandria Virginia just outside of Washington D.C. In the following letter, written some two weeks later on April 29th, the slowdown of the pace of life has given Richard the chance to regenerate some of his wry and more cheerful outlooks on life. He now has some things to look forward to in the coming weeks.

*Alexandria April 29th [65]*
*Dear Sister*

*I received your letter and was very much pleased to think that you received those two miserable pencil scratches and here is another of the same kind.*

*Well, about the papers, I don't think the Captain would receive them any quicker than I would and I do not care about stale news anyway.*

*In this I send a sheet of rebel note paper and a postage stamp, just as I captured them in Fort Mahone [sic] on the 2nd of April. I can tell you all about that day when I get home.*

*We expect to be discharged soon because the government does not want to many men now the war is about over and this corps has had as much if not more fighting than any of them.*

*A shell burst in the camp today by accident and wounded 6 or 7 men, none of our regt. fortunately.*

*I am feeling tiptop and am glad that the war is over. It was to bad about Mr. Lincoln and I was very sorry when I heard of it.*

*I received a letter from father the other day. It is full of cautions and lecturing the same as ever.*

*If I was home now, what a good time I would have. I did not know how to value it when I was there. Now every tree and every stone seem dear to me. I send my best wishes to Mrs. Gibson. Tell her I am the same Dickie as ever.*

*We can look from here over into Washington and see the capital and the whole city. I have not been to Richmond at all. Father directed his letter there. After we reached Petersburgh [sic], we traveled almost in an opposite direction from Richmond and now we have come back again.*

*When you write again, wont you send me 2 or 3 dollars in greenbacks for no others will pass here. I have not received any pay yet, none but that two dollar bill you sent me, but that's all right, it will be a biger [sic] pile when I get it.*

*I must quit now for the mail will go out in a few minutes. So I hope the young ones are quite well and all the old ones too, pigs, chickens, calves and every thing.*

*Dick*

The first message in the letter is clear.: when you have been at the center of making the "news," it doesn't make a lot of sense to read some reporter's version of how you fought the battle almost a month after it occurred. Whereas the old news was fine when the war was going on and the news came from a variety of different fronts, now the news was just a rehash of the two most important events: the surrender at Appomattox and President Lincoln's death.

The more recent camp tragedy of the exploding munitions is what is happening in the here and now for these soldiers. The vision of the fickleness of the angel of death has still not left the troops as they see survivors of the roughest of military battles becoming casualties in a simple accident.

Richard's enhanced appreciation for life and the natural world are evidence of how much he has matured in only nine months. Life has sobered his vision as compared to the gay party-boy days experienced during the Christmas holidays in Boston. He has learned to appreciate the small comforts in life.

It would appear from his comments that Federal money was in short supply. The paymaster hasn't yet caught up with the troops. Thus in an area that so recently had taken Confederate stamps and money freely, those bills were now only souvenirs to send home. They were no longer worth the paper they were printed on and new bills had to be reintroduced into the confederacy in order to stimulate commerce. Richard's sister has obviously been sending him a few dollars in her letters so that he had occasional spending money.

Richard is now beginning to put the battle of Petersburg into some perspective as it moves a bit more into the past and other incidents of a more recent nature take on new significance. He is glad the war is over and is now anticipating the point when he returns home and can tell what it was really like to the family.

# Chapter 8—The Grand Review and Brothers Reunited

Soldiers coming home from serving their country expect to be given a welcome by the nation that they have been serving. It is a tradition and Washington did its best to meet that expectation with the Grand Review of May 23 and 24, 1865.

The purpose of the Grand Review was not only to welcome soldiers home officially, but also to signal the end of the mourning period for assassinated President Lincoln. The affair spanned two days, with Richard participating in the first day's parade, as the full eighty thousand men of General Meade's Grand Army of the Potomac paraded down Pennsylvania Avenue in ranks of twelve men abreast. The second day was no less spectacular for the massed spectators of Washington, as General Sherman's Army of Georgia, composed of some sixty-five thousand men and many camp followers, paraded for six hours past President Johnson and General Grant who sat on the reviewing stand in front of the White House.

The two armies were camped on opposite sides of the Potomac River but still were able to meet in the city where they partied in the bars and taverns. It was at the end of the second day of the Grand Review that Richard finally encountered his brother, John Sherwin Clow. What a great end to the day that must have been for the two brothers, who were already charged up by the adulation of the thousands of Washingtonians cheering their parades.

**Rough Enough**

*The same Camp May 24<sup>th</sup> [65]*

*Dear Sister*

*I received your letter and thought as the grand review was coming off soon, I would wait until after that as I might possibly see Sher and I have seen him. I saw him last night.*

*We had our review yesterday and his was coming off today. After the review yesterday, I came along the road inquiring of Sherman's men where the 4<sup>th</sup> Minisota [sic] Regt. lay, but they told me it had gone across the river and would not be back again. Well, I went home to camp and felt tired enough. I was sitting in a tent when I heard someone inquire for Clow and looking up with a crust of bread in one hand and a canteen of water in the other. I saw the countryman standing in front of me. I knew him at once but the little fuz [sic] he had on his cheeks made him look so funny that I burst into a loud roar at him.*

*Well, we had a nice time and I went part way over to his camp with him. He looks younger than ever and is full of fun. We had a good swim before we parted and he told me all the news he knew. He had just got a letter and his wife and boy were getting along tiptop. He received the gun from father and likes it very well. He thinks I grow very fast, but I told him I was the same little black urchin he used to see. He says he boils weeds for greens and they give him such an apitite[sic] that he can't get enough to eat. He will be discharged in a short time now as he is only in for one year and has served 9 months of his time. He is ancious [sic] to get home to break up some more land that he has cleared. It is the best of land, clear black loam, but just as I suspected, four miles from a river. He didn't want to tell me that without some questions being asked. He's not had any pay since he enlisted 9 months. He don't seem to care much, there will be all the more when he gets it.*

*When you write again, send me $5. I suppose you think I am coming rather strong, but I would not spend it if I did not have to. We dress very nice now with our shoes blacked and white gloves, brasses shining and new clothes on parade every night.*

*Sher said his birthday was last Saturday and mine is tomorrow.*

*I am well today anyhow. Tell Alex I want to see him ever so much. I dreamed of that moose hunt the other night.*

*I hope you are all well.*

*Richard Clow*

*I have nothing to say to Mrs. Gibson now, but she don't know much. I love her that's all.*


In addition to the celebration of the Grand Review, the two brothers had their respective birthdays to celebrate together as well. This letter was

66

written the day before Clow turned eighteen years of age. He was finally legally able to make his own decisions about the military and his future.

Although many of the other units of both armies were disbanded and sent home following the Grand Review, The IX Corps remained near Alexandria awaiting further orders. Perhaps what Richard wrote was true, that Colonel Jarves (brevet General) was waiting until he could be officially promoted to the rank of General Officer.

One can only imagine the joy and surprise of these two brothers meeting. What a birthday reunion! Both men were in a party spirit, flushed from the victory of war, the grand review, and now the chance meeting. The afternoon spent at the swimming hole was a day to remember for the rest of their lives.

John Sherwin Clow "Sher" (fig. 5), had been with General Sherman's troops since the September of 1864. He had a one-year enlistment and, as a member of the 4th Minnesota Infantry Regiment, had managed to survive his own series of deadly battles while marching over two thousand miles across the deep South.

During this time these tough men were pushed to the extreme in the final months of the war. They were known to have covered over two hundred and fifty miles in the short period of only ten days in pursuit of Confederate troops. They had accomplished feats of endurance that would put even our modern athletes, with full rations and proper shoes, to a severe test.

Sher apparently enlisted in the military using his middle name rather than his given first name. Obviously, if he had been called Sher as a nickname all his life, his first name of John would not have held a lot of significance. Here again we see how the name a man puts on his enlistment record could confuse both military and historical records.

Following the war, Richard's brother returned home to Minnesota, his farm, and his wife. All we know of his farm is what is mentioned in this letter. The Clow family records indicate that Sher's wife, Celinda Warren Burnap Clow, remained on the family farm in Minnesota during the war. His son, Fredrick Redman Clow, had been born in 1863, making him a year old at the time of his father's enlistment. A previous daughter, Carrie Bertha Clow, born in 1862, survived only two months.

John Sherwin Clow and Celinda had three more children over the next few years following the war. Only two of his children were still surviving at the time of his death in 1909.

Note the mention of a "gun" that had been received by Richard's brother from his father. A number of men in the civil war armed themselves with additional weapons to those issued by the military. It is likely that Sherman's fast-moving final year of the war gave his men the impetus to acquire shorter barrel rifles. They were easier to handle while riding or marching long distances than the army issue Model 1861 Springfield rifles.

Also note the total change in lifestyle for the troops now that combat is over. The men are now on parade and guard duties in public which require them to purchase new uniform clothing. Richard appears to have been quite a dandy with expensive tastes. He would be the type to enjoy the spit, polish, and white-glove style of parade life.

There are no family records to identify the mysterious Mrs. Gibson who repeatedly crops up in Richard's P.S. notes. Her name appears again in this letter. His response appears to be with regard to a comment that his sister had passed along.

Over the next few weeks, the numbers of soldiers in the Washington and Alexandria areas dropped off dramatically as each unit was sent home with their severance pay. This was not the case with Richard's unit. Two weeks later, in the following letter, they are still outside Alexandria doing a bit of drilling and foraging for the spring fruits of the land. The excitement has now worn off and he is ready to go home.

*Camp near Alexandria June 15<sup>th</sup> 65*
*Dear Sister*

*I received yours of 28<sup>th</sup> May and I suppose you think it is hard I did not answer it before, but I don't always feel like writing, you know.*

*I am well and having a good time. We don't have anything to do but eat cherries and strawberries and drill a little.*

*I don't like to hear you say that Alex best days are over for hunting. I cant see that. I send you some money that came from Petersburgh [sic] when we entered on the morning of the 3<sup>rd</sup> of April.*

*I hear that there was an order issued from the war department that we could have our guns and equipments by paying $6 to the government. If so, I will certainly have mine as it is the one I had in Fort Mahone[sic] and fired more than two hundred shots in that fight.*

*I cant tell you anything about what we are going to do, but I rather guess we will all be home soon. When you write again send me a few papers at the same time. I think I will get them. Old papers will do, Frank Leslies and Harpers weeklys [sic]. That is the greatest trouble here, nothing to read.*

*You want me to send a message to the boys. Well, now, let me think what shall I say? Well, ask them if they have seen anything of a Babcock around there anywhere.*

*I tell you what I would like to do when I am out of this. That is, to come home and get a citizens suit and have some of you come out with me and I would take you where the big battles have been fought. You can see all the breastworks around Petersburgh [sic], the place where the mine blew up, all the graves and skulls and the pieces of shell and the last of all, the trees filled with bullets and some cut off with solid shot. I am acquainted with all the places along the line from Hatches run on the left up to the Appomatux [sic] on the right. I mean by that, all the places of fame. There is more to be seen there than you think for and it is worth going a great way to see. You will never see such forts and breastworks in any other country.*

*I have no more to say this time. Do you see anything about the regiment in the papers? I have an idea that this regiment never was heard of before and it has been out 18 months. The other regiments around here have all gone home and as our Colonel is acting Brigadier General, I suppose we wont go yet because he wants to get a star on his shoulder to take home.*

*You need not mind that necktie.*
*With best wishes to all your forever.*
*Dick*

With the return to normality, Richard's insatiable desire to read emerges once again. He has to have something to occupy his mind while they bide their time waiting for Col. Jarves to get his promotion. History tells us that the Colonel may have been an acting Brigadier General Officer while in the field, but he was never promoted and retired as a Colonel.

It's doubtful that Richard ever had the chance to show his family the historic sites which were still so fresh in his mind. The fact that many of these places are now historic parks indicates the significance that accompanies those sites even today. His communications and pictures taken later in life indicate that he did return to several of his old haunts in Idaho, the Dakotas, and Montana before his death.

The note from his sister indicates that Richard's brother in law, Alexander James Cruikshank, was already having health problems of some kind at age 36. Family records indicate that he continued to have children with his wife until at least 1871.

Richard's reference to a "Babcock" appears to be a colloquial joke of the times. According to family tradition, it refers to the male member of a mysterious group of ground living birds known as "Babs," which are very much akin to the "Snipes" that inhabit many local woodland areas. The females, called Babhens are dully colored, while the cocks, or more properly the Babcocks, are prized trophies because of their splendid plumage. Many a young man has spent hours waiting alongside a trail in hopes of snagging one of these to the amusement of more knowledgeable folks.

Another two weeks go by and Richard's unit has still not moved or been mustered out. Richard's letter indicates his boredom with the whole state of affairs and asks for more reading material. He appears to be indulging himself in hunting for pigeons and quail. He also continues to fantasize about the hunting trip with Alex on his return to the Boston-area farm. One can imagine the luxury of being able to gorge on blackberries after the monotony of military meals for an entire winter.

*Camp near Alexandria July 2, 65*
*Dear Sister*
*I am not used to writing with a pen so I expect to make a poor scratch of this. I wrote to you on the 15$^{th}$ and have not yet received an answer although I have looked for one every day. The letter I sent contained some rebel money and if you have not received it, I suppose somebody has taken it thinking it contained good money. If so, they got nicely sucked in.*

*When you answer this would you send me some papers, it is getting quite lonely here now and some papers would come in handy to pass away the time. Is Jessie and grandma with you yet? If they are, tell them to write to me. I hope Jessie did not get offended at me when I told her not to write to me as I would be moving and could not well answer them, but now I can all that will write.*

*It seems to me that this Regt. will never get home. Do you ever see anything about it in the papers? I don't suppose you do for I guess it is lost to all civilized parts of the country.*

*Tell Alex I have not forgotten that hunting trip yet, but just the opposite, it is becoming more and more impressed upon my memory, and if I get out of this by the first of September, I shall go without fail. You can tell Alex it is no use for him to back out now for I am going. I have not received an answer to that letter I wrote to father, and he told me if I would write he would answer it directly. Are the boys still with you on the farm? Tell me all the news next time about the place, and the folks in the place, and about everything in general. How is Alex crop? I don't mean whare [sic] he puts his bread, but the grass you know and such stuff.*

*I have been having a very good time. I thought there was black berrys [sic] on Paws farm but here they beat all I ever saw any-whare [sic]. I went out one day and picked four quartes [sic] in a very short time. There are any quantity of wild pigeons, and quails, here now.*

*I will bring home my musket when I come, as we can have them by paying $6 to the government, and I will willingly pay that for mine.*

*Tell the boys to write to me and I will answer them. Send me a few stamps in your letter as it is almost impossible to get them here for love nor money.*

*I can't think of anything more to write about this time only don't forget the papers, old ones will do just as well as any.*

*With best wishes to Alex*

*and love to all I am the same, Dick*

Soldiers are pack rats and tend to pick up mementoes and small souvenirs of the places they visit or do battle. Richard was no different from any other person and his letters occasionally contained small bits of rebel money, stationery, or stamps that he found. As he notes, the security of the mail system was poor and cash was probably stolen by clerks and handlers. They would have been looking for any sort of legal tender, as Richard's letters seem to indicate was his own situation.

The sizes of most foot soldiers' souvenirs were very small. The running battles between Petersburg and Appomattox would have given them very little time for looting or picking up trophies. More important for the men during that time was anything edible that they could carry in their pockets as they moved quickly towards their next objective. The supply troops following the infantry with their wagons had more space and time and thus did most of the looting.

This was probably Richard's last letter from the field before he finally was mustered out on July 12, 1865. Following his discharge, he returned home.

We must presume that Richard returned to the Boston farm owned by his brother-in-law Alex and his sister, Agnes. It was a hero's welcome from his family. Everyone wanted to hear his war stories and involvement in famous battles. Thus, at least for a period of time, Richard was the war hero at the center of everyone's attention.

What was it that happened to him during the following months to make him decide to reenlist in the Army again?

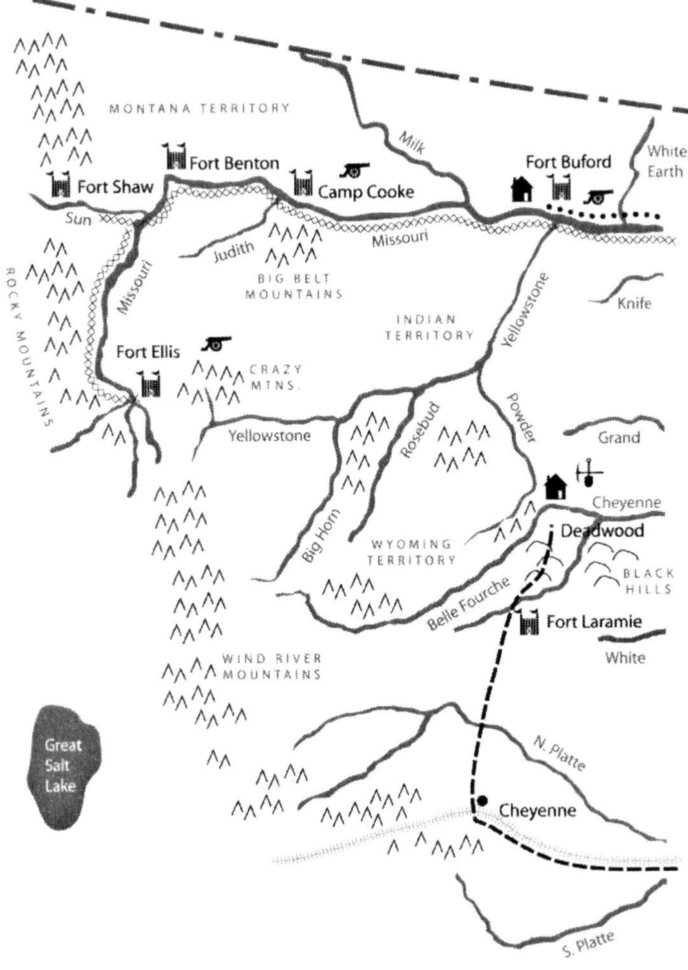

Richard Clow's
Travels on the Frontier
MONTANA TERRITORY
Milk
Fort Benton
Fort Shaw
Camp Cooke
Fort Buford
White Earth
Sun
Missouri
Judith
Missouri
BIG BELT MOUNTAINS
Knife
ROCKY MOUNTAINS
INDIAN TERRITORY
Yellowstone
Fort Ellis
CRAZY MTNS.
Yellowstone
Rosebud
Powder
Grand
Big Horn
WYOMING TERRITORY
Cheyenne
Deadwood
BLACK HILLS
Belle Fourche
Fort Laramie
White
WIND RIVER MOUNTAINS
Great Salt Lake
N. Platte
Cheyenne
S. Platte

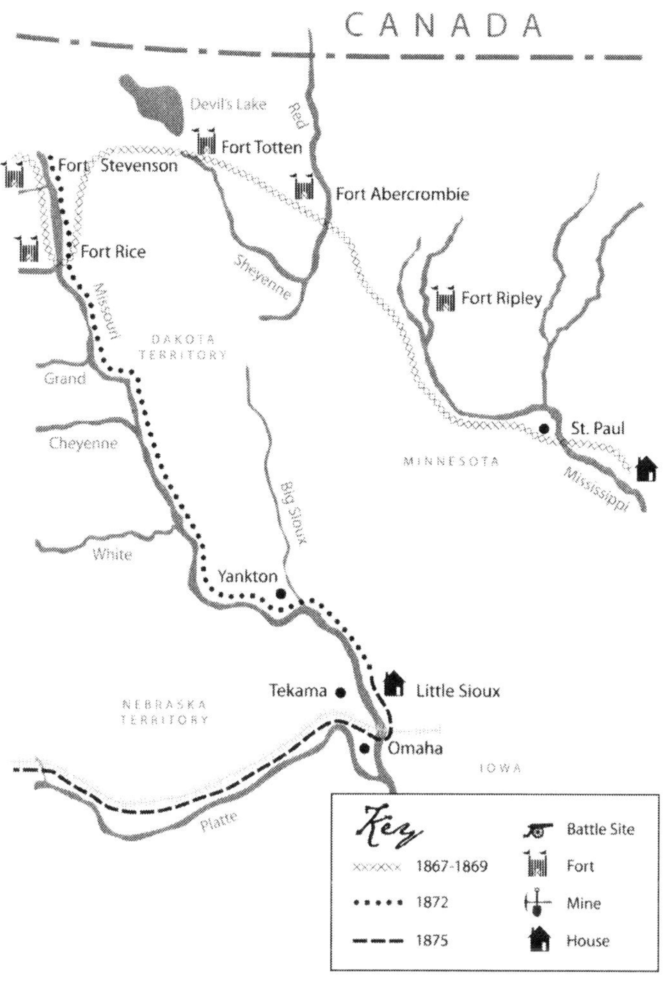


CANADA
Devil's Lake
Red
Fort Totten
Fort Stevenson
Fort Abercrombie
Fort Rice
Sheyenne
Fort Ripley
Missouri
DAKOTA TERRITORY
Grand
Cheyenne
MINNESOTA
St. Paul
Mississippi
Big Sioux
White
Yankton
Tekama
Little Sioux
NEBRASKA TERRITORY
Omaha
IOWA
Platte
Key
XXXXXX 1867-1869
••••• 1872
--- 1875
Battle Site
Fort
Mine
House

# Section 2: The Indian Wars

# Chapter 9—The Road to Reenlistment

Following his arrival home, Richard would have found himself to be a young man who had money to spend from his military bounty and a lot of friends and relatives who wanted to see him and hear his stories. He was the center of family attention.

This situation may have lasted for a few months as Richard got back into the work of the farm, and the autumn harvesting took most of the family time. During this time, he also would have caught up with all the friends he had left behind, heard all gossip that surrounded this group, and probably became reacquainted with his girlfriend Reina.

I suspect that by Christmas time, Richard had become a bit disaffected with life in Boston. On the farm, the conversation would revolve around the repetitive subjects of weather, crops, and animals. With his social group, by this time, he would have found that their lives were still caught up in the repetitive talk of parties, the theater, or the next ball. I suspect that by the time the festivities of Christmas rolled around, he was ready to stand up on the table and shout something like, "Don't you see that the world has been changed?" and "Aren't you interested in what really happened in the war?" But he knew he couldn't do that and if he did it would only spoil all the "fun."

I imagine that Richard had already noticed something that many soldiers, travelers, and adventurers find when relating their stories to others. That is, the listener wants to hear the big broad story idea and they want to focus on the "good parts."

By this I mean they want to hear about the point when the adrenaline was flowing and the climax of the event was reached. They really don't want to know about the rain and the mud, the closeness and smell of the dead, the dreams and fears brought on by exposure to too much violence and death, or the depression and tears that follow having a buddy die.

Richard had probably already seen the glassy eyed look of an audience being lost by something they didn't want to know. He had probably learned quickly to suppress talking about his dreams, emotions, and fears brought on by the war. He had probably learned to watch his audience for signs of boredom and close out the tale on a good note rather than telling about his real true feelings in a battle. He learned to repress the bad things and glorify things that really weren't all that glorious in order to please his audience.

In doing so, Richard was repressing exactly the feelings that needed to be let out for him to return to good psychological health. He may have found a few other war veterans to share his experiences a bit more closely with, but that wouldn't fix the gap that was growing between himself and his family and friends.

The consequences of the repression of Richard's war experiences would have been insidious and there were few persons interested in studying the mental traumas of war at that time. Almost fifty years later, Captain W. H. R. Rivers, M.D., addressed the Royal Society of Medicine in 1917 on "The Repression of War Experience." He noted that the patients dreaded recounting their experiences to friends and family who would not be able to comprehend the nature of the violence they had experienced. They described repeated instances of fear, anger, and reoccurring sweating nightmares about dead or mutilated friends to the point of actually dreading sleep. [13]

Ultimately Richard may have had similar symptoms. He might have tried to avoid some of these feelings by going off on a moose hunt with his brother-in-law, or by attending the theater, going to dances, or playing

---

[13] Rivers, W.H.R., Capt., An Address on The Repression of War Experience, *The Lancet, Feb. 2, 1918,* http://www.net.lib.byu.edu. 2012.

charades, and getting back into the "gay life" of Boston. Despite his efforts, his symptoms would have returned again and again as the ghosts of war continued to haunt his mind.

Richard's friends wouldn't have known how to deal with any changes in his behavior. In their own defense, they would begin to avoid him. They knew the war was over. They knew Richard had experienced some horrible things. But, so what, hadn't they all had tough times? Their lives had to go on. This was the life they led and enjoyed. Richard had to become a part of it again or move along somewhere else.

One of the pictures of Richard taken after the Civil War shows him dressed up with a friend contemplating a skull and a book (fig. 10). The note on the picture indicates that Richard and his friend are pretending to be medical doctors. Was this make-believe world of fancy dress and parlor games something that Richard tried to use to get back into synchronization with his friends?

By Christmas time, Richard had grown apart from his friends and family. He had to escape and find somewhere new to start life where the trivialness of Boston life wouldn't drive him crazy.

As the spring of 1866 appeared and bulbs began peeking through the snow, Richard left Boston and traveled west to stay with his older brother John Sherwin Clow on his farm in Minnesota. Here was a man he knew and respected who had military experience. His brother was someone he could communicate with because he been through the same kinds of experiences.

Richard probably stayed with the family and helped out over the summer with work on the farm and then assisted with the fall harvesting. Then, with the advent of fall, he realized that the small farm couldn't support him as well as his brother's family.

Leaving the Minnesota farm, he then traveled east to Milwaukee, Wisconsin, on the western shore of Lake Michigan to be with his father and another sister, Bertha Clow. This was an ideal place for him to spend Christmas and ring in the New Year.

After a long, cold, Wisconsin winter, Richard was probably ready to move on. This might have been especially important, considering his relationship with his father. Richard seems to have felt it necessary to rebel against his father who was quite probably a strong authority figure. By spring, the close quarters of the family house would have become too confining for both of them.

In addition to having conflicts with his father and running low on money by this time, Richard may have had another reason for taking another tour of duty in the military. He would still have been suffering from some of the traumas suffered during the Civil War. If old soldiers could understand how he felt, then joining the military again would put him in an occupation where he could communicate his feelings to people who would understand.

One might infer from some of Richard's letters about depression that he was suffering a variety of post-traumatic-stress disorder, or PTSD as it is commonly called. This particular syndrome had not been described at that time, but certain symptoms of it resemble a Civil War malady known as Soldier's Heart or DaCosta's Syndrome. This battle fatigue syndrome was most commonly treated by the soldier being removed from the front line and given ample rest and food to help them recuperate. [14]

With a realization that a return to military life was the only way he could find people with whom to relate, Richard went to the recruiter in Milwaukee, Wisconsin. On April 26, 1867, he signed a contract for three years' service in the 13th Infantry.

Richard's enlistment papers (fig. 12) are signed with a flourish by both himself and Bvt. Maj. John Christopher, Cpt. 26th Infantry Regiment, U.S. Army. They indicate that Clow had hazel eyes, dark hair, a dark complexion, and was five feet seven inches tall. His assignment was directly to the 13th Infantry Regiment.

According to the excerpts from *The Thirteenth Regiment of Infantry* by Lt. James B. Goe in 1867 the 13th Infantry Regiment already had men stationed in the far west. Some men were already working on the newly established Fort Buford, while others were several hundred miles upstream at Camp Cooke, which was being established on the west bank of the confluence of the Judith and Missouri Rivers. Even farther to the west and south of Fort Benton, the 13th was building Fort Shaw on the Sun River in order to protect the miners heading south through Helena to Virginia City and Nevada Cities and the gold fields.

As a newly reenlisted man, Richard Clow's first task was to get himself to his new unit. With this in mind, he probably departed Milwaukee,

---

[14] *Da Costa's Syndrome*, (Bionity.com, 2012), http://www.bionity.com/ en/encydopedia/ Da_Costa%27s_syndrome.html.

Wisconsin about the 1st of May 1867 to make his way across country to reach his first posting at Fort Shaw, Montana Territory.

# Chapter 10—The Route to Montana and the Forts

Richard's route to Montana in order to join Company C of the 13[th] Infantry was over land. Fortunately, spring was coming rapidly to the northern states by this time of the year and travel might have actually been enjoyable.

His path would have followed the traditional route of persons heading west to the gold fields from that part of the country (fig. 19). The first portion would have taken him northwest from Milwaukee through many scattered farms and small communities to St. Paul on the banks of the infantile Mississippi River.

After passing this population center, he would have entered more remote wilderness country as he headed northward along the Mississippi until he reached Fort Ripley. At this point his path would have turned westward, gradually leaving the wooded lakes area of Minnesota and entering the plains to reach the Red River and Fort Abercrombie, located on the eastern edge of the Dakota Territory. As a hunter, he undoubtedly enjoyed this country with woods and open glades where deer might be seen at any moment along the forest edge.

At Fort Abercrombie, Richard would then have joined a military unit or band of travelers for the safety afforded by large numbers. This was Sioux Indian country and hostilities were on the increase as the native peoples watched the large numbers of travelers trekking across their hunting grounds toward the west. The trip of just over a hundred miles to Fort Totten on the shores of Devil's Lake would have taken anywhere from four days to a week, depending on the speed of the group he was accompanying and whether they traveled by foot or horseback.

From Ft. Totten, it was still another 130 miles across increasingly isolated and more hostile wilderness territory to reach the Mandan Indian villages and Fort Stevenson on the banks of the Missouri River. Again, another week would have passed as they traveled while keeping a constant eye out for hostile bands of Sioux. Along the way, the landscape would have changed from forest to open grassland with lower bushes and small trees in the gullies. These areas of shelter would have afforded good cover for deer and Richard undoubtedly would have honed some of his stalking skills to bring in animals on occasion for food.

Upon reaching Fort Stevenson, the men may well have found that the Missouri River was still frozen with winter ice. May was generally the time of the spring breakup, which would allow river traffic to move up into Montana. Fort Rice was situated approximately fifty miles to the south of Ft. Stevenson. It was the Headquarters of the 13[th] Infantry and Richard would need to go down river to report in to that unit and get his assignment orders. If the river was already free of ice at this point, he could easily have taken a boat for the final fifty miles. If not, then he would have walked or ridden that last section of the route.

After reporting into the headquarters company of the 13[th] Infantry Richard would have joined the next group of soldiers headed up towards Fort Benton in central Montana. With the Missouri river running at full spring flood by this time, the journey aboard the sternwheeler must have been exciting.

It was a fascinating journey, with frequent stops at the forts and for wood as they pressed upriver. From the vantage point of the boat, the men would have had good views of the large Indian villages which neighbored Forts Stevenson and Berthold.

Beyond Berthold, the river banks would become more thinly populated. The sternwheeler steamboat (fig. 24) would regularly pull in at woodcutter sites where masses of cottonwood logs could be loaded for fuel as they churned upstream. Because of the current, it would have taken over a week to reach the confluence of the Yellowstone and Missouri Rivers. At this point, Richard would have first laid eyes on the post that was to become his home in another two years, Fort Buford.

While docked at Fort Buford, Richard saw how the men were building the new sections of the fort from adobe mud and sawn cottonwood planks. The dominant noise was the whine of the sawmill where cottonwood logs were cut into planks for the new construction.

Upon leaving this site, it was only another five miles before they came to the pier of Fort Union. This fort was in the process of being dismantled by soldiers and carpenters with all usable wood being taken to the site of Fort Buford for inclusion in that construction (fig. 13 and fig. 14).

It is possible that as they waited at the dock of one of these two sites, Richard got his first glimpse of the man who was to eventually become his father-in-law and employer, the renowned fur trader, Charles Larpenteur. Certainly he would have seen the massive teepee tent camps set up by the Sioux Indians on the banks of the Missouri opposite the forts. These served as the bases for the Sioux to trade skins with the traders as well as sites for launching hunting, raiding, or war parties. They were most certainly a formidable nation of people who dominated this section of the Indian hunting grounds.

Following these stops, the steamboat would have pressed on up the Missouri towards Fort Benton another three hundred miles away. It was a trip to remember. There were massive herds of buffalo blackening sections of the plains and hills in the distance. Prancing small bands of dainty brown and white antelope would have dotted the sagebrush hills. Richard would have had glimpses of the white rumps of elk and flashing tails of deer along the wooded brushy banks of the river. It was a paradise of wild game, a place that he would come to know and love in the next years as he traveled across this vast Montana territory.

For over a week, they navigated past the clutching fingers of giant tree snags jutting into the river and fingerlike sandbars waiting to trap the shallow draft boat at every bend. At narrows they were warned to be on their guard lest a band of passing Indians should take a pot shot at the boat.

As the steamboat passed the mouth of the Judith River, still a hundred miles East of Fort Benton the beauty of this big sky country would have begun to sink in. There were still miles to travel between sandstone cliffs and white badland columns of rock before the rolling sagebrush hills around Fort Benton appeared.

By the time they reached the booming river town of Fort Benton with its bare wood plank houses, wagons, teams of horses, and men readying for the gold fields, the newcomers would certainly have had a grand tour of the west.

Fort Benton itself was a bustling trading town built initially around the early trader fort that brought Indian pelts and hides out of this remote turnaround point for the steamboats on the Missouri. With the opening of the gold fields in southern Montana, it had grown into a supply and grub-stake town for the miners. In a few more years, as the herds of Whiteman's buffalo began to blanket the northern plains, it would become a burgeoning cow town with saloons and hotels.

At this point, the final leg of Richard's journey would have begun. Now, traveling on foot or by horse again, he would follow up the Missouri leaving the sagebrush plains and enter the foothills of the Rocky Mountains and the great pine and fir forests that cover this section of the country. At the point where the Sun River empties its clear mountain waters into the Big Muddy Missouri, Richard would have joined up with Company C of the 13[th] Infantry. Their task was to build and garrison Fort Shaw, Montana (fig. 15).

Over the coming months of the summer of 1867, he would have helped with the building of that new fort and the patrolling of the road leading southward to Helena and the gold fields.

The frontier and the scent of gold in Montana was a strong lure for many young men at this time in U.S. history. The discovery of gold in Montana had actually occurred prior to the Civil War.[15] In 1866, the discovery of large amounts of gold around Virginia City was brought down the Missouri River by miners in their flat bottomed mackinaw boats. When the news hit the headlines, the rush was on.

By the spring of 1867, the up-river rush to reach the gold fields around Virginia and neighboring Nevada Cities in Montana was in full swing. The military knew it was going to be called on to expand its system of forts in the west in order to provide some level of protection for miners travelling the roads that crossed Indian country.

---

[15] Huckabee, Rodger Lee *Camp Cooke: The First Army Post in Montana – Success and Failure on the Missouri (Boise State University Theses and Dissertations.* Paper 153, 2010), 2-3, http://scholarworks.boisestate.edu/td/153.

The best route to the gold fields at that time was the one which followed the course of the Missouri River past the navigable waters at Ft. Benton and then went overland through the mountains to the south. The trail passed through the area of present-day Last-Chance Gulch in Helena and then headed on south until it reached the Ruby Mountains. Here, among the gravels left by streams washing out of the old garnet-filled mica schist rocks of the Ruby range, was a giant pocket of placer gold waiting to be panned, sluiced or dredged. The easy gold seemed almost endless. It drew miners and businessmen like a magnet to the mountains of Montana.

There was a secondary route to the gold fields, which in straight-line distance was shorter than going all the way up around northern Montana: the Bozeman Trail, which went from Fort Laramie across the Wyoming plateau, dropped into the Yellowstone River valley, climbed over Bozeman Pass, and then passed through the Gallatin Valley into the Jefferson River drainage and on to Virginia City.[16] The problems with this route were two-fold. First, the trail cut right through large tracts of land that had been designated as Indian Territory, and the Indians were not happy about masses of intruders passing through their hunting ground. Second, because the travel was all overland, it required wagon trains to travel self-sufficiently through most of that wilderness country from start to finish. There were no stop offs to recuperate or resupply in the event of a problem.

The military chose to protect the longer, yet safer, Missouri route. In part, this had to do with the logistics of transporting men, supplies, and animals into the remote corners of Montana. It also had to do with their respecting the rights of the Indians by treaty to the lands that the government had ceded to them. In the end, they were forced into an invasion of Indian lands because of the government's inability to control the flood of headstrong miners eager to get to the gold by whatever route.

Steamboat navigation up the Missouri was ideal for military transport. The river was open to the passage of boats from the time of ice break-up at the end of May until it froze in November. The main danger to boat

---

16 Brown, Mark H., *The Plainsmen of the Yellowstone: A History of the Yellowstone Basin* (Lincoln: University of Nebraska Press, 1961), 152-156.

travel on the river was becoming stranded on one of the constantly shifting sand bars. This left the boat open to attack by hostile Indians, or damaged the boat as the men tried to winch, pull, or pry it off. Another problem for a stranded boat in the late fall of the year was the danger of being trapped in the ice over the winter. In such a case, the steam engine was removed from the hulk and saved on shore while the hull of the boat was destroyed by the ice and torrential floods of the spring.

The ever inventive steamboat companies and their captains had developed a system of leg-like poles called a grasshopper which could be used at times to pull a stranded steamboat across a bar and back into the main channel. In the process, two pairs of pole-like hinged legs were extended ahead of the boat. As they were lowered, the tip of the leading pole penetrated the sand and mud of the river bottom. At this point, the angles of the two double booms would have appeared like the hind legs of a grasshopper, hence the name.

Unlike a true grasshopper, the leg-like poles were not used to push the steamboat but rather to pull it over the sandbar. This was done by using a system of ropes and winches which pulled on the embedded pole and thus allowed the boat to inch itself forward over the sandbar. When the leading poles were near the boat due to its advance over the bar, they were once again withdrawn from the sand and re-extended. By repeating this process, the boat could be gradually pulled forward off the sandbar over a period of hours or days.

On occasion, this type of difficult procedure also required the men of the boat to take a hawser ashore and lend a hand by pulling physically on the rope. Since the only alternative to not freeing oneself from a jam was to abandon the boat and walk to the next fort, everyone participated in these efforts to keep the steamboat moving. A walk of fifty to a hundred miles through hostile Indian Territory was not something anyone anticipated.

Because of the treacherous changing bars and rocks in the rapids after the spring floods on parts of the river, few steamboats were able to make it up to Fort Benton and return in one piece prior to 1866. As the gold rush got into full swing by the summer of 1867, the number of steamboats plying the river increased from four boats in 1866 to over thirty. More operators were willing to take the risk of losing a boat for the chance of an enormous profit.

A regular steamboat service was in full-swing by the fall of 1867. A down river trip from Fort Benton to Sioux City, Iowa, a journey of approximately a thousand miles, could be done in 14 days on a sternwheeler. This voyage was considerably more comfortable and safer than floating in an open manpowered mackinaw boat or traversing Indian Territory by horse and wagon for several months on the Bozeman Trail.

In the spring of 1867, most of the companies of the 13[th] Infantry were stationed at the headquarters in Fort Rice. With the military mandate to protect the Missouri River route more effectively, the soldiers and their companies were assigned to new posts along the Missouri at the strategic sites of Camp Cooke and Forts Berthold and Buford. From these basic postings, the 13[th] Infantry then expanded its influence by sending Company C to establish Ft. Shaw on the Sun River in Montana during the summer of 1867.[17] From this point, Company C also moved south and east to be stationed in the Gallatin Valley at Fort Ellis in an attempt to protect the final portion of the Bozeman Trail.[18]

Because of this, Richard Clow's stay at Ft. Shaw was probably broken up with a number of assignments away from the fort. One of the first of these details was to establish a secure mail route connecting the Missouri River to Helena. The unit was then assigned to Ft. Ellis where the 13[th] Infantry was given the nearly impossible job of stopping Indian cattle raiding on early Gallatin Valley ranchers. Another nearly impossible job for this small band of soldiers was protecting the increasingly numerous settlers and travelers coming through the Bridger Mountains after having traversed Indian Territory all the way from Fort Laramie in eastern Wyoming

---

[17] Huckabee, Rodger Lee *Camp Cooke: The First Army Post in Montana—Success and Failure on the Missouri (Boise State University Theses and Dissertations.* Paper 153, 2010), 50, http://scholarworks.boisestate.edu/td/153.
[18] Goe James B., Lt., "The Thirteenth Regiment of Infantry" *The Army of the United States: Historical Sketches of Staff and Line with Portraits of Generals-in-Chief* (1896):575-585, http:// www.history.mil/ books.

# Chapter 11—Fort Ellis Protecting the Bozeman Settlers

Fort Ellis was established and garrisoned on August 27, 1867 by the 13[th] Infantry in Montana.[19] The fort had similar purposes as those of Fort Shaw and Camp Cooke: controlling Indian movements and livestock raiding, as well as protecting the ever increasing numbers of invading miners and settlers moving into Montana Territory.

Gold was first discovered in Montana prior to the Civil War, and by 1867 many miners were using the Yellowstone River route from Laramie to reach the gold fields of Montana instead of going far north along the Missouri. This overland route, initially called the Montana Road,[20] was formally established in 1863 by John Bozeman, for whom it is named. In fact, the Lewis and Clark expedition records going over the same pass on their homeward journey some fifty years earlier. A nearby route known as Jim Bridger's Pass had also been blazed through the mountains that bear Bridger's name to connect the Yellowstone Valley with the Gallatin Valley on the west.

In addition to miners, the route also suited a number of hardy settlers and cattlemen who found the Gallatin Valley to have excellent soils and grass for farming.

---

[19] Brown, Mark H., *The Plainsmen of the Yellowstone: A History of the Yellowstone Basin* (Lincoln: University of Nebraska Press, 1961), 172.
[20] Ibid., 152-156

Following the historic 1866 cattle drive from Kansas to Montana along the Bozeman Trail, commerce steadily increased along this route. This first drive was done by a miner turned cattleman named Nelson Story. Within a few short years, sizable numbers of cattle and horses were grazing across the broad hills of this delightful valley surrounded by shining mountains.[21]

As the numbers of settlers and animals increased, the remaining buffalo in the Bozeman area decreased rapidly. The Indian tribes in search of game quickly honed in on the Whiteman's Buffalo as an easy alternative food supply. The cattle herds were numerous, scattered over wide open ranges, and often ripe for the taking with little or no opposition. An advantage to this handy food supply also rested in the fact that cattle could be herded back to camp without needing to be slaughtered out on the prairie.

In addition to cattle, herds of horses often accompanied the cattle and were used by the cowboys to ply their trade. These beasts supplied the plains Indians in the area with an alternate source of supply for riding animals. It was far easier to snag part of a cow hand's string of horses and not have to chase down wild mustangs roaming the rough country.

The Bridger, Flathead, and Bozeman passes, which enter the western side of the Gallatin Valley, gave Indian rustlers and horse thieves numerous alternative routes for getaways. Once across the Bridger Mountains to the north and east of the valley, stolen animals could easily disappear into the rugged Crazy Mountains or be moved into the miles of rolling broken plains beyond.

As a consequence, the early Indian engagements by the troops from Fort Ellis were often in remote areas along the eastern flanks of the Bridger Mountains. In some cases, the mounted infantry even pursued the Indians into the Shields River Basin, whose source is high in the Crazy Mountains to the north of the present day town of Livingston.

Two relatively serious skirmishes with Indians occurred in the Fort Ellis area during the time that Richard Clow was stationed with the 13[th] Infantry in western Montana. There is no mention of his name in the written descriptions of the fights, but members of his Company C of the 13[th] Infantry were in on both of these engagements.

---

[21] Ibid, 168-169.

The first of these occurred on March 12, 1869.[22] A party of 34 enlisted men and ten civilians under the command of Capt. Clift and Lt. Wann pursued a band of Indians who had taken a number of cattle. As they rode out, they came across the badly mutilated bodies of two cattle herders who had tried to protect their charges.

When the men had ridden over the pass and were in view of the Crazy Mountains, they sighted a band of Indians. This was probably in the vicinity of the Shields River and according to the military report near a "Sheep Mountain."[23]

In his report, the Captain describes the Indians as being either Sioux or Nez Perce, evidenced by their fine mounts. The Indians obviously outnumbered the soldiers and came down to the east side of the river, beckoning for the soldiers to come across a small shallow part of the river and approach.[24]

Realizing that any closer approach to this large band might put his men in jeopardy, Captain Clift refused to cross. As the Indians prepared to cross towards the soldiers, the troops withdrew and found higher ground from which to defend themselves against this superior force.

The Indians, mounted on superb steeds, crossed the river and opened fire on the soldiers as they were seeking cover. The broken ground afforded the Indians ample cover in their advance, thus forcing the soldiers to change positions repeatedly. By constantly moving through the rough ground, the soldiers were able to prevent themselves from being flanked and the Indians were required to cross open ground in order to follow them.

The Indians finally withdrew following almost four hours of shooting at the small band of soldiers. They left behind four dead men and two dead horses, while the soldiers suffered the loss of only one horse. Their other horses were completely exhausted after having been forced up and down the steep slopes repeatedly as the men maneuvered to new

---

[22] Goe James B., Lt., "The Thirteenth Regiment of Infantry" *The Army of the United States: Historical Sketches of Staff and Line with Portraits of Generals-in-Chief* (1896):575-585, http://www.history.mil/ books, 581.

[23] Ibid., 581.

[24] Ibid., 591.

positions. As night fell, the exhausted troops withdrew back over the pass, reaching the fort the following day. The cattle were never recovered. [25]

In another engagement from Fort Ellis Captain Clift again went out on patrol to investigate the disappearance of seven head of cattle and a horse. On this occasion, he was accompanied by a Lieutenant and some forty men. [26]

After following the trail of the rustlers northward for a number of miles along the western side of the Bridger Mountains, they came to Flathead Pass. Here the trail crossed the low pass and dropped into the head of Sixteen Mile Creek. At that point, they met up with a band of thirteen Indians and the stolen animals.

Two of the Indians immediately fled, escaping with the stolen horse. The remaining eleven men fled up a stony ridge on the back side of the Bridger Range. Upon reaching a diff area, they took shelter behind piles of rocks and returned fire on the pursuing soldiers.

The soldiers were unsuccessful in dislodging the Indians from their high refuge after nearly two hours of shooting. At this point, Captain Clift split his forces, sending the Lieutenant to assault the east side of the rocky slope. Taking the remainder of the men, the Captain then made his assault from the west. [27]

This tactic was successful in that that nine of the Indians were killed quickly and only two were able to escape. The record notes that Captain Clift himself showed extreme courage while engaging the Indians with his pistol. When his ammunition ran out, he turned to throwing rocks as a means of drawing fire and distracting the Indians from the other group of advancing men. Near the end of the battle, one soldier, Private Conry, was killed by final shots from the Indians. [28]

Clow's mention of having been at Camp Cooke and Fort Shaw gives no indication of the length of time he was at either of those particular postings. It is possible that he simply passed through them on the way down river to Fort Buford from Fort Ellis or was stationed at them for an extended period and never reached Fort Ellis. Unfortunately, unless other materials and information surface, this may never be known.

---

[25] Ibid., 581.
[26] Ibid., 582
[27] Ibid., 582.
[28] Ibid., 582.

It is clear that the men of the 13th Infantry at Fort Ellis had a number of combat skirmishes. They stood firmly against numbers considerably in excess of their own and scoured the countryside in search of those disrupting the safety of the settlers, ranchers, and miners. The concept of small fortified enclaves and the gradual movement onto the reservations was still the basic policy in dealing with the Indians. In a few short years, it would change drastically to one of all-out warfare and annihilation. That the 13th Infantry was able to keep large areas of land relatively safe from Indian attack, while opening new roads and territory, is a credit to the men of that unit.

As with most enlisted men until they attained a considerable rank or were written about by their commanding officers, Clow's travels at this time remain hazy. He is not cited for either disciplinary action or for special bravery and deeds at any of his postings in Montana. It is unfortunate that only one of his letters to his sister, Bertha Clow, still survives, as he had a flair for describing both his assignments and duties.

The members of the 13th Infantry worked through the summer at Fort Shaw erecting a set of adobe buildings with no surrounding stockade in 1867. This type of construction system, which the army tried to import from their experiences in the southwestern desert states, was ultimately a failure. Whereas the hot arid climate of the southwest dried adobe bricks to a cement-like hardness, there was too much rain and not enough heat to cure the Montana adobe before the freezes of winter.

The moisture which remained in the bricks at the end of the summer tended to freeze and expand with the extreme cold of winter. Repeated freezing and thawing caused the adobe bricks to break apart. Within a matter of a few years of repeatedly being exposed to the cold arctic freezes of winter and the heavy spring rains, the bricks disintegrated. With this type of treatment, the forts very literally just fell apart.

Fort Shaw was rebuilt with lumber a few years after Richard Clow's time there and expanded into a set of buildings including wooden barracks, officers' quarters, and a parade ground. At the peak of its development, Fort Shaw had ample accommodations for over 400 soldiers. By 1892, Fort Shaw was no longer a military fort and had been turned over to the Bureau of Indian Affairs. It became the government operated Fort Shaw Indian Industrial School with 300 students housed in some 20 buildings in that year.

# Chapter 12—Camp Cooke the Rats' Nest

Following his assignment at Fort Shaw, Richard Clow and a portion of Company C of the 13[th] Infantry were assigned briefly to Camp Cooke on the Missouri River, about a hundred miles east of Fort Benton, for continued construction work and patrols.

This small but interesting Missouri River fort fulfilled several missions. Primarily it was built with the idea of stopping any renegade Indians from escaping military pursuit by crossing the U.S. border into Canada. Secondarily it was to help protect the overland settlers from marauding Indians as they plied the land and water routes to and from Fort Benton. As a consequence, the men of this fort ranged across the wide open spaces of northern Montana both on foot and by horseback.[29]

The Milk River plains to the east were said to have some of the best buffalo hunting of the entire West, according to journalist Yellowstone Kelly.[30] Because of his hunting skill, Richard Clow undoubtedly would have visited this area to help supply the fort with meat.

The site of Camp Cooke was near the confluence of the Judith and Missouri Rivers. Because of the constantly shifting river sands at that

---

[29] Huckabee, Rodger Lee *Camp Cooke: The First Army Post in Montana – Success and Failure on the Missouri* (*Boise State University Theses and Dissertations, 2010*), 2-20, http://scholarworks.boisestate.edu/td/153.
[30] Quaife, M. M., ed., *Yellowstone Kelly* (Lincoln: University of Nebraska Press, 1973), 69-74.

point and a nearby section of rapids known as Drowned Man's Rapids, steamboats were obliged to slow their progress along this stretch of the river. Doing this, however, made them vulnerable to Indian attack from the shore.[31] [32]

There isn't any solid factual evidence as to the origin of the name Drowned Man's Rapids. This rough water site was noted by Lewis and Clark who named it Ash Rapids. In later years this name was changed to Drowned Man's Rapids due to the drowning of an unnamed miner who apparently fell overboard from a boat in the mid 1800's. According to legend, the miner was travelling down-river from the gold fields and after falling or being pushed overboard sank rapidly due to a substantial amount of gold carried in his money belt. This is probably a fictitious elaboration of what happened in the drowning case as many frontiersmen were unable to swim. Thus, a chance fall into deep rushing water would have meant rapid drowning in any case. Apparently the miner's body was never recovered, so, we are left with one more fable to add to the lore of the frontier trails.

By the time that Richard Clow reached Camp Cooke in 1868, the fort, with its stockade and adobe buildings, was already in a sad state of disrepair. Despite it being only about two years old, the construction techniques were the same failed adobe construction methods used at Fort Shaw. It was another case of an adobe fort along the Missouri which, as noted earlier, fell apart due to uncured adobe bricks which could not withstand the cycle of thawing and freezing during the colder months.[33]

Compounding the basic problems due to poor construction was a much more serious one: Camp Cooke had become infested with rats. In fact, by early 1869, the rats had virtually overrun the entire fort, eating the stores of food imported for livestock and men alike.[34]

---

[31] Kane, L. M., ed. And transl., *Military Life in Dakota: The Journal of Philippe Regis de Trobriand* (Lincoln: University of Nebraska Press, 1982), 44.

[32] Huckabee, Rodger Lee *Camp Cooke: The First Army Post in Montana – Success and Failure on the Missouri (Boise State University Theses and Dissertations.* Paper 153, 2010), 16, http://scholarworks.boisestate.edu/td/153.

[33] Huckabee, Rodger Lee *Camp Cooke The First Army Post in Montana – Success and Failure on the Missouri (Boise State University Theses and Dissertations.* Paper 153, 2010), 21-22, http://scholarworks.boisestate.edu/td/153.

[34] Ibid., 98.

True rats are not native to Montana. There is an animal known as a bushy-tailed wood rat commonly called a pack rat which lives throughout the Rocky Mountains. These are solitary animals that may live near buildings, but do not invade and colonize human construction. The Norwegian rat, on the other hand, has a long and intimate history with humans throughout the world. These creatures seem to have invaded this northern climate via steamboat travel.[35]

Because of the cold winters, rats can only have reached Montana and Camp Cooke and survived by coming up river from warmer states and jumping ship whenever the steamboats docked. Because of their prolific breeding rate, they quickly multiplied inside holes in the adobe mud walls of the fort. The walls then acted as insulation to protect them from the cold of the harsh winters which would ordinarily have killed them off.

In the process of foraging for food around the fort, the rats ruined both human and animal foodstuffs by eating portions and then urinating and defecating on the remainder. Other Montana towns and forts also suffered from these furry immigrants, but not to the same extent that they afflicted the isolated enclave of Camp Cooke.

On approximately May 22, 1869, the majority of the troops stationed at Camp Cook, including Richard Clow, were pulled out of the fort and departed for Fort Buford aboard the steamboat Deer Lodge. Approximately thirty men were left behind to man the isolated post.[36]

By the late summer of 1869, the rats had multiplied to such an extent that the adobe walls were crawling with them. An article in the *Helena Daily Herald* of April 3, 1869 had already made the fort the laughing stock of Montana with a portion of its headline stating "Ravenous River Rats Raiding Ruinously."[37]

It was reported that rats ran along the tops of the fort's walls at all times of the day and night. The fort was apparently in such poor condition and smelled so badly that the local Indians wouldn't even go near the buildings. At this point, in desperation, the remaining soldiers finally became so fed up that they declared all-out war on the furry invaders. The *Helena Daily Herald* of August 15, 1869 again reported on the dilapidated fort using the word "engagement" to describe the actions

---

[35] Ibid., 99.

[36] Ibid., 101

[37] Ibid., 99.

over a period of four days that were reported to have disposed of 1,400 of the creatures. Reports from the local Indians indicated that it sounded like a small war was going on inside the stockade. [38]

Apparently, as legend has it, the last day of the rat-killing campaign had just been completed when Major General Hancock arrived for an inspection of the conditions at the fort. Word had gotten out about the atrocious condition of the fort and had finally reached Fort Shaw over two hundred miles away. General Trobriand, the new commander of troops in the Montana District, had authorized the inspection. General Trobriand had recently been transferred from Fort Stevenson and had the task of cleaning up a previously mismanaged command.[39]

When Hancock arrived, he apparently found that the men had just completed their mini-war against the rats. Over a thousand dead animals were stacked in a giant pile on top of a wooded pyre. The men were in the process of cremating their dead opponents. The stench of the smoke from these burning animals was terrific and obviously affected the Colonel's report. The uncomplimentary comments by Hancock, concerning both the men and the fort, resulted in the closure of the fort by the end of the summer of 1869. It was abandoned and sold in 1870 and never reopened.[40] [41]

During its short lifespan, Camp Cooke was the site of a number of encounters between hostile Indians and members of the 13th Infantry.

There is no way for us to know if Richard Clow participated in some or all of these incidents, as his name is not mentioned in descriptions of actions written by the officers in charge. At the same time, it is very likely that he was involved in some of the engagements based on his letter from Fort Buford in 1869. Additionally, during the period from May 1867

---

[38] Ibid., 103.

[39] Kane, L. M., ed. And transl., *Military Life in Dakota The Journal of Philippe Regis de Trobriand* (Lincoln: University of Nebraska Press, 1982).

[40] Ibid., 44.

[41] Huckabee, Rodger Lee *Camp Cooke: The First Army Post in Montana – Success and Failure on the Missouri (Boise State University Theses and Dissertations.* Paper 153, 2010), 106, http://scholarworks.boisestate.edu/td/153.

through May 1869, Clow was assigned to the 13[th] Infantry in the upper Missouri River area of Montana so it makes his participation likely.

The most aggressive Indian attack on Camp Cooke took place on May 17, 1868. On this day, approximately 2,500 warriors surrounded and attacked the post at about 1:00 PM. The two companies of infantry returned fire immediately.[42][43]

Captain Auman of Company B realized that the fort's herd of horses was in a corral some 400 yards away from the stockade and would be run off if not rescued. Taking at least one other man, he managed to reach the herd of horses and open the corral to release them. Then, mounting several of the horses, the men drove them back and straight into the Camp Cooke corral which was under the protecting fire of the guns of the fort. During this time the Indians were within two hundred yards of the fort.[44][45]

Later, during the battle, several small cannons were put into action against the Indians causing them to keep their distance from the fort. In this part of the action, the same Captain Auman was wounded, shooting himself in the foot, as he was running to the powder magazine to procure a fuse knife.[46]

The total engagement lasted over six hours, during which time the officers' wives requested that they be placed inside the fort magazine. This was done with the intent that the magazine was to be set on fire and blown up in the event of the fort being taken. Although this would have meant a rather gruesome ending for the women, it was deemed to be

---

[42] Goe James B., Lt., "The Thirteenth Regiment of Infantry" *The Army of the United States: Historical Sketches of Staff and Line with Portraits of Generals-in-Chief* (1896):580, http:// www.history.mil/ books.
[43] Huckabee, Rodger Lee *Camp Cooke: The First Army Post in Montana – Success and Failure on the Missouri (Boise State University Theses and Dissertations.* Paper 153, 2010), 75-76, http://scholarworks.boisestate.edu/td/153.
[44] Goe James B., Lt., "The Thirteenth Regiment of Infantry" *The Army of the United States: Historical Sketches of Staff and Line with Portraits of Generals-in-Chief* (1896):580, http:// www.history.mil/ books.
[45] Huckabee, Rodger Lee *Camp Cooke: The First Army Post in Montana— Success and Failure on the Missouri (Boise State University Theses and Dissertations.* Paper 153, 2010), 76, http://scholarworks.boisestate.edu/td/153.
[46] Ibid., 76-77.

preferable to their falling into the hands of the hostiles.[47] Fortunately by the end of the day, the Indians withdrew and did not return.

Two days after this major engagement, members of Companies B and H of the 13[th] Infantry again engaged hostiles near the mouth of the Musselshell River in Dakota Territory. Then, on the 24[th] of May, they had another small skirmish, presumably with some of the same group that had been involved with the larger engagement. In neither case were any casualties reported.[48]

---

[47] Ibid., 77-78.

[48] Goe James B., Lt., "The Thirteenth Regiment of Infantry" *The Army of the United States: Historical Sketches of Staff and Line with Portraits of Generals-in-Chief*, (1896):581, http://www.history.mil/ books.

# Chapter 13—Fort Buford

Near the end of Richard Clow's second year of enlistment, the command of the Montana District and Fort Buford underwent a complete shake-up. As the Missouri River ice began to break up in May of 1869, General Trobriand reshuffled the companies of the 13[th] Infantry. Fort Buford, formerly considered as part of the Dakota Command, was transferred to the Montana Command.[49] It was following this change that First Sergeant Richard Clow appears to have been transferred to Fort Buford. He would have arrived at his new post on May 26, 1868 with the rest of Company C of the 13[th] Infantry aboard the steamship *Deer Lodge* to take charge of Fort Buford, Dakota.[50]

The problem causing the change in command at Fort Buford had been brewing for quite some time. The officers of the fort, including the commander, Lt. Col. Bowman, had a record of extreme drunkenness.[51] The notes and reports to General Trobriand and those sent by him from his headquarters at Fort Stevenson, indicate that all the officers were

---

[49] Goe James B., Lt., "The Thirteenth Regiment of Infantry" *The Army of the United States: Historical Sketches of Staff and Line with Portraits of Generals-in-Chief*, (1896):581, http://www.history.mil/books.

[50] Casler, Michael M., ed., *The Original Journal of Charles Larpenteur: My Travels to the Rocky Mountains between 1833 and 1872* (Lincoln: The Museum Association of the American Frontier, 2007), 216.

[51] Kane, L. M., ed. And transl., *Military Life in Dakota: The Journal of Philippe Regis de Trobriand* (Lincoln: University of Nebraska Press, 1982), 352-354.

preferring charges against each other. Trobriand refers to the whole lot of officers at Fort Buford as an "Augean Stable."[52] With this reference to the fifth of Hercules' twelve labors, he was clearly pointing to the need for Fort Buford to be thoroughly cleaned up.

According to various accounts, one of the incidents which brought the whole thing to a head was the 1868-69 New Year's Eve party for the officers of the fort. Apparently a Lt. Leonard in a drunken argument, threatened his superior officer, Captain Dickey with a pistol. The Lieutenant was put out of the officer's room and charges were drawn up against him and sent to Fort Stevenson for General Trobriand's action.[53]

The other incident was actually a series of weeks in which the commander of the fort, Col. Bowman was reported to be in a continuously drunken state. His inebriation, which included drunken orgies lasting ten to twelve days at a stretch, was such that he was unable to leave his quarters and papers had to be brought to him to sign in bed.[54]

Finally, official charges were documented and brought against Colonel Bowman by Major Little who was the next in command. These were to be sent by courier to General Trobriand at Fort Stevenson but were intercepted by Col. Bowman and destroyed. Fortunately, Major Little had the forethought to send a copy of the same charges to Adjutant General Greene of the Dakota Territory. These were forwarded to General Trobriand who, as a man of temperance took direct action.[55]

Subsequently, Lt. Col. Bowman was relieved from his duty and given a recommendation for immediate retirement. Three other officers of the fort, Captains Rankin, Wainwright and Piatt, were also relieved of their duties and referred to General Trobriand on similar charges with recommendations that they be discharged.[56]

At the same time that this smaller shuffle was occurring at Buford, major changes were taking place in the army as dictated from Washington. General Sherman had become the new general-in-chief of the military and a reduction in units was being mandated throughout the army. In this

---

[52] Ibid., 354.

[53] Ibid., 351.

[54] Kane, L. M., ed. And transl., *Military Life in Dakota: The Journal of Philippe Regis de Trobriand* (Lincoln: University of Nebraska Press, 1982), 352.

[55] Ibid., 352.

[56] Ibid., 353.

reorganization, many units were to be combined, others would be discontinued, and twenty regiments would be phased out.[57]

One of the units to be changed was the 31st Infantry (not to be confused with the 13th Infantry) which had been at Fort Buford and would now be combined with the 22nd Infantry and moved elsewhere. As a consequence, the men of the 13th Infantry who had been farther up the Missouri River in Montana, would now be assigned to Fort Buford as the regiment in charge of that post. In this same administrative move, General Trobriand was reassigned from Fort Stevenson on the Dakota Plains to Fort Shaw on the Sun River in Montana.[58]

In that order, Fort Buford was transferred into the District of Montana from the Dakotas. Thus, for the final year of his duty in the military, Richard Clow, First Sergeant of Company C, 13th Regiment of Infantry was technically still assigned to duty in Montana. He arrived at Buford on Wednesday, May 26, 1869 with the other members of the 13th to relieve the 31st Infantry of their duties.

The three new companies of the 13th Infantry found Fort Buford to be somewhat in disrepair upon their arrival, not unlike the problems they had seen at Camp Cooke and Fort Shaw. In addition to the lack of maintenance due to the malfeasance of the officers commanding the fort, they found once again the same adobe construction that was falling apart. Because the original construction of the walls had taken place in 1866, the weathering was as bad as or worse than had taken place at other forts with this type of construction.[59]

Fortunately, the men had some time to make repairs over the summer before winter would once again turn the walls of the barracks into ice cubes. Some of the materials used in the original construction included planks, poles, and logs hauled down river from the old Fort Union fur trading post only ten miles away.[60] [61] These older wooden materials plus

---

[57] Ibid., 371.

[58] Ibid., 367-368.

[59] Remele, Larry, ed., *Fort Buford and the Military Frontier on the Northern Plains 1850-1900* (Bismarck: State Historical Society of North Dakota, 1987), 47-48.

[60] Ibid., 44.

[61] Brown, Mark H., *The Plainsmen of the Yellowstone: A History of the Yellowstone Basin* (Lincoln, University of Nebraska Press, 1961), 85.

new sawn planks would have aided the men in patching up the fort over the summer.

The history of the garrisoning of Fort Buford prior to 1869 is one complicated by the numbers of men available for manning the fort at any one time, as well as by the rotation of men out of the military as they completed their terms of service. Initially the fort had been built by Company C of the 13th Infantry, which arrived in June 1866, one year after the end of the Civil War.[62] They had used many of old Fort Union's timbers to construct the first stockade and also to act as reinforcement for the adobe walls of the single story officer's quarters and enlisted men's barracks. Planks had also been sawn from cottonwoods, which at that time were still plentiful along the banks of the Missouri.

In 1867, the garrison at Fort Buford was turned over to the 31st Infantry and the 13th Infantry then moved up into Montana to build Fort Shaw, Fort Ellis, and Camp Cooke. The new units at Fort Buford started the first expansion of the fort. This was to accommodate the anticipated larger body of soldiers to protect this portion of the route to the Montana Gold Fields. The 31st Infantry soldiers departed Fort Buford in May of 1869 at the change in command and were subsequently consolidated with the 22nd Infantry. Following this, the 13th Infantry once again took over full command of the fort.[63]

For the next twelve months, beginning in May of 1869 through May 1870, the garrison at Buford was completely made up of members of the 13th Infantry, Companies C, E, and H. The actual numbers of soldiers varied between 89 and 193 enlisted men, depending on recruits and departures due to the completion of tours of duty. At one time during that summer, the commander, Lt. Col. Morrow, actually anticipated that he would have no more than twenty nine enlisted men by the beginning of 1870. Fortunately, eighty-six new recruits arrived but unfortunately had no rifles. Thus for a time, the fort had insufficient arms to properly carry

---

[62] Remele, Larry, ed., *Fort Buford and the Military Frontier on the Northern Plains 1850-1900* (Bismarck: State Historical Society of North Dakota 1987), 44.

[63] Ibid., 44.

out the functions of guard duty and still have a protecting force for itself.[64]

At one point, the shortage of soldiers was so great that Morrow informed his superiors that only sixty men remained for actual military action after the regular work details were filled. Clearly these numbers were insufficient to carry out the full mission of the fort.[65]

Fort Buford had been the center of serious Indian raids and harassment for more than a year by this time. The reduction in force made them much more liable to attack. Sitting Bull's warriors were fully aware that there were only limited numbers of soldiers for the guarding of hay wagons and horses and the cutting and hauling of wood.

Even today it can be seen how the terrain around Fort Buford (fig. 18) made it an ideal target for Indian attack. Along the banks of the Missouri are the remains of the dense thickets of brush and willows, which could conceal quite large bands of men. To the north of the fort, away from the river, are relatively flat plains. These plains butt up against foothills with arroyos and gullies that could also conceal ambushers. The present day tourist can see that while the fort proper was a defensible position, soldiers or civilians travelling through the surrounding countryside in 1869 would be liable to attack.

The distance to Indian Territory in 1869 was only a few hundred yards from the fort. Early photos show that directly across the Missouri, on the south bank, was a large Sioux encampment. With this in mind, one can well understand the tension and worry about attack that prevailed throughout the fort during this period. Indians from several tribal groups came to the fort on a regular basis to trade and buy supplies from the three trading post which were just outside the actual fort proper. Thus there was the constant knowledge that hostile Indians could be within those groups of traders and be using their cover to observe and plan further attacks.[66]

During the winter of 1868-69, reports noted that the soldiers were virtual prisoners inside their own fort. They were unable to venture out beyond the walls for wood or water due to continuous hostile activity.

---

[64] Ibid.,46.

[65] Ibid., 46.

[66] Kane, L. M., ed. And transl., *Military Life in Dakota: The Journal of Philippe Regis de Trobriand* (Lincoln: University of Nebraska Press, 1982), 358-359.

Fortunately, the stockade had a twenty-foot-deep well inside and a good supply of wood on hand to last the winter. The solid stockade and the fort's cannon were the two features that probably saved Fort Buford from being overrun by a large war party during these early years of its existence.[67][68]

A visit to the present-day site of Fort Buford helps the reader understand the exponential growth of this fort. Over the seven year period from 1866 to 1873, the fort expanded rapidly from its original rustic square stockade to become a model fort with a full parade ground.

By 1873, the ten original inner buildings, which had two corner bastion towers surrounded by a stockade of cottonwood posts, had been fully replaced. The original walls, which extended some 360 feet on each side with the inner buildings, and the adobe barracks, had been demolished. The fort had grown in a series of incremental jumps. By the end of 1868, it was a new rectangle some 600 ft. by 1100 ft. on a side with six barracks. Ultimately by 1872, it had the approximate shape of a square with walls, parade grounds, barracks, houses, and stables extending about 2000 ft. on a side.[69]

During the next seven year period, the garrison itself grew from barely a hundred men to nearly a thousand. By 1872, the garrison included actual cavalry units and was deemed so powerful that a stockade was no longer needed to deter Indian attack. The wooden barracks complex that housed only infantry units covered an area that was almost equal to the area of the entire original fort. There were eighteen sets of officers' quarters, a library, hospital, guardhouse, and magazine. When the fort was officially abandoned by the military on October 1, 1895, it had seen many more

---

[67] Athearn, Robert G., *Forts of the Upper Missouri* (Lincoln: University of Nebraska Press, 1967), 243-246.

[68] Remele, Larry, ed., *Fort Buford and the Military Frontier on the Northern Plains1850-1900* (Bismarck: State Historical Society of North Dakota, 1987), 43.

[69] Remele, Larry, ed., *Fort Buford and the Military Frontier on the Northern Plains1850-1900* (Bismarck: State Historical Society of North Dakota, 1987), 48, 70-75.

changes. Truly, it was a far cry from the fort in which 1st Sergeant Richard Clow spent the summer and winter of 1869—1870.[70]

---

[70] Ibid., 70-75.

# Chapter 14—Sitting Bull Near Fort Buford

One cannot write about Fort Buford without including a section about Sitting Bull, the main leader of the hostile Sioux forces that lived in and controlled all of the lands surrounding Fort Buford. In 1869, this land was still definitely Indian Territory. It had not been ceded by the Indians to the encroaching white population and was still regarded by both sides of what was to become a decisive conflict as being Indian land. Sitting Bull, as a guerrilla warrior and leader of his own people, was destined to play a major role in the eventual development and growth of Fort Buford itself.

Sitting Bull was also known by the name of Lame Bull due to an old wound that made him limp. As a key Indian leader, he is often described as a stocky, well-built man who was well known for being a great story teller. He was also reckoned to be a highly intelligent natural military strategist. Being somewhat of a linguist, he spoke English and some smattering of French, as well as the language of the nearby Assiniboine tribes. Additionally, he was classed as being a notorious liar and had reputation for being extremely cruel. This latter attribute may have been overstated as the lore of his prowess grew to legendary proportions in the years following the Custer Massacre. In at least one instance he was known to have shown compassion and actually prevented his band of warriors from killing three sleeping whites on the Dakota prairies in 1873.[71]

Other authors praise him for his great skill as a warrior and for having a good-natured sense of humor. He was said to be a phenomenal rider with great endurance for the hunt or chase. His quality of fearlessness surely applies to his raids on Fort Buford, as these were at times of an almost audacious nature. In later years he was said to be one of the most powerful medicine men of the Sioux, preparing warriors for battle but no longer participating in battle.[72] [73]

There is no complete documentary list of Sitting Bull's exploits in the Fort Buford area. The attacks mentioned in Richard Clow's letter would appear to have been by a substantially large enough force to indicate that a leader of Sitting Bull's capacity was with them. Most of the attributions of his involvement in attacks were due to Indian scouts actually identifying him in a mass of warriors. Additionally, the local Indian rumor mill would often report that he was responsible for a particular attack after the fact.

The first attack attributed to Sitting Bull in the Fort Buford area occurred in the early winter of 1866, soon after the construction of the fort. In the fall of that year, Captain Rankin reported that there were more than ten Sioux Indian camps along the banks of the Missouri River near the fort and that an attack appeared to be imminent. This apparently was due to the breakdown of talks with the Army over safe passage routes through Indian Territory at Fort Laramie.[74]

At Buford, the first major attacks commenced in November 1866 and came to a head on December 21 with a surprise attack on the infrastructure of the fort. On that day a series of raids captured both the saw mill and icehouse where parts were stolen and a pump destroyed.

---

[71] Johnson, W. Fletcher: *Life of Sitting Bull and History of the Indian War of 1890-91: The Red Record of the Sioux* (New York: Edgewood Publishing, 1891), 40-64.

[72] Ibid., 4-64.

[73] Kane, L. M., ed. And transl., *Military Life in Dakota: The Journal of Philippe Regis de Trobriand* (Lincoln, University of Nebraska Press, 1982), 289.

[74] Rankin, William G., Capt., "Letter from Fort Buford" in Dingle, Susan, ed., At the Confluence: Now and Then: Papers presented at the Symposium Held in Williston, N.D., June 29. 2002 (Bismarck: State Historical Society of North Dakota, 2003), 90.

Then, for the next two or three days, the raiders appear to have had almost complete run of the area outside the fort, holding the soldiers prisoner in their own fort because of their large numbers.[75]

At the point when the attackers began firing into the fort and actually staged a war dance in the captured fort saw mill in a show of contempt for the soldiers, Captain Rankin turned his two cannon on the mill and counterattacked, driving them off. Following this, the warriors burned all the haystacks of the fort and retreated back to the other side of the Missouri after having lost only one member of their raiding party.[76][77]

During the following month, repeated raids prevented the soldiers from collecting wood and water outside the fort or receiving mail. They were fortunate to have had a good stock of wood, but were required to dig a well in order to keep supplied with water. The excavators of the well were a group of miners passing through the area and as luck would have it, they struck gold-bearing sand at about twenty feet deep, yielding about ten cents of color for every quart of dirt extracted.[78][79]

During this period rumors about the condition and safety of the troops and families were so rampant that in early references, books such as *Sitting Bull and the Indian War*, it was printed as fact that Captain Rankin had actually shot his wife to prevent her falling into the hands of the Sioux.[80][81]

---

[75] Athearn, Robert G., *Forts of the Upper Missouri* (Lincoln: University of Nebraska Press, 1967), 232.

[76] Waldo, Edna LaMoore, *Dakota* (Caldwell: The Claxton Printers Ltd., 1936), 110.

[77] Remele, Larry, ed., *Fort Buford and the Military Frontier on the Northern Plains 1850-1900* (Bismarck: State Historical Society of North Dakota, 1987), 30, 43.

[78] Remele, Larry, ed., *Fort Buford and the Military Frontier on the Northern Plains: 1850-1900* (Bismarck: State Historical Society of North Dakota, 1987), 43.

[79] Athearn, Robert G., *Forts of the Upper Missouri* (Lincoln: University of Nebraska Press, 1967), 233.

[80] Johnson, W. Fletcher, *Life of Sitting Bull and History of the Indian War of 1890-91: The Red Record of the Sioux* (New York: Edgewood Publishing, 1891), 60.

Sitting Bull's warriors were not able to keep up their heavy pressure on Fort Buford after the river reopened in the spring of 1867. Three new companies of the 13th Infantry arrived in May and work on expanding the fort commenced in earnest throughout the summer. Despite the increased troop strength, attacks on unwary civilians or small groups of soldiers at work or while hunting continued as Indians harassed the Buford surroundings.[82]

Throughout the following year of 1868 and into the next, hostilities continued with several more serious incidents, including the loss by the army of some 200—250 head of cattle which were driven off by Sitting Bull's warriors. Additionally there were further attacks on work details, hunting parties, and travelers throughout the area.[83] [84]

The cattle raid was a masterpiece of planning and execution on the part of the Indians. It had the mark of Sitting Bull all over it and the chief probably reveled in his success for months afterwards. The report sent to General Trobriand at Fort Stevenson noted that 200 head of the total fort cattle herd of some 250 animals were stolen on the afternoon of August 20, 1868.[85] [86] In the description it was noted that the raid began with a band of over one hundred warriors making an abrupt charge at the cattle herd from several of the deep ravines that came out of the badland slopes

---

[81] Waldo, Edna LaMoore, *Dakota* (Caldwell: The Claxton Printers Ltd., 1936), 118.

[82] Remele, Larry, ed., *Fort Buford and the Military Frontier on the Northern Plains: 1850-1900* (Bismarck: State Historical Society of North Dakota, 1987), 44.

[83] Coues, Elliott, ed., *Forty Years a Fur Trader on the Upper Missouri: The Personal Narrative of Charles Larpenteur, 1833-1872* (Minneapolis: Ross and Haines, Inc, 1962), 390.

[84] Harvey, Mark, "Securing the Confluence: A Portrait of Fort Buford, 1866 to 1895," in Dingle, Susan, ed., At the Confluence: Now and Then: Papers presented at the Symposium Held in Williston, N.D., June 29. 2002 (Bismarck: State Historical Society of North Dakota, 2003), 36.

[85] Kane, L. M., ed. And transl., *Military Life in Dakota: The Journal of Philippe Regis de Trobriand* (Lincoln, University of Nebraska Press, 1982), 331.

[86] Casler, Michael M., ed., *The Original Journal of Charles Larpenteur: My Travels to the Rocky Mountains between 1833 and 1872* (Lincoln: The Museum Association of the American Frontier, 2007), 205.

not far from Fort Buford. As they raced towards the herd, the twenty mounted infantrymen and herdsmen made every effort to turn the herd towards the safety of the fort and to get them whipped into a run.[87]

As the warriors gained on them, the herdsmen were forced to turn and confront their enemy with returned rifle fire. At that point they had the herd moving in the right direction and should have been able to repel the warriors long enough to save the herd, except for the appearance of another band of warriors from the opposite direction.[88]

These warriors had come out of another set of ravines and were positioned between the herd and the fort. This band, also consisting of one hundred or so warriors, was armed with blankets and noise makers in addition to their rifles. They swung their noise makers as they charged and discharged their rifles over the heads of the herd. The commotion was such that the herd turned completely and stampeded in the opposite direction. The fear-crazed beasts charged right through and past the herdsmen who had halted to repel the force to their rear. A small number of yelling Indians continued right past them and continued to haze the beasts on into the hills.[89]

At this point, the herdsmen found themselves trapped between two groups of over one hundred Indians each. The men were surrounded by club-swinging Indians, all attempting to kill or count coup and gain prestige by touching their living foe. In their desperate situation, the soldiers could do nothing about the escaping animals and had to concentrate on fighting their way back towards the fort from whence infantrymen were streaming on the double.[90]

When the Indians saw the reinforcements, they dispersed and let the herdsmen through to the fort. Then they raced after the main herd, shooting any straggling animals as they rode past. The hoard of yelling Indians hazed the main body of the herd along for several miles while the men inside the fort frantically dropped their construction tools, grabbed their weapons, saddled up, and gave chase.[91]

---

[87] Kane, L. M., ed. And transl., *Military Life in Dakota: The Journal of Philippe Regis de Trobriand* (Lincoln, University of Nebraska Press, 1982), 331.

[88] Ibid., 331.

[89] Ibid., 331.

[90] Ibid., 331-332.

[91] Ibid., 332.

A body of mounted infantry followed at a gallop within a few minutes and upon catching up with the herd, engaged the Indians in a wild running skirmish for several miles. At this point, the heavier army mounts began to play out from the wild chase. The mounted infantrymen then fell off the chase and concentrated on gathering the remaining strays and herding them back to the fort for the night.[92]

By the next day, when a full mounted force could be readied to follow up on the herd, it had already been moved south of the Missouri and deep into Indian country. Not one animal was recovered on this expedition. In a single raid, the entire meat supply of the fort, designed to last through the winter months, had been cut to a size that would scarcely last until November.[93]

In addition to the loss of cattle, the men at the fort were lucky to get off with only three men killed and three seriously wounded. Several others were injured from the blows of war clubs and it was reported that Lt. Cusick was saved from death by one of his men who threw himself into the fray when the Lieutenant was grappling with several Indians. That man subsequently died of his wounds.[94] [95] [96]

Despite Sitting Bull's successes on a small scale, on the larger scale his force was continually dwindling as more and more tribes moved onto reservations. In the late fall of 1868, Chief Red Cloud signed a peace treaty with the U.S. that would allow safe passage of whites through Indian Territory. This treaty left Sitting Bull's followers as pariahs with even some of their own people.[97]

---

[92] Ibid., 333.

[93] Ibid., 333.

[94] Ibid., 332.

[95] Coues, Elliott, ed., *Forty Years a Fur Trader on the Upper Missouri: The Personal Narrative of Charles Larpenteur, 1833-1872* (Minneapolis: Ross and Haines, Inc, 1962), 391.

[96] Casler, Michael M., ed., *The Original Journal of Charles Larpenteur: My Travels to the Rocky Mountains between 1833 and 1872* (Lincoln: The Museum Association of the American Frontier, 2007), 205.

[97] Remele, Larry, ed., *Fort Buford and the Military Frontier on the Northern Plains: 1850-1900* (Bismarck: State Historical Society of North Dakota, 1987), 45.

Sitting Bull and his warriors were angered by the treaty and stepped up their attacks in the Fort Buford area. Thus even during the fierce cold of midwinter in 1869, there were further attacks on the fort. These were directed at every aspect of the fort: buildings, cattle, civilians, and the soldiers. Nothing was safe outside the fort.[98]

Any man who let down his guard for even the shortest period of time was at risk of violent death. These levels of attack continued throughout 1869 and into early 1870. During this period the garrison of the fort was particularly low in numbers and soldiers were unavailable to do anything other than guard their own backs and the fort.

By 1870, change was in the wind as far as the reinforcements coming to Fort Buford. Additional companies of infantry were assigned to the fort to better confront Sitting Bull's constant threats. By the time of the departure of the 13[th] Infantry from Fort Buford in April 1870, attacks on the fort itself had dropped off completely.

Sitting Bull seems to have recognized that the newly constructed walls and expansion of buildings at Fort Buford made it much more impregnable to any direct assault. As a consequence, he directed his hostilities against the railroad surveying parties, woodcutters, and civilians who were away from the fort. This former group was especially hated by the Sioux as they realized that the advent of the railroad would spell an end to not only the buffalo, but to their nomadic way of life.[99]

Sitting Bull moved his actions away from Fort Buford around 1874 to concentrate more on the stream of settlers coming across the Dakota and Montana plains. He also attacked other Sioux clans in hopes of getting some of them to leave the reservations and join his band.

Following the 1876 success of Sitting Bull's warriors, along with those of Gall and Crazy Horse against Custer's men at the Little Big Horn, the military pressure against the Indian tribes increased substantially. The tribes scattered and Sitting Bull sought refuge in Canada as the other warring tribal groups were forced to surrender through continual troop pursuit and harassment during the winter of 1876-1877.[100]

---

[98] *Ibid., 46.*

[99] Johnson, W. Fletcher, *Life of Sitting Bull and History of the Indian War of 1890-91: The Red Record of the Sioux* (New York: Edgewood Publishing, 1891), 64.

[100] Ibid., 139.

During this same time, General Hazen and his soldiers at Fort Buford were the key to getting supplies out to the far-flung units of soldiers fighting the winter campaign under Generals Miles and Crook. Without a constant flow of food, these soldiers could not have kept up with the light traveling Indian villages. [101]

Sitting Bull's final years play out as a tragedy for a man who had been such an independent and strong leader of his people. Right up to the last year of his campaign, his charisma could still attract large numbers of warriors to his cause. His force of personality motivated his warriors to deeds of great heroism in battle. With the mind of a military leader, he recognized the whites' intent to eventually dominate all of Indian Territory and worked to prevent that takeover. Although his ultimate goal was not achieved, his campaign prevented the domination of the Northern Plains by whites for almost fifteen years.

When Sitting Bull retreated into Canada, he did so in the hopes of finding a new and permanent home for his people. This of course did not happen. His move took his people away from the harassment by troops, but put them in a place where they slowly starved. Already the Northern Plains had been depleted of their life-sustaining herds of deer, antelope, and buffalo, and the nomadic hunter-gatherer way of life on the plains was coming to a close. With insufficient game to sustain his people, Sitting Bull finally listened to his daughter's pleas for surrender. [102]

In the spring of 1881, after all the other Indian leaders had surrendered in the field, Sitting Bull was finally persuaded to bring his last remaining supporters back into the United States. In an ironic ending, on July 19, 1881, fifteen years after he had become a scourge to the travelers, soldiers, and settlers crossing this very section of the Dakota plains, Sitting Bull officially surrendered at Fort Buford. [103]

In attempting to understand the anger and concerns of Sitting Bull and other Indian leaders concerning the treatment of their peoples and the destruction of their way of life on the northern plains, we set the stage for

---

[101] Remele, Larry, ed., *Fort Buford and the Military Frontier on the Northern Plains 1850-1900* (Bismarck: State Historical Society of North Dakota, 1987), 50-51.
[102] Ibid., 53.
[103] Ibid., 54.

a better understanding of Richard Clow's next letter which was written to his sister Bertha in 1869.

# Chapter 15—A Letter from Indian Country

*Fort Buford D.T.*
*September 28th 1869.*
*Dear Sister Bertha,*

*I received your letter dated June 20th and had to laugh when I read about you receiving mine a year ago.  I am almost sure that that is not the last one, but there is a great deal of trouble with the mail out here as you can see, for I only received your letter yesterday.*

*I am never sick, so you are mistaken about that, but my life has some slight events such as going on a Buffalo hunt or some little promotion, or on an Indian scare, all of which I have been lucky enough to enjoy.*

*I sent my discharge of claim to Father,  as even if I did not get the whole of it, it had already been given him by an old English law and,  supposing the rest to have done the same,  I did so also,  but at the same time,  I like to see Father have it, and we should have given him some if we had got it all,  and I think it is best as far as I'm concerned that he has got it, for when we get money in our hand we hate to give it up. He was cross with me for spending my bounty when I came home from the war,  and said I should have put it where I could derive some benefit[sic] from it,   now is my time,  I will see where he puts his.*

*Well, Berth, I wish you could see me now, I am the prettiest [sic] thing you ever saw, with a black whisker and such a nice white face. Well I won't have any trouble to get married when I come home anyhow.  I want to know if you have got that girl picked out for me yet and if not,  you had better get about it, for I am coming very soon now, remember the 26th of April.*

# Rough Enough

*We had four men killed here the other day, they left the post and went two miles in a wagon and the Indians came on them on the open prairie and killed them all, but not without a loss for the men were armed with sixteen shooters and one man had an eighteen shooter. This man wore a red shirt, and when the Indians came with a rush they wounded his three companions, but he would not leave them (although they were helpless) but stood there and gave them his assistance by killing ten, and wounding twenty of the Indians, but at last they fixed him and then fired fourteen arrows into him and scalped them all and I saw them in this condition, and it made me think of the time when I and two others killed four of them and I only wished it had been ten times four.*

*The same day that they killed our men, they attacked the hay party of this post and one young fellow of E. Company (a particular friend of mine), named Waterhouse showed the greatest bravery I ever heard of, fighting back eighteen of them while the men were getting the mules unhitched from the mowing machines. He is a very quiet fellow and I would almost lay down my life for him. He has been promoted to Sergeant for that act and his name has been sent to Washington, he may be better paid in the course of time.*

*In speaking of homesickness, I don't get that, but I have a continual feeling as if I would like to be near somebody that thought something of me, and I could look at and love, and this yearning for something, I don't know what, makes me very quiet sometimes, even sorrowfull[sic] but I shake it off and start again.*

*I have plenty of time to think no for I am 1st Sergt [sic]. of the Company and have a room to myself with not much to do but dress up in full uniform and go on guardmount[sic], and call my Roll at the proper hours, it is a gay life if it were in the world, but out here it isn't much, but I can make out anywhere.*

*You want to know if I get any strawberrys [sic], but I don't as we don't have them here. I had one peach, but no other fruit (except dried) in my three years. You must remember this is no farming country, there is nothing here except barren plains and no timber except on the river and that is cotton wood, it is something like Poplar, the leaves are much the same and the wood is poor unless very dry.*

*We are at Fort Buford now and will be likely to stay here the rest of my time. Your letter went to Fort Shaw and then to Camp Cook and then here, it followed me just as I went.*

*Bertha, I have no more to say at present only that you need not put my rank on the outside of the letters you send me as a man may be Sergt.[sic] today and Pvt. tomorrow according to his deeds. You may think this strange, but it is me, so good bye, Berth from the same old boy.*

*Richard Clow*

*Richard H. McBee Jr.*

*Fort Buford D.T.*
*Oh! Bertha give my respects to Mrs. Pitman.*

By the time Richard Clow wrote this letter, he would already have been at Fort Buford for nearly five months, having arrived in late May of 1869. As the 1[st] Sergeant at the fort, he was immersed in his daily duties of assigning and supervising details, drilling the men to keep them fit for duty in the field, and acting as advisor and counselor to the less experienced enlisted men under his command.

First Sergeant Clow appears to have had quite a bit of leisure time, which allowed him to go out hunting. A contemporary of Clow's, Luther (Yellowstone) Kelly, notes that in the vicinity of Fort Buford there were large numbers of buffalo, antelope, and elk.[104] Given that Richard Clow was described by trader Charles Larpenteur as a "renowned hunter,"[105] it is likely that Clow was out hunting whenever the opportunity presented itself. In that Kelly was in the Fort Buford vicinity several times during this period, it would not be at all surprising if Dick Clow, Kelly, and another hunter named "Longhair Smith" didn't hunt together on occasion.[106]

Clow's letter mentions two specifically documented confrontations between hostile Indians and civilians or soldiers. The main incident—the killing of the four men by a band of nearly two hundred warriors—appears to have been a deliberate ambush set to attack the hay-cutting party that was due to go out from the fort later in the day. In the second attack, it was probably the same war party (or more likely a portion of it) with the warriors taking advantage of an opportunistic situation.[107] [108]

---

[104] Keenan, Jerry, *The life of Yellowstone Kelly* (Albuquerque: University of New Mexico Press, 2006), 32.

[105] Casler, Michael M., ed., *The Original Journal of Charles Larpenteur: My Travels to the Rocky Mountains between 1833 and 1872* (Lincoln: The Museum Association of the American Frontier, 2007), 225.

[106] Keenan, Jerry, *The life of Yellowstone Kelly* (Albuquerque: University of New Mexico Press, 2006), 39.

[107] Hesser, Genia, Letter by author, Fort Buford State Historical Site, N. D., April 21, 2006, 1-2.

The full description of the first incident as it was worked out by the soldiers, who rode out to assist, appears to be as follows. The four men were transient civilian residents of the fort who had come down from Fort Peck a few days before. They were planning on going out to the first hay fields near the Little Muddy River, about eight miles from Fort Buford, to help cut hay.[109] Thus it is likely that they could have been accompanied by a larger group of men if they had only been a bit more patient. Captain Moffit's hay crew had come in from the fields and was unloading hay wagons. According to the records, Captain Moffit himself had advised them to stay and go out with the larger hay group that would be leaving when they had finished unloading.[110] The four men had been warned of the dangers and should have known about precautions against attacks, since they had been as far north as Fort Peck and recently crossed a large expanse of hostile territory to get to Fort Buford.

Being impatient, the four of them set off in a double-seated wagon with one horse trailing behind on a lead. One man, an Italian reported to be named Ranaldo by one source, (the tombstone actually says "Joseph Araldo") was (fig. 21) reportedly wearing a red shirt. According to their tombstones at Fort Buford, the other three men were named James MacLane, Adam Jones, and Peter Dugan. According to another source, these last three men were simply named: Dugan, McLean, and "Dutch" Adams.[111] (One wonders if this "Dutch" is the same man who was associated with Yellowstone Kelly as a courier from Fort Buford at an earlier date).[112] [113]

---

108 Innes, Ben, *Interments at Fort Buford 18996 to 1895,* (Fort Buford: 6th Infantry Reg. Assn. Publ., 1996), 11.12.

109 Ibid., 11.

110 Hesser, Genia, Letter by author, Fort Buford State Historical Site, N. D., April 21, 2006, 1-2.

111 Hesser, Genia, Letter by author, Fort Buford State Historical Site, N. D., April 21, 2006. 1-2.

112 Quaife, M. M., ed., *Yellowstone Kelly* (Lincoln: University of Nebraska Press, 1973), 40.

113 Keenan, Jerry, *The life of Yellowstone Kelly* (Albuquerque: University of New Mexico Press, 2006), 33.

When the four men were approximately a mile-and-a-half from the fort, yet still within sight of the flag, they were ambushed by between one and two hundred Indians who were apparently waiting for all of Moffit's crew to come down the road. [114] [115]

The warriors were well-concealed in a narrow, dry creek bed that cut through one of the bluffs and therefore were invisible to the approaching men until they sprang from ambush. They were a well-armed war party with rifles, bows, and lances, and were stripped down to travel 'light' for the war path. [116] [117]

The first volleys of rifle fire killed all three of the horses instantly. The blood trails on the ground indicated that several members of the hapless small band of white men were wounded when they left the wagon. They made a wild dash to a buffalo wallow several hundred yards away. Here they hoped to find sufficient cover to hold off their attackers until help arrived from the fort. [118]

The four men had repeating rifles which gave them the advantage of superior firepower. But despite this slight advantage, there were obviously too many warriors pitted against them. In addition, the warriors were coming at top speed on horseback and could easily overrun the low-profile defenses of the buffalo wallow. Within thirty minutes, all four men were dead with the Italian, Joseph Araldo (Ranaldo), being the last to fall. [119]

By the time the first assistance arrived, the men were dead, scalped, and mutilated. Their bodies were taken back to the fort where the surgeon noted that he removed thirteen arrows from one single man. The rumors that came back to the fort over the following days indicated that at least

---

[114] Innes, Ben, *Interments at Fort Buford 18996 to 1895,* (Fort Buford: 6th Infantry Reg. Assn. Publ., 1996), 11.

[115] Hesser, Genia, Letter by author, Fort Buford State Historical Site, N. D., April 21, 2006. 1-2.

[116] Ibid., 1-2.

[117] Innes, Ben, *Interments at Fort Buford 18996 to 1895* (Fort Buford: 6th Infantry Reg. Assn. Publ., 1996), 11.

[118] Innes, Ben, *Interments at Fort Buford 18996 to 1895* (Fort Buford: 6th Infantry Reg. Assn. Publ., 1996), 11.

[119] Ibid., 11.

ten warriors died of wounds, although only one man's body was left behind as the warriors fled from the belated rescue attempt.[120]

The four men were buried in the fort cemetery where their tombstones can still be seen by visitors to the reconstructed fort (figs. 20, 21, 22, 23).

Apparently this same band of warriors, or a smaller cohort of them, circled around to another hay party that was working at Painted Creek. This is the site of Clow's second description of an attack which was successfully repelled by his friend Waterhouse who again probably had a repeating rifle for defense. [121]

Clow's descriptions give us a very personal perspective on the state of security on the Northern Plains during this time. There were obviously some very good reasons for travelers to only go outside a fort in the company of a larger body of armed persons. In addition, he describes other aspects of isolation at the fort which made life seem almost unbearable: the lack of contact with the outside world, loneliness for family and friends, the lack of fresh fruit or vegetables, and also the transient nature of even a promotion in rank. Similar conditions to these would not have been uncommon experiences for frontier soldiers stationed in many other remote forts, sometimes for years on end. It is no surprise that depression, melancholy, and suicide were problems within the ranks.

When one reads the graphic descriptions recorded by various observers who apparently saw the mutilated bodies of the dead persons it is easy to understand the fears and nightmares that probably haunted many men. Charles Larpenteur recorded the unearthing of the already buried Indian, Running Bear in which they "...cut him to pieces, scalped him and great dances went on in the camp."[122] Lt. Col. Bowman noted in the death of a black civilian named Tom, that he was found "...divested

---

[120] Ibid., 11

[121] Hesser, Genia, Letter by author, Fort Buford State Historical Site, N. D., April 21, 2006. 1-2.

[122] Innes, Ben, *Interments at Fort Buford 18996 to 1895* (Fort Buford: 6th Infantry Reg. Assn. Publ., 1996), 11.

of all clothing and dead, scalped and horribly mutilated and pinned to the ground with 27 barbed arrows."[123]

The fears of the men were not only about what would happen to them after they died, but also in the manner of their treatment prior to death. Joseph Henry Taylor observed that in the deaths of two men, "a search party found the hay loaded, the teams gone and the mangled bodies of the two hay haulers nearby. They had been beaten to death with whiffle trees…," the oak cross pieces that attached the mules to the wagon tongue.[124] Certainly that would not have been a quick or pleasant way to die.

As winter approached, even Clow's better situation as First Sergeant (with superior quarters (fig. 26) containing a stove for personal heating and his heavier uniform and buffalo robe (fig. 25)) would not have warded off the depressions that apparently still haunted him. Life in a frontier fort was subject to privations that went beyond just keeping warm.

---

[123] Ibid., 9
[124] Ibid., 9

# Chapter 16—Winter and Spring Come to Buford

When winter arrived on the Dakota Plains in 1869, it was probably the same ferocious animal of a season reported by General Trobriand during the winter of 1867—68 at Fort Stevenson. His reports show temperatures below zero early in November, with the Missouri River already carrying large chunks of ice. By February of that year temperatures had dropped to a bitter thirty degrees below zero. We can assume that only a few hundred miles away, any early arctic front would also have had soldiers scurrying to make the final preparations for a long winter at Fort Buford with similar extreme conditions.[125]

Temperatures often fluctuated wildly into December, with one week having temperatures of nearly twenty below and the next a balmy forty-five above. By January and February, the forts along the Missouri had become completely isolated, having very little communication while drifts and blizzard conditions blocked the men into their quarters for extended periods of time. At this time, the river also froze over completely so that any communication with the outside world became almost non-existent. The few couriers who attempted to pass from one fort to the next often

---

[125] Kane, L. M., ed. And transl., *Military Life in Dakota: The Journal of Philippe Regis de Trobriand* (Lincoln: University of Nebraska Press, 1982), 232.

returned with crippled horses, and they and their Indian guides often lost their way due to the gigantic drifts which changed the face of the landscape.[126] In some cases they left their horses in the stables and resorted to walking or running with their dog sleds across the arctic-like wilderness.[127]

During this period, the men at Fort Buford suffered under the terrible conditions of cold and isolation. The barracks were like icehouses inside. Carrying wood and stoking the red-hot stove became a major duty as the men tried to keep the temperatures in the long narrow adobe building above freezing while the wind whistled through cracks in the walls.

Dr. Kimball, the post surgeon, describes the winter situation in the barracks as "totally inadequate for the needs and warmth of the troops."[128] The men often resorted to lying in their bunks under whatever covers they could find to try to keep warm. Men at the distant ends of the barracks away from the stove often resorted to doubling up in bed with their buddies in order to fight off the terrible ache of the cold. Buffalo robes became a necessity for any warmth both in and out of bed, as the army issue blankets were still of Civil War vintage and made from very thin wool or a felt-like material. The trading posts made extra money from men needing to buy the heavier blankets, which they supplied to the Indians as well.[129]

The men's uniforms were also totally inadequate for the awful winter cold. Troops had been issued medium-weight wool uniforms, also of Civil War vintage.[130] They often had to face the bitter cold of arctic fronts in these completely unsatisfactory garments, which had been barely sufficient for east coast winters. Buffalo robes and heavy blankets became the dress of the day for going outside for any kind of duty. Being assigned to a duty in one of the smaller wooded buildings, such as the jail or library with their small stoves, would have become a prized location of warmth. Men would have readily volunteered for kitchen duty just to get near the

---

[126] Ibid., 225.

[127] Ibid., 220-224.

[128] Remele, Larry, ed., *Fort Buford and the Military Frontier on the Northern Plains: 1850-1900* (Bismarck: State Historical Society of North Dakota, 1987), 47.

[129]Ibid., 28.

[130] Ibid., 28.

cook stoves for an extra bit of warmth. Even feeding and cleaning duties in the stables with the dozens of warm horse bodies and the warmth of exercise were preferable to remaining in the icy barracks.

In reading a portion of Col. Trobriand's diary in which he describes his own feelings on March 1, 1868, as winter seemed to relapse onto the Dakota plains during that year, the reader can better understand the cabin fever which must have pushed some of the enlisted men in their pitiful quarters to the edge of sanity.

> *"How tired I am of this interminable winter! Of this everlasting snow which for more than three months has hidden the color of the earth from us and blinds our eyes with its unchanging whiteness…of these monotonous days which follow each other and are just alike, with no variety, no incident, like large drops of boredom falling one after the other into the dead sea of the past…of an existence where the hours of sleep become hours of deliverance…of this absence of all distractions of society which keeps me in my miserable log hut…alone during the day, and alone in the evening… "*[131]

The first sergeant's quarters at Fort Buford, occupied by Richard Clow, were almost luxurious by comparison. The twelve-by-fifteen foot space had its own small stove continually radiating warmth. There was at least the possibility of warming one's hands enough to be able to flex the fingers and write out the interminable lists of duties required by this position. In his confined room, the first sergeant might actually have enjoyed a higher standard of comfort than the officers might in their high-ceilinged wooden quarters. Plus he had his duties to occupy his time.

One of the most serious problems during the winter was human waste disposal. There were no inside latrines in the barracks and it was a good distance to the outhouses. Going this distance through drifts while being battered by bitter blowing winds and near-zero temperatures was not feasible. As a consequence, the men were forced to use slop buckets at one end of the barracks throughout much of the winter. [132]

---

[131] Kane, L. M., ed. and transl., *Military Life in Dakota: The Journal of Philippe Regis de Trobriand* (Lincoln: University of Nebraska Press, 1982), 237.

[132] Harvey, Mark, *"Securing the Confluence: A Portrait of Fort Buford, 1866 to 1895,"* in Dingle, Susan, ed., *At the Confluence: Now and Then: Papers presented at the Symposium Held in Williston, N.D., June 29. 2002* (Bismarck: State Historical Society of North Dakota, 2003), 39-40.

Every morning one of the men on detail duty was to empty these buckets outside. As the severity of winter encroached on the fort and drifts shut down human movement outside the buildings, the buckets were dumped closer and closer to the barracks door.

When temperatures were below zero with a whipping wind, the chill factor outside froze the slop almost instantly, leaving no smell. Subsequent blizzard snow and drifting would cover the frozen waste and leave a fresh covering upon which the next layer of waste could be deposited. Thus each day produced a new layer of frozen human waste which lingered quietly under the cold blanket of snow until the onset of spring.

However, life in the fort during the middle of winter was not all work and no play. The men had their cards or dice and a game was always in progress. A few men who had learned how to read could actually check books out from the fort library, which had been established in 1867. With nearly four hundred volumes, the library provided avid readers with ample materials to satiate their desires in mid-winter. In addition, the fort had built a small theater for plays. [133] First Sergeant Clow's interests and education would surely have led him to be involved in both of these diversions. All of these activities kept some of the men away from the heavy drinking that was the major problem in this and other isolated frontier forts. [134]

The drinking generally occurred in the one final place outside the barracks for men to find a bit of entertainment: the trading posts. These establishments provided the soldiers with ample opportunity to spend money on drink while playing cards, dice, or generally carousing outside the barracks on a payday spree. [135] The posts acted like a safety valve on a

---

[133] Remele, Larry, ed., *Fort Buford and the Military Frontier on the Northern Plains: 1850—1900* (Bismarck: State Historical Society of North Dakota, 1987), 29, 45.

[134] Harvey, Mark, *"Securing the Confluence: A Portrait of Fort Buford, 1866 to 1895," in* Dingle, Susan, ed., *At the Confluence: Now and Then: Papers presented at the Symposium Held in Williston, N.D., June 29. 2002* (Bismarck: State Historical Society of North Dakota, 2003), 40.

[135] Remele, Larry, ed., *Fort Buford and the Military Frontier on the Northern Plains: 1850—1900* (Bismarck: State Historical Society of North Dakota, 1987), 28-29.

pressure cooker at times, allowing soldiers to escape from the confined quarters and the same persons in the middle of winter. Unfortunately, the excessive drinking often led to fights, and occasionally to the robbery or murder of a man who flashed too much money. This appears to have been the fate of Private John Caffrey who was murdered on the evening of July 4, 1868. [136]

It would seem that part of the motivation behind Charles Larpenteur's idea of putting a ten pin bowling alley into his post was to give the soldiers a positive indoor activity to enjoy during the winter rather than just drinking. This particular source of entertainment was completed in the fall of 1870, and became a source of constant entertainment for the men even on Sundays. [137]

With the spring thaw, the fort became a more pleasant place from the aspect of the men being able to get outside, get a bit of sun, and not have to be constantly fighting off the terrible cold. Outdoor wrestling matches and foot races could be held and the men relaxed as they had more room to get away from the crowds in the barracks. [138]

Of course, the warm weather also brought about the progressive revelation of layer upon layer of human waste which had been dumped just outside the barracks during the height of the winter cold. As the last deposits of white snow melted, they brought to light yellowed ice and increasingly the smells of urine and feces. These odors must have wafted across the fort with each warm breeze and become almost unendurable as temperatures shot well above freezing on spring days. At such times the entire fort very likely smelled worse than an open pit latrine.

Spring waste removal details were some of the first orders of duty that First Sergeant Clow assigned as the men emerged from their confining winter barracks. Although not particularly appealing to the nose, everyone could appreciate the need for the speedy removal of this offensive

---

[136] Innes, Ben, *Interments at Fort Buford 18996 to 1895*, (Fort Buford: 6th Infantry Reg. Assn. Publ., 1996), 9.

[137] Casler, Michael M., ed., *The Original Journal of Charles Larpenteur: My Travels to the Rocky Mountains between 1833 and 1872* (Lincoln, The Museum Association of the American Frontier, 2007), 220.

[138] Remele, Larry, ed., *Fort Buford and the Military Frontier on the Northern Plains: 1850—1900* (Bismarck: State Historical Society of North Dakota, 1987), 29.

material. A pit was dug and everything buried to remove the smell from this permanent dwelling area. Unfortunately, because the men had little knowledge of modern sanitation, the fort's well eventually became contaminated and had to be abandoned.[139]

Also with spring came the start of parade drills and exercises supervised by the first sergeant and junior officers in order to weld the troops back into disciplined fighting units. The emergence of spring grass meant there was a need for the men to drive horses and any remaining cattle out to graze each day and to guard them from Indians. During the shortage of manpower at the fort through the winter of 1870, the stock was grazed only a few hundred yards from the fort to protect it from marauders.

The end of the month of March generally brought about the breakup of ice on the Missouri.[140] The first mackinaw boats and dugout canoes with miners headed back to civilization would pass the fort headed downriver. Soldiers who had received a discharge for time in service over the middle of winter impatiently waited for this time to set out for home. Many discharged soldiers preferred to brave the high waters and floating debris of the "Big Muddy" in April to escape Fort Buford, rather than hanging around until late May waiting for the first downriver steamboats.[141]

Spring also brought in scores of Indians to trade at one or more of the three trading posts associated with Fort Buford in 1869. All were vying for the same business and spring was the time for the best furs, collected over the winter by the Sioux and Assiniboine tribes in the area. Spring also brought with it the first influx of travelers and settlers passing

---

[139] Kelly, Carla, *"The Buffalo Carcass on the Company Sink: Sanitation at a Frontier Army Fort"* in Dingle, Susan, ed., *At the Confluence: Now and Then: Papers presented at the Symposium Held in Williston, N.D., June 29. 2002* (Bismarck: State Historical Society of North Dakota, 2003), 52-54.

[140] Kane, L. M., ed. And transl., *Military Life in Dakota: The Journal of Philippe Regis de Trobriand* (Lincoln: University of Nebraska Press, 1982), 254-255.

[141] Casler, Michael M., ed., *The Original Journal of Charles Larpenteur: My Travels to the Rocky Mountains between 1833 and 1872* (Lincoln: The Museum Association of the American Frontier, 2007), 211-212.

through this area, with a consequent upsurge in the frequency of Indian scares and raids.

The trading posts at Fort Buford were operated by five competing groups: the military sanctioned government sutler (the head trader of a post), the North West Fur Company, a private company named after its owners (Durfee and Peck), a fourth private company run by John Gerard, and lastly, the private trading post owned and operated by Charles Larpenteur.[142] Consequently, competition was heavy for soldier, civilian, and Indian trade. Charles Larpenteur seems to have had a flair for developing new trade ideas which made his store very successful.

Larpenteur had already been a fixture in the northern plains for over thirty-five years by this time. He had first worked as a clerk for the American Fur Company under the early traders, Sublette and Campbell, and later worked as a clerk and sutler for The North West Trading Company at Fort Union, ultimately moving to work for the Company of Durfee and Peck prior to setting up his own trading post at Fort Buford in 1868.[143] Thus he knew the trade business from bottom to top and was able to be successful by finding niches not already filled by his competitors.

The Larpenteur trading post was a building made partially of logs and adobe that was nearly 120 feet long.[144] It was slightly separated from the main fort by approximately fifty yards (fig. 17). The trading post was divided into living quarters, a storage room for inventory, a store sales area for the Indians to purchase goods, and another store area for the civilians and soldiers. In addition, there was a root cellar, an attached dwelling, and finally, a large common area with tables for drinking, talking, and playing games.[145]

The trade business was cut-throat. Since each store was vying for trade with the same Indians, miners, soldiers and travelers in the area, the

---

[142] Ibid., 236(2).

[143] Ibid., vi-vii.

[144] Coues, Elliott, ed., *Forty Years a Fur Trader on the Upper Missouri: The Personal Narrative of Charles Larpenteur, 1833-1872* (Minneapolis: Ross and Haines, Inc., 1962), 389.

[145] Casler, Michael M., ed., *The Original Journal of Charles Larpenteur: My Travels to the Rocky Mountains between 1833 and 1872* (Lincoln: The Museum Association of the American Frontier, 2007, 178-197,

quality of the trade goods was extremely important. The Indians of this area had been associated with trade goods for almost fifty years by this time. Thus, they knew which trader had the best quality goods for sale and drove hard bargains for their furs and pelts.

Although it was illegal to sell liquor to the Indians during this period, all of the traders, at one time or another, smuggled illicit alcohol into their establishments and peddled it to the Indians. The sale of alcohol to the Indians was for the obvious reason that it would befuddle the bargaining process and give the trader the upper hand in making a deal to buy the best skins for the least amount of money.[146]

Liquor sale to the Indians was one of the main reasons several traders ran into problems with the government at Fort Buford. From all accounts, the sale of liquor to the Indians was a part of the risk of doing business and all the traders, with the possible exception of Charles Larpenteur, seem to have been willing to run that risk at one time or another. Trader J. B. Gerard was expelled from Fort Buford in 1869 for stealing grain from the fort in order to make liquor which he was selling to both soldiers and Indians.[147]

In contrast, the sale of liquor to the soldiers doesn't seem to have been well-regulated at Fort Buford. Based on the problems Col. Bowman and other officers had with alcohol abuse, as well as the deaths of several enlisted men associated with drinking, it would have been wise for everyone at the post to keep alcohol under much tighter supervision.[148]

Based on the temperance philosophy of General Trobriand and the conduct of the previous commanding officers at Fort Buford, the fact that

---

[146] Harvey, Mark, "Securing the Confluence: A Portrait of Fort Buford, 1866 to 1895," in Dingle, Susan, ed., At the Confluence: Now and Then: Papers presented at the Symposium Held in Williston, N.D., June 29. 2002 (Bismarck: State Historical Society of North Dakota, 2003), 41.

[147] Kane, L. M., ed. And transl., *Military Life in Dakota: The Journal of Philippe Regis de Trobriand* (Lincoln: University of Nebraska Press, 1982), 359.

[148] Harvey, Mark, *"Securing the Confluence: A Portrait of Fort Buford, 1866 to 1895,"* in Dingle, Susan, ed., *At the Confluence: Now and Then: Papers presented at the Symposium Held in Williston, N.D., June 29. 2002* (Bismarck: State Historical Society of North Dakota, 2003), 40.

Richard Clow was not a heavy drinker may be one of the reasons why he was promoted to the position of First Sergeant in 1869. The new commanding general of the Montana district, being a believer in temperance, may well have wanted to instill some of this into his soldiers.

# Chapter 17—Leaving the Army at Ft. Buford

According to his military record, First Sergeant Richard Clow mustered out of the military on April 16, 1870 at Fort Buford (fig. 27 & 28). As a new civilian, Mr. Clow apparently stayed on at the fort and did not return to see his sister Bertha as he had mentioned in his letter. The reason for this stay could very well have been because he had finally fallen in love with a girl named Mary.

During the previous year when the fur trader, Charles Larpenteur, returned from his home near Little Sioux, Iowa, he brought his family along. The family was comprised of his third wife, Rebecca, son Louis (by Rebecca), daughter Elizabeth (by Larpenteur's deceased second wife), and step-daughter Mary Bingham. They all lived in the newly constructed home attached to the trading post. Larpenteur had finally decided that he would operate as a trader at Fort Buford for the rest of his life. [149] [150]

Mary Bingham (fig. 29) was the natural-born daughter of Larpenteur's third wife, Rebecca, by her former husband, Lucius Bingham. Bingham had died in July, 1852, and his daughter, Mary Bingham was born early in

[149] Coues, Elliott, ed., *Forty Years a Fur Trader on the Upper Missouri: The Personal Narrative of Charles Larpenteur, 1833-1872* (Minneapolis: Ross and Haines, Inc., 1962), 304-305.

[150] Casler, Michael M., ed., *The Original Journal of Charles Larpenteur: My Travels to the Rocky Mountains between 1833 and 1872* (Lincoln, The Museum Association of the American Frontier, 2007), 76, 79.

the following year, 1853. Mary had grown up in the Larpenteur family for virtually her entire life, as her mother Rebecca, married Charles Larpenteur in 1855.[151]

Mary was never officially adopted into Larpenteur's family, although he apparently treated her like his real daughter. At her marriage, the information indicates that Mary Bingham was joined to Richard Clow, thus an official adoption and name change never occurred. Despite this, on the rare occasions when Larpenteur refers to Mary, she is mentioned as "daughter," "Mrs. Clow," and "Lady," sometimes misspelled as "Laday."[152]

Mary's stepsister, Elizabeth Larpenteur, was the daughter of Larpenteur's Sioux wife who had been killed by Pawnee warriors in the early 1850s.[153] She was almost ten years older than Mary. Mary's half-brother, Louis, was the biological son of Rebecca and Charles Larpenteur. Based on the date of his tombstone, he was approximately nine years of age at this time in 1869.[154]

We will never know exactly when Richard Clow met his future wife, Mary Bingham, but it probably happened during the winter of 1869 and the spring of 1870. It may well have been at the Larpenteur trading post where Richard would have gone for a drink and a song with other soldiers for an evening of relaxation. Or it may have been at a play performed by various members of the Fort Buford garrison in which Richard had a part.

In any case, by the time First Sergeant Clow was ready to become a civilian in April of 1870 he seems to have changed his plans about going home to find his girl. Clow's whereabouts for the next seven-and-a-half months are unknown, but his name suddenly appears in Charles Larpenteur's journal on Saturday, December 3, 1870. The note, which describes Clow as "the clerk who is a renowned hunter," is brief and gives no clue as to when he actually started working at the trading post. He may

---

[151] Ibid., 76, 69.

[152] Ibid., 241-256.

[153] Coues, Elliott, ed., *Forty Years a Fur Trader on the Upper Missouri: The Personal Narrative of Charles Larpenteur, 1833-1872* (Minneapolis: Ross and Haines, Inc., 1962), 305.

[154] Casler, Michael M., ed., *The Original Journal of Charles Larpenteur: My Travels to the Rocky Mountains between 1833 and 1872* (Lincoln: The Museum Association of the American Frontier, 2007), 315.

have stayed put in Fort Buford after mustering out and started work almost immediately as a laborer for Larpenteur on his bowling alley and other buildings.[155]

Richard Clow's first official employment as a clerk for Charles Larpenteur occurs sometime before December 3, 1870. It would seem that after that time, Richard Clow begins to figure more closely with Larpenteur's life as some of his activities, such as chopping wood or going out hunting ducks and antelope, are mentioned in Larpenteur's journal. Because of this, I would suspect that Clow married Larpenteur's step-daughter, Mary Bingham, somewhere prior to this date.[156]

There is no mention of the wedding in Charles Larpenteur's published journals. The wedding probably took place during the summer of 1870 based on the fact that it is not mentioned in Larpenteur's journals which have a gap from June 1869 until the beginning of August 1870.[157] Another piece of evidence for this date comes from the back of the tin-type photo of Mary Bingham (fig. 29) which has a note indicating that this is her photo taken about the time of her wedding in 1870.

The tranquil life for Richard Clow and his new family soon took a turn for the worse. Mary's stepsister, Elizabeth Larpenteur, died of consumption on February 27, 1871. She had married a recently discharged soldier and friend of Clow's, Alf Knott. This tragedy, coupled with the fact that Larpenteur's broken thigh from the previous year was not healing, complicated life for the entire extended family.[158] [159]

The death blow to the Larpenteur trading post venture came as a surprise. It occurred soon after Larpenteur had requested and received permission from the government to expand his trading post to include a

---

[155] Casler, Michael M., ed., *The Original Journal of Charles Larpenteur: My Travels to the Rocky Mountains between 1833 and 1872* (Lincoln: The Museum Association of the American Frontier, 2007), 225.

[156] Ibid., 227-233.

[157] Ibid., 217.

[158] Ibid., 230.

[159] Coues, Elliott, ed., *Forty Years a Fur Trader on the Upper Missouri: The Personal Narrative of Charles Larpenteur, 1833-1872* (Minneapolis: Ross and Haines, Inc, 1962), 392, 394.

"home of entertainment."[160] This, along with his ten pin bowling alley, would have made the Larpenteur establishment a very profitable business and guaranteed that the family would remain permanently at Fort Buford.

Instead, out of nowhere came a blow that would eventually destroy his business. The problem began in Washington with the Congress's approval of an expansion of the Fort Buford Military Reservation. At the same time, this expansion was followed by a bill in 1870 that forbade more than one trading post being on a military reservation. The trader was not designated, but was to be appointed by the Secretary of War, William W. Belknap, whose corrupt methods guaranteed that an honest trader would not be picked for the new position.[161] [162]

When Charles Larpenteur sent in a request to be the solitary trader at Fort Buford, his forty-plus years in the field made him the obvious pick for the position because of his experience, honesty, good relations with the Indians, military, and his reputation for temperance with alcohol. Despite all of this, his request was denied and the appointment went to a totally inexperienced man named Alvin C. Leighton, who apparently had a route to appointment through Secretary Belknap's pocketbook.[163]

With Leighton's arrival in Fort Buford in the spring of 1871, all of the trading posts including Larpenteur's were closed.[164] Larpenteur

---

[160] Casler, Michael M., ed., *The Original Journal of Charles Larpenteur: My Travels to the Rocky Mountains between 1833 and 1872* (Lincoln: The Museum Association of the American Frontier, 2007), 237.

[161] Ibid., 238.

[162] Coues, Elliott, ed., *Forty Years a Fur Trader on the Upper Missouri: The Personal Narrative of Charles Larpenteur, 1833-1872* (Minneapolis: Ross and Haines, Inc., 1962), 393.

[163] Casler, Michael M., ed., *The Original Journal of Charles Larpenteur: My Travels to the Rocky Mountains between 1833 and 1872* (Lincoln: The Museum Association of the American Frontier, 2007), 238.

[164] Coues, Elliott, ed., *Forty Years a Fur Trader on the Upper Missouri: The Personal Narrative of Charles Larpenteur, 1833-1872* (Minneapolis: Ross and Haines, Inc., 1962), 394.

fortunately managed to make a deal to sell out his remaining trading goods only four days before departing. [165]

On Monday, May 15, 1871, Larpenteur and his remaining family, including Richard Clow and his wife Mary, loaded all their belongings aboard the sternwheeler Andrew Ackley and departed from Fort Buford for the final time. [166]

It must have been a heart-wrenching situation for the entire family and also for Richard Clow. This sensitive young man had grown to full maturity following the Civil War here on the western frontier. He loved hunting and the excitement of the life that surrounded the fort and trading post. He had moved into a position that allowed him to use his education as well as his skill as a frontier hunter. Now his life and that of his family had been turned upside down. He was faced with having to fall back on the good will of Charles Larpenteur in order to become established in a new home.

As the extended family departed Fort Buford, there is a good chance that Clow's wife, Mary, already knew she was pregnant. Now they were headed down the Missouri where Clow would try his hand at becoming a family man and a farmer near Little Sioux, Iowa.

---

[165] Casler, Michael M., ed., *The Original Journal of Charles Larpenteur: My Travels to the Rocky Mountains between 1833 and 1872* (Lincoln: The Museum Association of the American Frontier, 2007), 235, 239.
[166] Ibid., 235.

# Section 3: After the Wars, The Diary

**Author's Note:** It is due to a fortunate quirk of fate that Richard Clow's small diary survived when my father's mother, Cora Cochran Clow, burned most of her father's old letters and diaries when she moved from her home in Eugene, Oregon to live near my parents in Bozeman, Montana. This one booklet survived because it remained inside a small box specifically labeled as being things that Grandpa Clow wanted my father to have. Along with Richard Clow's Civil War knife and powder horn were his few letters and his small diary. One wishes that he had put a few more of his letters into that box.

I have transcribed the entire diary and placed it in the appendix of the book so that readers may be able to use some of its information in their own further research. The entries all appear to be within the time frame of 1871 to 1875. My editorial in-text notes are in brackets. Readers will also note that at times, a year, e.g. [1874], has been inserted in the diary text by me. These dates have been deduced using the universal calendar. Because of the short year span of the diary, wherever Clow puts in the actual day of the week along with the month, the year can be accurately determined.

I have included specific sections of the diary, such as Clow's songs and poems, within the next chapters of the book where they are indispensable to the story line. The lists of ducks killed, logs chopped, supplies bought, etc., if referred to in the text, are obscure points that are referred to by diary page number so that the interested reader can locate them easily in the appendix. The original diary and letters are still in my possession.

# Chapter 18—Leaving Fort Buford

Prior to departing Fort Buford, Richard Clow had been working at Charles Larpenteur's trading post as a clerk since his mustering out of the Army in 1870. Although there is no exact location noted for Larpenteur's trading post, when one visits Fort Buford, the guides will point to an area just a hundred yards west of the current main Fort Buford post where it believed this one-hundred-and-twenty-foot-long building may have been situated.

The departure from Buford must have been an extremely emotional event for the family. Certainly Charles Larpenteur knew that his forty years in the upper Missouri River region were over. He could see that an era had passed. The free trappers had almost disappeared and the whole country's attitude about the Indian tribes was changing.

There was no longer a feeling of cooperation between the Indians and the trading groups. The rivers and streams were being cleaned out of their last wild fur resources and the Indians had begun to understand that their way of life was disappearing as well. They were realizing the inevitability of their being dominated by the encroaching masses of white ranchers, farmers, and businessmen. The resistance that they offered, although substantial, could not hope to stem the tide of immigrants and the loss of their primary source of food and materials: the buffalo.

The more the paramount chiefs like Crazy Horse and Sitting Bull resisted the white invasion, the more harshly their peoples were treated. Racial discrimination was rapidly showing its ugly face in the treatment of the native Indians by the government and the settlers. It was becoming an ingrained institution throughout the West through the management and perpetuation of the reservation system. Today, over a century-and-a-half later, we have still not broken free of these prejudices.

At times one can't help but wonder how things might have turned out very differently if men like Charles Larpenteur and General Trobriand had been in charge of dealing with the Native Americans. Here were men of their word who had dealt honestly with the Indians for years. They learned their languages and, in Larpenteur's case, even married into the tribes. These men would probably have taken a very different stance in coming up with a solution for Indian Territory. It might have been more akin to what eventually occurred in Canada with a consequent lower level of hostility.

The Larpenteur Family's steamboat ride down-river to Little Sioux, Iowa was a leisure journey in many ways. They had ample time to sit on the upper decks at the stern and watch the massive drive wheel churn the muddy waters of the Missouri. From their lounge chairs on the second deck, they could watch the workmen pushing their giant wheelbarrow loads of cottonwood fuel aboard the boat whenever they pulled into wood cutters cabins for refueling. Additionally, their privileged position as paying passengers allowed them to visit the wheel house and talk to the Captain. They could use their high perch on the second deck to spot game and wave at other boats churning up the Missouri towards the frontier or flying past them when they stopped to take on more fuel.

When they tired of the rear view, they could pass to the front and pick out key landmarks ahead. Larpenteur certainly must have been familiar with a number of these, considering the numerous times he made this passage for supplies and to visit his southern home. They would have passed piles of cottonwood logs stacked by wood cutters in readiness for the next sternwheeler, Mandan villages, decrepit old forts, and new bustling communities. Rapid changes were taking place all along the Missouri and soon this territory would be split up and accepted as the states of North and South Dakota.

If the sun beat down too fiercely during those spring days or a cold wind swept across the outer decks, they could always retreat into the glass-windowed sitting room and converse, embroider, or write notes. Meals were exquisitely served to these full board passengers, and the menu probably included soups, entrees, and desserts of the finest caliber.

An afternoon nap would also have been a possibility in the small cabins, listening to the throb of the massive steam pistons.

One can almost see the twenty-five-year-old Richard Clow sitting next to the aging Charles Larpenteur and listening avidly to the older man recount tales about each bend of the river. Larpenteur would have been certain to mention significant wood stops or the sites of incidents on the river. As he spoke, the two men would have pulled out their pocket watches to consult the passing of time while also jotting a few words for remembrance in their respective journals before resuming conversation and tales of the day.

As we imagine all this, we can understand why Richard Clow's diary notes parallel those of Charles Larpenteur almost exactly. Those persons reading *The Original Journals of Charles Larpenteur* will see the uncanny similarity of the following Journal section written by Clow in comparison to Larpenteur's own description of the down river boat trip. [167]

**Diary Page 4:** *May the 14th (1871) making packs of robes & peltries. The steamer Ackly [Ackley] arrived at ten AM. Made arrangement to go on board of it and started up work.*

*Firm Don*
*Bumber & Sqim           3.15*
*Nails              .54*
*Friday night and meals (followed by numbers 2, 3, 6 and several illeg.)*
**Page 5:** *May the 15th (1871) Left Buford at 12 and stop at the [illeg.] White earth (illeg.) The day was quite warm and L [illeg.]*

White Earth is very likely the White Earth River which had been a key focal point for early fur traders as early as 1825 when James Kipp founded a post for the Columbia Fur Company at this point.[168] Charles Larpenteur certainly had known Mr. Kipp, who in 1835 was working at Fort

---

[167] Casler, Michael M., ed., *The Original Journal of Charles Larpenteur: My Travels to the Rocky Mountains between 1833 and 1872* (Lincoln: The Museum Association of the American Frontier, 2007), 235.
[168] Thompson, Erwin N., *Fort Union Trading Post: Fur Trade Empire on the Upper Missouri* (Williston: Fort Union Association, 2003), 9-10.

McKenzie near the Marias River in Montana, and came to Fort Union in April of that year to bring in a load of hides and pelts. [169]

**<u>Page 6</u>:** *May the 16[th] (1871) St [orm] y wind is gust [illeg.] day and making [illeg.]. Reach Berth [old] at 2 PM Stevenson at 3 PM Reach [illeg.] Curry [Carie] & Koontz about 12 [illeg.] The Far West 25 miles below Stevenson. Stop for the night [illeg.]*

Storms along the Missouri River could cause real problems for the steamboats. With a high superstructure sticking up above the water and almost no keel, a boat could easily be blown off course in a high wind and ground itself on a bar without keen attention to any drift of the boat. In addition, the rains that accompanied storms could unleash masses of floating debris into the river with consequent fouling of the paddle wheel or worse yet, causing a collision of the hull with an unseen log. Colonel Trobriand notes that floating stumps were classed by the boaters into two groups: "snags," which float with the current, and "sawyers" that float counter to the current, as in an eddy or whirlpool. A boat struck by one of these could founder in a matter of minutes if the hull were punctured. [170]

Fort Berthold was another of the early Missouri River trading forts which was already in decline by this time, rendering it of little use to the military in their attempts to guard wagon trains headed west. When Colonel Sackett arrived at this fort on his 1966 inspection trip, he noted that it might be better for the military to no longer guard the small Mandan and Gros Ventre villages from the aggressive Sioux tribes who were taking over the region. His statement of, "I hardly believe in using troops to protect Indians from Indians, as we have as much as we can do to protect white men from Indians," bears out his thinking. He found the

---

[169] Coues, Elliott, ed., *Forty Years a Fur Trader on the Upper Missouri: The Personal Narrative of Charles Larpenteur, 1833—1872* (Minneapolis: Ross and Haines, Inc., 1962), 79.

[170] Kane, L. M., ed. And transl., *Military Life in Dakota: The Journal of Philippe Regis de Trobriand* (Lincoln University of Nebraska Press, 1982), 26.

quarters to be small and not well-lighted and the food so poor that several men were down with scurvy.[171]

Fort Stevenson was the 1867—1869 command center for General Trobriand, who was in charge of the military forts within the Dakota Territory and by this time had been transferred to Fort Shaw, Montana, from which he commanded the Montana military troops.[172] Fort Stevenson was built to fill help fill in a 200-mile gap of protection along the Missouri River between Fort Rice and Fort Buford. It was also the supply center for Fort Totten, which lay almost 150 miles to the northeast and protected the Red River Trail for travelers coming west from St. Paul, Minnesota.[173] Fort Stevenson received few direct Indian attacks, perhaps due to the better discipline and higher quality of the commanding officers.

**Page 6 (Continued):** *May the 17[th] (1871) Wed. Strong headwinds all day Took in 25 cords of wood at George Ba [kers] wood yard at painted [illeg.]*

Based on the fact that the steamboat, Andrew Akley, was recorded by Richard Clow on the previous day as having stopped for the night about 25 miles below Fort Stevenson, it would appear that they moved downriver another five or so miles the next morning before stocking up on wood. The densely forested Painted Woods was about thirty miles from Fort Stevenson and had been used extensively since 1868 as a source of wood for steamboats.[174] Although the site no longer exists, it was along the river at about the present-day site of Bismarck, North Dakota.

The Painted Woods area was a hot spot for potential Indian problems. The Sioux objected to all the wood cutting because they used this area for winter camps. The cottonwood bark was a staple food for Indian ponies in the winter months, but the wood cutters were more interested in what

---

[171] Athearn, Robert G., *Forts of the Upper Missouri* (Lincoln: University of Nebraska Press, 1967), 224.

[172] Kane, L. M., ed. and transl., *Military Life in Dakota: The Journal of Philippe Regis de Trobriand* (Lincoln, University of Nebraska Press, 1982), 371-372.

[173] Athearn, Robert G., *Forts of the Upper Missouri* (Lincoln: University of Nebraska Press, 1967), 251.

[174] Kane, L. M., ed. and transl., *Military Life in Dakota: The Journal of Philippe Regis de Trobriand* (Lincoln: University of Nebraska Press, 1982), 359-360.

they could sell to the steamboats than leaving some trees for winter horse food. This conflict meant that there was a constant threat of attack along this portion of the river. The Painted Wood area had originally been controlled by the Mandan and Rees Indians, who were driven out by the Sioux as they moved west due to pressure from pioneers. In 1869 there were approximately 4,500 Sioux camped at this site. [175] [176]

    ***Page 7:*** *May the 17th Wednesday Remained at Rice the balance of the night waiting on the Bay [liff]*

Fort Rice had a ten-foot stockade with two towers and a saw mill. It had been constructed as a part of the 1865 extension of military influence up the Missouri River in order to protect settlers. [177] By this time it had become a non-factor in the control of lawlessness in the area due to the small numbers of soldiers posted there. The land had been denuded of trees by wood cutters to the point of near sterility, and there were no settlements or large Indian camps near the post. Fort Rice had been the command center for the 13th Infantry when Richard Clow first went out to the frontier in 1867, but now had few duties to occupy it. The center of commerce and military strength for this part of the Missouri River had moved approximately thirty miles to the north to Bismarck and Fort Abraham Lincoln. [178]

    ***Page 7 (Continued):*** *May the 18 (1871) Thursday Still strong headwinds met the Nellie [P]eck at about nine AM Reached Grand River Agency at eleven AM left at 3 PM Stoped [sic] for the night about ½ hour befor [sic] Sun Set on account of a heavy Storm*

---

[175] Ibid., 359-360.

[176] Athearn, Robert G., *Forts of the Upper Missouri* (Lincoln: University of Nebraska Press, 1967), 258.

[177] Remele, Larry, ed., *Fort Buford and the Military Frontier on the Northern Plains 1850-1900* (Bismarck: State Historical Society of North Dakota, 1987), 11.

[178] Athearn, Robert G., *Forts of the Upper Missouri* (Lincoln: University of Nebraska Press, 1967), 264.

The Grand River drains the area north of the Black Hills and its headwaters were a hunting ground for the Sioux. Today it runs through the center of the Standing Rock Indian Reservation, on which Chief Sitting Bull is buried.

By 1871 the Indian agency at this confluence was a major source of food and equipment supply for the members of the Sioux Nation who had decided to settle on the reservation. These agencies often became sources of intertribal conflict as more aggressive bands of non-reservation Sioux raided the rations and supplies given out to the reservation Sioux who were attempting to live a peaceful farming lifestyle. [179]

**_Page 8_**: *May the 19 (1871) Friday the day was beautiful[,] reached shienne [sic] at quarter after nine AM [.] left at one reached Sully at 2 [illeg.] and left at five [.] Stop for the night about 25 miles below Sully in Company with the Steamer May Lowery who left Sully about 2 hours before us*

The mouth of the Cheyenne River was another site for wood cutters and a hot spot for conflicts with the Cheyenne and Sioux Nations that occupied much of this area. There was a small military post there in 1870 (which was later named Fort Bennett). [180] Today this river runs along the southern border of the Cheyenne River Indian Reservation.

By 1871, pressures were mounting in this area due to repeated violation by miners and settlers of the treaty of 1868, which designated the lands west of the Missouri River and the Black Hills as Indian Territory. In the ensuing years, surveyors for the railroads, more clandestine miners, and large military survey expeditions into the area would continue to aggravate the situation until it exploded into open warfare. [181]

Fort Sully was another of the 1865 line of military expansion into the west as military campaigns against the Indians increased and more settlers required protection along the migration trails. [182] The fort had been

---

[179] Ibid., 273.

[180] Ibid., 273.

[181] Remele, Larry, ed., *Fort Buford and the Military Frontier on the Northern Plains: 1850-1900* (Bismarck: State Historical Society of North Dakota, 1987), 45-48.

[182] Ibid., 11.

recommended for abandonment by Colonel Sacket in 1866, and during that summer it was rebuilt by the 13th Infantry at a new site some thirty miles up-river, a more suitable location for steamboat landing, timber, and grass.[183] The following year, this fort was the site of much of the final negotiations and wrangling that went on between the U.S. and the Sioux Nation to establish the treaty of 1868 which defined safe routes through Indian Territory and a cessation of warfare. In 1871, Fort Sully was reinforced with more troops in order to extend the military protection for the railroad surveyors who were working along the Missouri River up as far as Fort Buford.[184]

**Page 9:** *May th[e] 20ᵗʰ (1871) Saturday Left very early reached the Brule Agency at 9[illeg.] Left the agency at half past 10 May Lowry passed us at the Agency. Passed the May Lowry again stuck on a bar near White River. Reached Whet Stone at half past six when we fell in with the Miner She left about 1 hour before us an we lef[t] at dusk and stoped at P Martin Near Randall*

The White River is the first main tributary flowing into the Missouri River to the north of the Niobrara River, which runs just south of and parallel to the Dakota/Nebraska border.

General Trobriand mentions in his 1867 journal, while aboard the steamboat Deer Lodge, how this portion of the Missouri was very wide with many sandbars and had dead-end passages that required the boat to retrace its route. The Deer Lodge eventually had to use its grasshopper poles on the front of the boat to drag itself over a bar to reach the main passage of the river. This is probably the kind of thing that happened to the grounded May Lowry in Clow's description.[185]

---

[183] Athearn, Robert G., *Forts of the Upper Missouri* (Lincoln: University of Nebraska Press, 1967), 220.

[184] Ibid., 208, 272.

[185] Kane, L. M., ed. and transl., *Military Life in Dakota: The Journal of Philippe Regis de Trobriand* (Lincoln, University of Nebraska Press, 1982), 22, 29.

P. Martin's was another Missouri River wood cutter site where the boat would have refueled. [186]

Fort Randall was a gradually decaying remnant of the 1860 military frontier defense line. [187] It was long past having any real usefulness in protecting pioneer travelers. When visited by a Colonel Sackett in 1866, it was already falling down, filled with rats, and the men had not been properly drilled and trained as fighting units. He recommended that the soldiers be transferred to truly hostile Indian Territory up near Fort Benton, Montana. By 1867 there were only sixty-three men available for duty and due to their inability to defend themselves against Indian cattle raids the fort was considered a liability to the military. [188] By 1871 it would have been a site for Charles Larpenteur to point out and relate old adventures, but it was not a major factor in the later Indian wars.

**_Page 10_**: *May the 21 (1871) Sunday Passed Panca [Pancaw] Agency at 7 A.M [,] Running Water at ½ [?] Seven where we D [illeg. possibly Docked][,] met the [illeg. possibly boats] K[o]ontz and the Mollie Maser[.] reached Yankton at ¼ after 11[.] Landed to put out one passenger & Wife [.] Miner left at the same time.*

Running Water is the point at which the Niobrara River enters the Missouri. An early pioneer trail followed up the Niobrara taking early miners on a route south of the Black Hills to the Powder and Yellowstone Rivers and from there to the Montana gold fields.[189]

The town of Yankton was approximately 30 miles farther down the river. It had been designated as the capital city of the Dakota Territory. There was also a Dakota Indian agency at this point. It is described by

---

[186] Casler, Michael M., ed., *The Original Journal of Charles Larpenteur: My Travels to the Rocky Mountains between 1833 and 1872* (Lincoln: The Museum Association of the American Frontier, 2007), 235.

[187] Remele, Larry, ed., *Fort Buford and the Military Frontier on the Northern Plains: 1850-1900* (Bismarck: State Historical Society of North Dakota, 1987), 10.

[188] Athearn, Robert G., *Forts of the Upper Missouri* (Lincoln: University of Nebraska Press, 1967), 215, 237.

[189] Athearn, Robert G., *Forts of the Upper Missouri* (Lincoln: University of Nebraska Press, 1967), 214.

General Trobriand as having a number of cabins and also being at approximately the point where the hilly bank country of the Dakotas to the north give way to the monotonous flat plains which spread out into Nebraska.[190] After 1876, Yankton became one of the centers for miners traveling to Deadwood in the Black Hills.[191]

The steamboat arrived at Sioux City on May 21, 1871. From here the final segment of the trip was overland with the ultimate destination of the journey being Larpenteur's former family home. Originally named Fontainebleau by Larpenteur, it was situated just outside Little Sioux, Iowa. This was the place where he had farmed for a number of years, raised his children, and watched his former Sioux wife be brutally murdered by Pawnee warriors. He knew a number of local people, including the Driggs family who are mentioned repeatedly in his journals. It was near to where he had met Mary Bingham's mother, Rebecca, and where his son Louis and stepdaughter Mary had been born.[192] [193]

---

[190] Kane, L. M., ed. and transl., *Military Life in Dakota: The Journal of Philippe Regis de Trobriand* (Lincoln, University of Nebraska Press, 1982), 26.

[191] Parker, Watson, *Gold: In the Black Hills* (Pierre: South Dakota State Historical Press, 2003), 19.

[192] Coues, Elliott, ed., *Forty Years a Fur Trader on the Upper Missouri: The Personal Narrative of Charles Larpenteur, 1833-1872* (Minneapolis: Ross and Haines, Inc, 1962), 1-395.

[193] Casler, Michael M., ed., *The Original Journal of Charles Larpenteur: My Travels to the Rocky Mountains between 1833 and 1872* (Lincoln: The Museum Association of the American Frontier, 2007), 1-259.

# Chapter 19—Life in Little Sioux; The Tragedy of Winter

The steamboat Ackley, carrying Richard Clow, his wife Mary Bingham, and the Larpenteur family, reached Sioux City, Iowa on the 21st of May, 1871. Here they disembarked and settled business for a day before heading overland to home. The trip from Sioux City to Fontainebleau would take a full day making the journey a total of nine days in length. [194]

At this point, according to Charles Larpenteur's journal, the family stayed in temporary quarters near the Driggs family. Rebecca's sister had married into that family and Richard helped haul the Larpenteur family goods from the nearest river landing to the home. Larpenteur bought a span of horses and a wagon for the sum of $415 so that the family could move to a better home site. A few days later, the whole family moved south of Little Sioux to live with another set of friends who had their home along the Soldier River. [195]

Charles Larpenteur spent a few days searching for a suitable piece of land for his new home and registered his claim just over a week after reaching Fontainebleau. He also arranged with the Clows to have them

---

[194] Casler, Michael M., ed., *The Original Journal of Charles Larpenteur: My Travels to the Rocky Mountains between 1833 and 1872* (Lincoln: The Museum Association of the American Frontier, 2007), 241.

[195] Ibid., 241.

stay on and help with the work. Then he quickly got down to the business of planting a garden which would assure at least part of their food supply for later in the year. This was done by planting corn and potatoes on the Driggs' property.[196]

By this time it was already June first, which is a bit late for planting a large garden dependent on the spring rains. Time was imperative in getting the seeds into the ground. Richard Clow returned to the home after completing the planting of the potatoes and corn at the Driggs place only a week later. The success of their dry land farm depended on the area receiving sufficient rain over the coming weeks to bring the corn and potatoes out of the ground and get them established before the hot summer weather began.[197]

Some produce would have already been available. Lettuce and onions are planted as soon as the soil can be worked in the spring. These would already have been sprouting and growing well on local farms. The family was very fortunate to have relatives with ample food to share while they got on their feet.

At this point, Larpenteur made a decision to move closer to town. He realized that moving to the Soldier Creek area was going to be very difficult. They would be fifteen miles from town and the stores upon which they were going to have to rely heavily. Consequently, they moved back to Little Sioux and bought land much closer to town.[198]

This decision may have been swayed by two other considerations as well. Mary Clow was in the early stages of her pregnancy and Charles Larpenteur still was unable to walk well, due to the poor healing of his broken thigh (which had occurred more than a year previously). Without supplies, starting up from scratch was going to be too big of a challenge for the family to take on this late in the spring.

Clow apparently did a lot of the travelling at this point in time, going up to Onawa to collect supplies, and also to negotiate for land and the purchase of animals. The distance was nearly twenty miles which meant almost two full days of travel going there and back.[199]

---

[196] Ibid., 241-242.
[197] Ibid., 241.
[198] Ibid., 242-243.
[199] Ibid., 243.

During this period of time, Richard Clow was buying not only for Larpenteur but also for himself and his wife, Mary. He was digging deeply into his severance pay from the military, as well as any savings earned while working for Larpenteur at Buford, in order to set up a family home on their farm. He also seems to have had an agreement with Larpenteur to continue working for him.

By the time they were finished with their purchases the family had acquired 200 acres of rangeland along several miles of river frontage. The land appears to have been split ownership according to the phraseology of Larpenteur's journal, with Charles owning 120 acres and Richard owning 80. In addition to the cows and several head of cattle, they also purchased chickens and two ewes. Evidently, raising sheep was also a part of their plan.[200]

By the end of June, all seemed to be going well. With the Fourth of July approaching, festive preparations were made and Clow and Charles Driggs went off to hunt and fish. Larpenteur records that they returned with seven ducks, a quail, six doves, and a large Buffalo fish.[201]

Buffalo fish are of the genus *Ictiobus sp.* and come in both largemouth and smallmouth varieties. They are the largest of the sucker family of fishes and have been known to weigh over 50 pounds. A single fish of this size would be an excellent contribution to an Independence Day celebration.

The initial family house was partly made of sod blocks with a pine lumber roof.[202] This type of construction was warm in the winter and cool in the summer. Although similar in some respects to the failed adobe buildings of Clow's northern forts, it probably held up better in this southerly climate which was considerably less onerous than that in Montana.

During this period of time Clow came down with a severe fever to the extent that he could hardly work. He even had to have help loading and hauling the lumber from the rail head. A few days after recovering, around July 20, Clow evidently had an argument with Larpenteur about wages and quit working for him. Following this, and during the next month, Clow and his wife, Mary, travelled north to Minnesota to visit with his family.

---

[200] Ibid., 245.

[201] Ibid., 244.

[202] Ibid., 245.

This must have been a festive reunion itself, since Clow had not seen his family for more than four years. Upon his return to Iowa in mid-August, he apparently reconciled his disagreement with Larpenteur and went back to work for him again.[203]

The repeated mention by Larpenteur of numerous mosquitoes, and the fact that Clow appears to have come down with a severe fever, may be an indication that malaria was present this far north along the Mississippi River during the spring and summer.

Larpenteur records that Clow actually went into Little Sioux for "ague" medicine during the month of August.[204] Ague was recognized by repeated bouts of chills, sweating, and fever, all of which are symptoms of malaria. If not malaria, then this may have been at the beginning of one of the large influenza-like epidemics that swept across the United States during the years of 1870—1872.

Clow's fevers are the first hint that sickness is in the wind for the entire family in their new home. As fall comes and the crops mature, not only do the building projects have to be completed, but the crops also have to be harvested. There just isn't time for anyone to be sick in a subsistence farming life.

The preparation for winter during the fall of 1871 would have entailed a mountain of heavy work. They were still building fences, chicken coops, hog pens, and a stable, while also trying to complete the family houses. These projects also required numerous trips to town to pick up feed, hardware, lumber, and nails.[205]

Cattle and sheep needed to be fed throughout the winter so the cutting, raking, and stacking of hay was of primary importance before the rains came. Other crops had to be harvested as well to feed the family and the animals. It appears that the vegetable crop was fairly good despite the late planting date. Bushels of potatoes, onions, corn, and squash were collected and placed in the root cellar where a constant cool temperature kept them from freezing or rotting over the winter.[206]

The months of September through December brought on the duck hunting season with the vast migration of birds passing through the

---

[203] Ibid., 244-245.

[204] Ibid., 47.

[205] Ibid., 247-249.

[206] Ibid., 249-252.

central fly-way of the States. Hunting was an extremely important task for building up the winter food supply. Larpenteur records large numbers of both deer and ducks being shot to build up the family food supply. During the month of September 1871 alone, the men brought in 152 ducks, with the largest number killed on a single day being 48. Although the women are not mentioned during this period of time with chores, they probably spent a good share of their time dressing the animals out and then smoking and drying the venison and duck meat to preserve it for the long cold winter to come.[207]

Clow's diary has columns of total ducks killed on other hunting trips. His figures are probably for the two following years and indicate how important a source of food these animals could be. During the three year period from 1871 through 1873, it would appear that the men killed over 350 ducks during approximately 30 hunting trips for these animals alone (See Appendix 1, Diary pp. 13 & 14).[208]

It was an energetic life, one that wouldn't allow them to slow down, even as the first snows and freezing weather began in November. Larpenteur records that in between hunting trips during the months of October and November, Clow went to town several times, collected potatoes and corn, cut and hauled stable logs, stacked hay, plowed, chopped willows to make a pig pen, bought and hauled pigs, calves and cattle, hauled bricks and put in stoves.[209] Theirs was a rough outdoor life and they knew how to prepare ahead in order to prevent the possibility of starvation at the end of winter. Clow had already shot quite a number of deer by January and the skins were likely kept and tanned for clothing. His tanning recipe (See Appendix 1, Diary p. 12) is one that might be expected in any notebook of a man who plans to tan his own hides. Large crockery vats would hold the skins for curing in the acid bath. Then, after being washed, the skins would be allowed to partially dry. Finally, the stiffening skins would be pulled back and forth repeatedly over a post to make the hide flexible and soft. On Sept. 19, 1871 Richard and Mary Clow went to Little Sioux to consult a "renowned" doctor for some kind of "perfect cure all…"[210] This was probably the same Dr. Garmalds of

---

[207] Ibid., 248-253.
[208] Ibid., 248-253.
[209] Ibid., 251-255.
[210] Ibid., 258.

Clow's diary in which he notes that "Mary Clow 1871 Comensed [sic] taking Dr Garmalds medisen [sic] on the 18th of September" (See Appendix 1, Diary p. 12).

The good doctor may have been prescribing medicine for Richard with regard to his recurrent fevers, but the diary would appear to be saying that he was actually seeing Mary about her pregnancy. Based on the baby's birth date of January 19, 1872, Mary Clow was about five months pregnant at this time.

The winter's illnesses started when young Louis Larpenteur suddenly fell ill. It appears to have been abrupt, and within two days, he died. This may be an indication that the influenza epidemic of '71—'72 had begun. Louis's illness and death appears to have been caused by an inflammation of the lungs, and apparently there was nothing that the local doctor could do for him.[211]

There are two entries in the aging fur trader's journal not long after Louis's death that may give us clues about the deaths of Mary Clow and her baby in the coming months. Their deaths may not have been due to influenza, but perhaps due to an infection brought home by Richard Clow himself.

On December 23, Clow had gone hunting and managed to kill a large buck. Unfortunately, when he cut it open, he found that the fat and joints were all filled with fluid, indicating some type of infirmity. Clow took the deer's hide, but left the rest of the carcass.[212] Obvious to us, but not to a person living in the pre-antiseptic era, would be probable bacterial contamination of Richard Clow's hands and clothing while he was handling and skinning the animal. When he returned home, he may have unknowingly passed a potentially lethal bacterium to his wife.

By January 10, illness struck Clow's house-hold again, which caused him to go to Little Sioux again for medicine. This time it was specifically for his wife, perhaps being an ominous indicator that all was not well with Mary who was near term in her pregnancy. Nine days later, when baby Bertha (Bertie) was born, there was no indication of further illness and life appeared to have returned to normal for the family.[213]

---

211 Ibid., 253.
212 Ibid., 254.
213 Ibid., 255-256.

The onset of an early thaw in February found the men in the midst of splitting numerous posts, apparently for the fencing that was planned for the coming spring and summer months. Driggs' sow had eight piglets and, in his notes, Larpenteur is already calculating that when they grow up and weigh two hundred and fifty pounds apiece. He calculates that there will be about two thousand pounds of hog meat to sell at three cents per pound. The thought of sixty dollars makes him literally cheer 'out loud' in his journal.[214]

The nearby lake supplied Larpenteur's new ice house with thirteen loads of ice to be kept under sawdust over the coming summer.[215] One can see how the entrepreneur in Charles Larpenteur emerged as he used his years of experience on the frontier to direct the younger men of the extended family and turn his dreams into reality.

Then suddenly, just as the winter cold was about to break and the warmth of spring began to appear, the Clow's baby daughter, Bertie, died on the night of March 4, 1872. Clow went to Little Sioux the next day, collected a coffin, and on the 7th of March she was buried.[216] Winter had brought tragedy to this new young couple who had started off so positively with their life in a new place.

One can imagine the grief that struck the Clows, sending them both into a deep depression. As spring progressed, Mary Clow also fell ill. She followed her baby in death almost exactly a month later on April 6, 1872.[217] In one fell swoop, with the death of his wife and child, Richard Clow's life and dreams for a bright future had fallen apart.

---

[214] Ibid., 257.

[215] Ibid., 258.

[216] Ibid., 258-259.

[217] Ibid., 210.

# Chapter 20—Settling Accounts, A Love Poem, and Moving On

For all intents and purposes, the life that Richard Clow had come to know briefly—the joy of a family, a loving wife, and a new child—had come to an abrupt end. One can imagine the grief that he experienced over the next months following the burial of his wife only a month after the burial of his first born child.

At this point, he must have gone to the Larpenteurs to help him find comfort in his sorrow. It would not have been a happy party with Rebecca, the mother of Mary, now having seen the death of her first husband many years earlier and now the death of her daughter, Mary. Alongside all of this would be laid the sorrows of old man Larpenteur as well, who had seen the deaths of his first two wives, two sons, a daughter, and now his step-daughter. One can imagine the bleakness with which they all viewed the future.

Immediately following the death of his wife, it appears that Clow stayed on living near the Larpenteurs and ran errands and even paid a number of bills for them. He even witnessed Charles Larpenteur's final will and testament written on May 15, 1872.[218] This period of time would have lasted at least through July 1872 (See Appendix 1, Diary pp. 18—19).

---

[218] Casler, Michael M., ed., *The Original Journal of Charles Larpenteur: My Travels to the Rocky Mountains between 1833 and 1872* (Lincoln, The Museum Association of the American Frontier, 2007), 275.

Then there is a gap in those accounts which may indicate that he worked elsewhere for the rest of the summer.

By mid-November of 1872, Richard Clow's mentor, father figure, and guiding light, Charles Larpenteur, had also died.[219] [220] Rebecca, Mary's mother, was suddenly alone and would have needed a lot of help to prepare the farm for the winter, and then spring planting, in order to keep everything from falling apart. It is thus likely that Clow stayed on for the winter to aid her in those tasks.

Certainly, based on further notes of accounts with the Larpenteurs, following the death of Charles Larpenteur there were still various sums owing. It appears that when he finally settled up all of his accounts with his mother-in-law on December 12, 1872 that it was for a total of $156.62, (See Appendix 1, Diary p. 19).

The time was coming when Clow would have to either dig in his heels and tough it out as a farmer on the Little Sioux property or move on with his life. My guess is that Richard Clow already had made contact with a Mr. John Kellogg in Laramie City, Wyoming Territory, (See Appendix 1, Diary p. 11). After grieving for the death of his wife and mentor, new opportunities were opening up for him on the frontier.

At this point, having settled all of his accounts with his mother-in-law, Rebecca, Clow likely moved out of his house and moved up to live with the Driggs family. He continued to plant the spring crops and work the family farms until they could be put up for sale the following summer.

At this juncture in his life, we find several interesting entries that may or may not be related to this period of time chronologically. The first of these is his brief list of Spanish or Mexican Spanish words with their English meanings next to them (See Appendix 1, Diary p. 13).

The purpose of this list of words is obscure because they have no date attached. They may have been from years earlier to help him deal with the Mexican wood cutters and sojourners who passed through Fort Buford during his work at the trading post in 1870. Or they could be just

---

[219] Ibid., 315.

[220] Coues, Elliott, ed., *Forty Years a Fur Trader on the Upper Missouri: The Personal Narrative of Charles Larpenteur, 1833-1872* (Minneapolis: Ross and Haines, Inc., 1962), 395.

scribbling made over a few drinks with some Mexicans passing through the Little Sioux area. Another possibility would be that they were linked to his future return to the frontier and the need for a horse and trappings. In any case the spellings are Richard's phonetic renditions of the words. His spelling may also have been modified by Latin which he had most likely studied to some extent while at school in Boston.

Lists such as this one are not uncommon. Many travelers try to keep a few words of a foreign language in their notebooks. Occasionally, persons who are a bit more exacting even compile small dictionaries of those words. Charles Larpenteur did this with the English and Assiniboine languages, probably both to help him communicate with his Indian wives and also to deal with the tribes that came to his post for trading. [221]

It appears that Clow's source was someone who may have been illiterate and thus used very colloquial Spanish terms instead of proper dictionary names for things, as seen in the first term on his list "Causo Testia" with Clow's meaning of "Horse." Very probably this would have properly been translated as a "Cayuse" referring to an Indian pony and "Testia" relating to bad tempered thus becoming "a bad tempered Indian horse." On the other hand, that may have been the name our unknown source person used for all horses. This would be especially so if he had been bucked off a few times leading him to consider all horses as being somewhat "Testy Cayuses."

Following this brief list is another interesting section of diary with the words for the song "Waiting for Thee."

Did Richard Clow write some of these poetic words himself, or is it copied from something he read or heard sung while in Fort Buford, Iowa or in Laramie, Wyoming? It may even have been sung when Richard was wooing Mary at Fort Buford, or it may have been seen by him as a lament for the death of Mary? The chronological sequence of the diary suggests that it was written at about the one year anniversary of Mary Bingham's death.

---

[221] Casler, Michael M., ed., *The Original Journal of Charles Larpenteur: My Travels to the Rocky Mountains between 1833 and 1872* (Lincol: The Museum Association of the American Frontier, 2007), 267-270.

Whatever the purpose, the lines would still be quite appropriate for young men and women today who are separated by war or distance for lengthy periods. I have been unable to find an exact reference for this version of the song. A similar version is found at the beginning of a tantalizing article about lost and reacquired love which appears in the *Naples Record* of October 13, 1873.[222] This version is shortened and uses some different words, so it is possible that a portion of the song below was written by Richard Clow himself.

----------------------------------------------------------------

**<u>Diary Page 14:</u>**
Waiting for Thee
**[1]** I've been waiting for more than a year love
Yes waiting and watching for thee
Hopeing [sic] and praying youd [sic] come love
To Keep your true promise to me
Cho [rus]
By the lilies that float down the river
And the cowslips that grow by the lee
By the roses that bloom in the forest
Im watching and waiting for thee
**[2]** I've waited for more than a year love
For that promise from you to receive
So surely you'll not break your word love
And leave me your absence to grieve
Cho [rus]
**[3]** So Ill wait another year love
In hopes of your coming this way
When the daintyist [sic] shades of th[e] twilight
Will shut out the dawn of the day
Cho [rus]

----------------------------------------------------------------

That Clow did move away from Little Sioux is a given. He departed in the spring of 1874 and worked on his own for various ranchers in

---

[222] Naples Record, Vol. 5, No. 42, *"Waiting My Darling for Thee"* (NY), October 13, 1873. http://fultonhistory.com/Newspaper%2013/ Naples%20NY%20Record/Naples%20NY%20Record%201870- 1874/Naples%20NY%20Record%201870-1874%20-%200647.pdf

Wyoming. The exact location of these ranches is uncertain, but it is likely that they were in the vicinity of Cheyenne, Wyoming, where he seemed to have purchased some supplies (See Appendix 1, Diary p. 16).

By 1874, the city of Cheyenne had grown up rapidly from the time when the first survey and sales were completed in 1861. The Union Pacific Railroad had reached Cheyenne in 1868.[223] It was a town built on the solid commerce of easy-to-mine coal which lay near the surface of the ground in great seams. The railroad line coming in from the southeast made the transportation of this solid black gold back to the eastern states quite simple. The great industrial giant of the East was going full steam on development and needed fuel.

Cheyenne also became a center for ranches to ship out their cattle to stockyards in Iowa, Kansas, and Illinois. It was a bustling center of life and energy. It was the ideal place to locate a burgeoning frontier town because of the nearby coal fields and miles of rangelands, which would support sheep and beef cattle. The boom town of Cheyenne was a breadbasket of meat for the nation, in addition to being the supplier of cheap coal energy used to fuel the nation's industries and trains.

This would have been new country for Richard Clow, but it still had similar familiar vistas like the prairies of Montana. Sagebrush, antelope, deer, and elk were again plentiful and easy to hunt. It would also have been a good summer for him to work outdoors and ride the hills scouting out the land. In this manner he was able to garner important information about the Indian tribes and trails into the Black Hills as he prepared to explore for gold.

In 1874, when Clow went out to scout out the country around Cheyenne and Laramie, his first order of business was to find a job. Ranch work would have seemed the easiest place to start that search, a place where his skills as a rider, soldier, and farmer would be put to good use. From his notes, it also appears that he found a niche splitting rails, cutting poles, and shearing sheep for a number of ranches in the area (See Appendix 1, Diary pp. 15 & 16).

---

[223] Keenan, Jerry, *The life of Yellowstone Kelly* (Albuquerque: University of New Mexico Press, 2006), 72.

The brief notes in his diary would indicate that he spent at least a month riding from place to place, working at hard labor for about two dollars a day. His overhead was probably nil since most ranches would have provided meals and a place to throw a bed roll. A pair of shears is a lightweight piece of equipment to carry on horseback to augment one's resume of stock-working gear. By the end of the summer he had probably put aside a pretty good nest egg working for Sprague, Hutton, Keller, and others.

The summer of 1874 also saw the Custer expedition into the Black Hills of the Dakota Territory, with its intentions to confirm whether there was sufficient gold to justify changes to the treaty of 1868 that put this area as off limits to miners.[224] The expedition of some 1,000 men and over 100 wagons brought back enough information, indicating small amounts of gold in the Black Hills, to further fuel the gold fever. Publication of gold made the job of the army, detailed to keep miners out of Indian Territory, more difficult.[225]

By the time Dick Clow returned to the Driggs place around October 10, 1874, he would have had enough money to pay for room and board for the winter (See Appendix 1, Diary p. 31). Upon arriving home, he could not have failed to hear more about the gold rush to the Black Hills. In nearby Sioux City, the gold rush was being actively pushed by Charles Collins, the editor of the Sioux City newspaper. At that time it was estimated that five men could outfit themselves completely for the trip to the Black Hills for $569.85.[226] The lure for a single man to strike it rich had begun to draw him in.

During the winter months he would also have helped out on the Driggs farm to offset his keep, and also have been able to help his former mother-in-law, Rebecca, who still lived nearby. By winter's end, Richard had solidified his decision and made final preparations to return to the Dakota Territory to hunt for gold. His diary (see Appendix 1, pp. 19—31) shows a large number of purchases of equipment, materials, and clothing,

---

[224] Remele, Larry, ed., *Fort Buford and the Military Frontier on the Northern Plains: 1850-1900* (Bismarck: State Historical Society of North Dakota, 1987), 48.

[225] Parker, Watson, *Gold: In the Black Hills* (Pierre: South Dakota State Historical Press, 2003), 23-26.

[226] Ibid., 22, 29.

which he planned to use on his journey as well as his final settling up of accounts with the Driggs family.

# Chapter 21—The Road to Deadwood, Plans for Mining

On the morning of April 28, 1875, Richard Clow left the Driggs' family farm near Soldier Creek, Iowa for good (See Appendix 1, Diary p. 31). In all likelihood it was his friend, Don Driggs, who took him to the railway depot in Little Sioux. There he boarded the train headed south to Council Bluffs and Omaha, Nebraska. In Omaha, he would have switched to the Union Pacific Railway's transcontinental line that followed the Platte River across Nebraska into Wyoming. Finally, changing trains in Cheyenne to a branch line, he would then have traveled north another seventy miles to Fort Laramie.

With his gregarious nature, Clow probably found other travelers with whom to share the news of the country. Much of the talk probably centered on the prospects of finding gold in the Black Hills. As they talked, civilization and the farms of eastern Nebraska would have receded while the train sped westward onto the open plains.

Richard Clow was an obvious candidate to participate in a gold rush. He was a widower and seemed to have no close ties to family other than by post. As a former frontier military man, he understood the lay of the land in Indian country. He would know how to cross into the sacred hills without leaving a lot of signs if travelling alone. He would know not to ride on the ridge lines or have sparkling conchos on his saddle. He would know how to keep camp signs to a minimum and know when it would be smart to have a cold camp and lay low. In addition, he had developed strong shoulders, hands, and arms during his years of farming and splitting rails. He could face the back breaking work of digging day after day in the dirt for his pay. Finally, as a military veteran, he knew how to handle his weapons and although not an aggressive man, had the experience to use them if it became necessary.

Discussions with other passengers on the train would have brought out more information about the gold fields in the Black Hills, much of which was probably rumor. The summer of 1874 had been rife with the rumors of gold which were passed by word of mouth. The exaggerations of these stories could only grow as they spread. Some came from returning clandestine miners who had violated army orders to stay out of the Black Hills, which were Indian Territory. These men would have brought back stories of riches for the taking, but very few could actually show much for their months of hard labor.

Other rumors of gold came from the exaggerations based on Army scouts and soldiers who had been out with General Custer on his geological and surveying expedition into the Black Hills. The actual reports of the expedition had gone by courier to Fort Laramie on August 3, 1874. The offshoots of these initial small reports of a few flakes of gold brought a rash of newspaper articles. From Bismarck to New York, rumors were published within the coming months indicating placer gold finds of up to $50 per day. [227]

By the beginning of May 1875, the most recent rumors would probably have come from the miners of the Gordon expedition who had illegally entered the hills the previous summer. These men had been released from military custody upon reaching Fort Laramie and told stories which only served to fuel the fever of other prospective miners. [228] In addition, the soldiers made up their own tales after having listened to the gripes, curses, and bitterness of these captured men. It was rumored that some miners even offered gold nuggets for the soldiers to forget that they even existed.

Finally, the most convincing rumors would have come from the group of professional miners and surveyors who had accompanied the Custer expedition. These were the men who had actually looked carefully at the sands of the creeks and the quartz veins in the rock outcroppings. They

---

[227] Parker, Watson, *Gold: In the Black Hills* (Pierre: South Dakota State Historical Press, 2003), 26.

[228] Ibid., 35-36.

had actually seen indications of silver deposits and panned a few flakes out of the streams. Thus, it was theorized, they would know, with some certainty, where the greatest potential for a big bonanza of gold existed.[229]

From all accounts, there was going to be a flood of miners entering the Black Hills with or without government permission during the summer of 1875. The government was leaving it up to the military to decide how best to handle the incursions of whites into the sacred land of the Sioux known to them as *Paha Sapa,* or "Hills That Are Black."[230] They had come to the realization that stopping the masses would become impossible. There truly was "gold in them there hills."

Richard Clow had likely already picked out several places to stay when he returned to the Wyoming Territory to prepare for his mining expedition. In his writing folder was a business card for a Cheyenne boarding house which he probably collected during the previous year while working in that area (See Figs. 30 & 31). Places in Fort Laramie probably cost less than the seven dollars a week advertised for that room and board. Based on the card's mileage list and the fact that Fort Laramie was 70 miles closer than Cheyenne, he had only about 180 miles of trail riding ahead of him to reach the Black Hills and Deadwood.

The price of a boarding house was well worth it. A good night's sleep in a place to relax, think, and write was important for making good plans. In some ways, his organized life as he prepared to depart for the Black Hills was like being in a military campaign all over again. He had to plan for all the supplies he would need to establish a mining camp and build a winter shelter. At the same time, he didn't want to be overburdened with extra junk that would slow him down as he explored the hills. Then, in addition, he would need a few emergency essentials to be able to survive in the event that he was robbed or things were destroyed in a fire or accident along the trail. A man couldn't be too careful.

Overland roads from Laramie to Rapid City and Deadwood were first opened in 1874, but transport was dangerous from two standpoints. The Sioux Indians had been stirred up by the encroachment of white gold miners and then by General Custer's survey trip into their sacred grounds in the Black Hills. In addition, the narrow badland canyons of the Dakotas were a haven for robbers and holdup men. The depredations of

---

[229] Ibid., 25.
[230] Ibid., 3.

these bandits only grew worse with the flood of tenderfoot miners moving into the Black Hills. The reverse traffic coming out of the Hills was no safer because any traveler might be carrying large amounts of cash or gold.

The route Richard Clow followed into the Black Hills in early 1876 very likely followed along the same dangerous route taken by many other would-be miners and entrepreneurs during this same year. The journalist, Leander P. Richardson, who passed over this rough trail in July 1876 while travelling from Fort Laramie to Deadwood, documented the following nightly stopping places for that wagon train as being: 1. Rawhide Buttes, 2. Hat Creek, 3. Indian Creek, 4. Cheyenne River, 5. Red Canyon, 6. Custer City, 7. Spring Creek, 8. Rapid Creek, and finally, 9. Deadwood.[231] He also noted that Red Canyon was an especially narrow and dangerous point in the journey. It was the site of the massacre of the Metz family by Indians in April of that same year.[232] [233] One can be certain that a veteran infantry soldier such as Clow would have been certain to travel with a large enough band of men to thwart or scare off any attack. He had seen first-hand what could happen to small bands of travelers on the frontier.

Following the Custer Massacre in 1876, the Indian threat to the Black Hills area became even more treacherous as the Sioux celebrated their victory with major raids on whites throughout the west. In some cases, the highwaymen capitalized on this fact and became more aggressive in their own robbery tactics, sometimes masquerading as Indians so that the blame could be pushed off onto someone else.[234]

Richard Clow was neither the first man nor the last to ride the treacherous trail from Laramie through Rapid City and on to the gold fields. Like many men, he probably rode out of Laramie with a good-sized wagon train. If he needed to travel alone any distance, did probably so in a

---

[231] McLaird, James C., "I Know… Because I Was There: Leander P. Richardson Reports the Black Hills Gold Rush," in *Gold Rush : The Black Hills Story, ed. John D. McDermott* (Pierre, SD: South Dakota State Historical Society Press, 2001), 58-63.

[232] Ibid., 62.

[233] Parker, Watson, *Gold: In the Black Hills* (Pierre: South Dakota State Historical Press, 2003), 135.

[234] Ibid., 135-136.

manner designed to prevent observant Indian eyes from ascertaining his route. In such a case, while on the trail, he would have slept off the main route in a fireless camp to avoid detection by either Indians or other night riders on the wrong side of the law, also known as owl hoots. His rifle and pistol would have been half-cocked, near-at-hand, and ready for use, his ears intently listening for the slightest odd noise that might mean danger was approaching. He was a man with a goal and he truly meant to arrive in Deadwood in one piece.

# Chapter 22—Days of Work and Spanish Songs in the Gold Fields

The Gold fields of the Black Hills were definitely open to all comers by the summer of 1876. Richard Clow was not the first man to arrive and stake a claim, but he was by no means a late comer. Once the rumor got out to the general population, there was no way for the army to stop the encroachment by thousands of men on this remote part of the frontier. The few men who were detained by the army and taken to towns outside Indian Territory were soon free to make another try. [235]

The small towns around the Black Hills had neither the facilities nor the authority to hold these men. In any case, the only real solution would have been to lock them up permanently, but of course that would not have been a fair punishment for the simple crime of trespassing. No other crime had been committed. In many cases, as soon as the detained miners were set free, they were purchasing new equipment for another prospecting attempt within hours of having been brought to jail. In the end, it became a farce with a frustrated army becoming the laughingstock of the local civilians as it was trying to do an impossible job. [236] [237]

---

[235] Parker, Watson, *Gold: In the Black Hills* (Pierre: South Dakota State Historical Press, 2003), 66.

[236] Ibid., 66, 69.

[237] Keenan, Jerry, *The Life of Yellowstone Kelly* (Albuquerque: University of New Mexico Press, 2006), 73.

During the summer of 1875 hundreds of prospective miners seemed to arrive in the Black Hills almost overnight. Small unincorporated towns sprang up along any stream that seemed to show a bit of color. A gathering of several hundred to a thousand men could be expected within days of the announcement of a new strike. Then, within another few days, they could be gone again following the winds of chance that generally only favored the first few on a strike or the extremely lucky.[238]

The first true towns to be incorporated like Deadwood, Hill City, and Custer attracted the largest numbers of men. Their methodology for finding gold was simple: if there was a creek nearby, the men would populate both sides of the stream and build their sluice boxes. Then, they would dig into the nearby hillside, angling their tunnels downwards in hopes of striking the layer of gold bearing gravel and sand just above the bedrock. This material would be laboriously hauled up to the surface and shoveled into the sluice box to separate the gold from the debris.[239] It was backbreaking labor.

With the influx of the masses of gold seekers came numerous freeloaders, including gamblers, outlaws, thieves, and prostitutes. They all became a part of the small towns, just as much as the honest merchants, miners, blacksmiths, mule skinners, and lawmen.[240]

The tent cities along any creek that began showing a bit of color soon sprouted log cabins. These rough buildings were soon followed by sawn plank buildings. Almost, as if by magic, small towns appeared out of nowhere. They included all the amenities from bath houses to sport saloons, general stores, boarding houses, seamstresses, and eateries.[241]

The miner's job of working with a pick and shovel and then wading into the icy water to pan or sluice for gold was not easy. As one miner is reported to have said, "There's gold from the grass roots down, but more gold from the grass roots up."[242] It soon became apparent to large numbers of would-be miners that their bodies could not handle the back-breaking labor day after day. It was no place for a weak, lazy, or sickly

---

[238] Parker, Watson, *Gold: In the Black Hills* (Pierre: South Dakota State Historical Press, 2003), 71.

[239] Ibid., 54-55.

[240] Ibid., 143-144.

[241] Ibid., 141-149.

[242] Ibid., 65.

man. Within the first few weeks, the grueling work weeded out the losers. Either they died from overwork or exhaustion, switched to less physical work, or packed up and went home.

For Richard Clow, hard labor and a tough life were nothing new. He'd seen every form of human suffering while fighting in the trenches of Petersburg, building forts in Montana, and hacking out a farm in Iowa. His hands were hardened from carrying a rifle, straining on the handles of a plow, and from swinging an ax. At twenty eight years of age, he rode into the mining camps around Deadwood and went to work. During the month of October 1876, he struck gold!

Clow staked his claim to the "Golden Seal Lode" as he called it, by right of location and discovery on October 19, 1876, according to the Location Certificate first filed on March 16, 1877 in Deadwood.[243]

Initially, this claim would have been regarded as an illegal claim under the laws of the United States. At that time, the United States had still not negotiated a change to the 1868 Treaty of Laramie, which included the Black Hills in the Sioux Reservation. Until the ratification by Congress on February 27, 1877 of a new treaty which ceded the Black Hills to the United States, Richard Clow and all the miners, businessmen, and other settlers within the Deadwood area were nothing more than trespassers on Indian lands. They really had no legal rights to the gold they were mining from the sands and quartz rocks around Deadwood.[244] This would explain a portion of the wording in Richard Clow's claim which states that it is: "to show present ownership and claim and to cover any Illegality that might attach to making mining locations on an Indian Reservation."[245]

The actual location of Clow's Golden Seal Mine is quite vague in his initial location certificate, giving only dimensions and the fact that it is "situated west of the Lewella Mine."[246] In a later deposition made when selling a quarter of his claim on June 2, 1879, Clow notes the location a bit

---

[243] Clow, Richard, "Location Certificate: Golden Seal Lode," *Book of Deed, vol. 3, no. 2870,* (Deadwood, Lawrence County, SD., 1880, 1.

[244] Parker, Watson, *Gold: In the Black Hills* (Pierre: South Dakota State Historical Press, 2003), 139-140.

[245] Clow, Richard, "Location Certificate: Golden Seal Lode," *Book of Deeds, vol. 3, no. 2870,* (Deadwood, Lawrence County, SD., 1880, 1.

[246] Ibid., 1.

more completely by stating that it "is situated at the head of Packrat Gulch and is joined on the east by the Esmeralda Mine and on the west by the Central #2 Mine and on the north by the Ocean Wave Mine."[247] Then later in December of 1879 in another deposition he describes another section of the mine as being "situated on the west side of Blacktail Gulch opposite placer claim numbers six (6), seven (7), and eight (8), being fifteen hundred (1500) feet in length and three hundred (300) feet in width and is in the Whitewood Quartz Mining District, Lawrence County, Dakota Territory."[248] One final location due as to the mine's exact location comes from an affidavit filed in January 1880 by Clow which describes the location of the mine as "situated on the divide between Blacktail and Hidden Treasure Gulch." [249]

The placer claim #8, which is listed in Clow's affidavit above, may be related to one short note on page 38 of his diary that says "No. 8 below J. S. Collins" (See Appendix 1). The only mention of a J. Collins in Deadwood around this time is in a "Quit Claim Deed" for June 1876, showing the sale of "Lot No. Fourteen and one half (14½) situated on Main Street in the City of Deadwood, Territory of Dakota" by Charles Van Alstyne to a James Collins for the sum of two hundred dollars.[250] There is one other apparent mining claim note on this same page of Clow's diary for "No. 41 below P. J. Grounds" for which there appears to be no Deadwood reference.

If there were a friendship between Richard Clow and the miners on placer claim numbers 6, 7, and 8 below J. S. Collins, it may have been for one very good reason: water. The complete description of Clow's mine places it on the top of a small ridge between two creek drainages. This means that any ore from the mine had to be hauled to a stream and then run through a sluice-box to remove the gold. Perhaps he was negotiating

---

[247] Clow, Richard, "Mining Deed: Golden Seal Lode," *Book of Deeds, vol. 12, p. 409* (Deadwood, Lawrence County, SD., 1880, 1.

[248] Clow, Richard, "Mining Deed: Golden Seal Lode," *Book of Deeds, vol. 3, p. 431* (Deadwood, Lawrence County, SD., 1879, 1.

[249] Clow, Richard, "Affidavit of Richard H. Clow: Golden Seal Lode," *Book of Deeds, vol. 3, no. 2871* (Deadwood, Lawrence County, SD., 1880, 1.

[250] Van Alstyne, Charles, "Quit Claim Deed" *Book of Deeds, vol. 5, p. 337* (Deadwood, Lawrence County, SD., 1879), 1.

with the placer mines near him for access to the water for his sluice-box. It may explain the manner in which he chose to develop the mine over the next four years.

As the winter of 1876—77 began, Richard Clow did what any successful hard rock miner would do to speed up the development of his mining: he hired some help. By this time he would have been working his mine for two months, long enough to show that it could bring out "pay-dirt." In his affidavit filed on January 16, 1880, he legalized his hiring of a man named Dugdale during the 1876—77 winter. It states, "sometime during the winter of 1876—77 he [sic] conveyed an undivided one fourth interest in said Golden Seal Lode to one Dugdale for running a tunnel twenty feet in length."[251]

In addition, since hard rock mining requires equipment, Clow began to raise money by selling off other shares in his mine for real cash. The same affidavit indicates that, in addition to the deeding of one quarter of the mine for hard labor, he also sold another quarter of the mine. His continuing statement from above reads, " . . . and afterwards I sold and conveyed another undivided one fourth interest to one Cast, and these two afterwards sold and conveyed their interests to Wlm. W. Foster to my knowledge."[252]

From these records it is evident that Richard Clow was one of the lucky ones who got into the Black Hills early enough to stake a viable claim. Additionally, once he struck it rich, it is apparent that he had the acumen to develop his claim in a sensible manner as the wild life of Deadwood and the scrabble for gold swirled about him.

Of course, all the while that Richard Clow was breaking his back either sluicing crushed ore for gold or burrowing through solid rock in his mine, Deadwood continued to grow and prosper. New stores and warehouses were going up while giant stamp mills were erected to crush the ore. As the town grew, street vendors peddled their wares, gambling houses took money from the suckers, and grocery stores prospered with the burgeoning population. Farms and ranches developed in the surrounding grassy hills and transportation improved immensely with the advent of better roads and stagecoach lines. The railroad pushed ever closer as it

---

[251] Clow, Richard, "Affidavit of Richard H. Clow: Golden Seal Lode,"
*Book of Deeds, vol. 3, no. 2871* (Deadwood, Lawrence County, SD., 1880), 1.
[252] Ibid., 1.

was extended across the pacified plains, but would not reach Deadwood until 1890. People came and went in the town and much of the high life and hyped violence could be heard or read about in the newspaper after the fact, but wasn't witnesses by the majority.[253][254]

It is most probable that on the fateful day of August 2, 1876, when Wild Bill Hickok was murdered by Jack McCall, that Richard Clow, like many other honest and hard-working men, was up to his elbows in the icy water of a sluice box somewhere in Packrat Gulch searching the black sands for small nuggets or shining flakes of gold. At that time, he may have had an inkling of the vast riches that lay beneath his feet, but he certainly had not discovered them.

In August 1878 another frontier veteran, who very well may have met Richard Clow some ten years previously, arrived in Deadwood for a brief visit. Yellowstone Kelly and a small detachment of soldiers had been given the assignment of following the Tongue River out of Montana eastward towards Deadwood, with the idea of establishing a mail route between that city and the Yellowstone River. This would provide a shorter route for mail to reach southern Montana than the Missouri River route up through Fort Buford. Kelly gave an interview to a reporter in Deadwood to explain his assignment, and it is tempting to hypothesize that he also met with Richard Clow to reminisce about their hunting days on the frontier near Fort Buford.[255][256] In subsequent years, the Golden Seal Mine continued to produce gold and because of this, the value of Richard Clow's remaining half of the mine continued to grow. By 1879, though, his interests seem to have taken a turn towards other goals. During that year, Clow began to sell out the remaining shares in his mine.

---

[253] Lee, Bob, "It Started with a Mining Boom," in *Gold Rush: The Black Hills Story, ed. John D. McDermott* (Pierre, SD: South Dakota State Historical Society Press, 2001), 84-95.

[254] Parker, Watson, *Gold: In the Black Hills* (Pierre: South Dakota State Historical Press, 2003), 41, 151.

[255] Quaife, M. M., ed., *Yellowstone Kelly* (Lincoln: University of Nebraska Press, 1973), 208-209.

[256] Keenan, Jerry, *The Life of Yellowstone Kelly* (Albuquerque: University of New Mexico Press, 2006), 128.

On June 2, 1879, he sold another quarter of his mining shares to a Martin E. Posh for the sum of five hundred dollars. [257]

This sum may sound like a fairly paltry amount when compared to our present day wages, but one must realize that mining did not pay much as a job. According to the displays in the Mining Museum in Lead, South Dakota, the ordinary wages for a miner were around $2.00 per day while an experienced miner might make $5.00 a day. [258] Thus, Richard Clow was making a sum equivalent to between 100 and 250 days of hard labor through this one transaction alone.

Following this sale, the mine must have hit a rich vein for a period of time, or mines such as the nearby Esmeralda may have hit a lode that caused the value of shares in the Golden Seal to soar. At this point, Richard Clow took advantage of this increase in value and on December 27, 1879, sold the final quarter share in his original mine to a group of four men: William Woodruff, W. H. Hibbard, Jabez Chase, and Alexander Dunbar, for the tidy sum of two thousand five hundred dollars. [259]

With this sum, equivalent to almost three years of hard rock mining wages, Richard Clow left mining, purchased land, and began cattle ranching. Although he had departed from the actual mining scene, he still remained in close contact with other owners of nearby mines, especially the main owner of the Esmeralda Lode, William Story, who, along with Alfred Mahler, had discovered that mine which was on a ridge adjacent to Clow's in June of 1876. [260] William Story was to remain as an important friend and figure in Richard Clow's life, as we shall see in coming chapters.

---

[257] Clow, Richard, "Mining Deed: Golden Seal Lode," *Book of Deeds, vol. 12, p. 409* (Deadwood, Lawrence County, SD., 1880), 1.

[258] Parker, Watson, *Gold In the Black Hills* (Pierre: South Dakota State Historical Press, 2003), 92.

[259] Clow, Richard, "Mining Deed: Golden Seal Lode," *Book of Deeds, vol. 3, p. 431* (Deadwood, Lawrence County, SD., 1879), 1.

[260] Story, William and Mahler, A., "Location Certificate: Survey & Plat, Esmeralda Lode," *Book of Deeds, vol. 3, no. 2884, p. 365* (Deadwood, Lawrence County, SD., 1880), 365-367.

Clow's diary has an interesting drawing of what appears to be a method for shoring up the entry into a mining tunnel, along with the phrase, "A monkey in every fork nigger spurs." The drawing (See Appendix 3, p. 44) shows bricks stacked to make two columns with an archway between and perhaps a lintel on top. This may have been what the entry to the Golden Seal Mine looked like after several years of work on the shaft.

Today if you were to search for the Golden Seal Mine you would find that virtually no record exists of it except in the legal records of Deadwood and in this book. It was apparently dissolved and melded into adjoining larger mines soon after the 1879 sale of Clow's final portion of the original claim. The present day physical location of the original Golden Seal Mine has also changed drastically from those early days. It now rests under the houses, roads, and further mining excavations which make up a part of Lawrence County, South Dakota, in what is now officially known as Central City. Central City itself is halfway between the current towns of Deadwood and Lead, which are separated by approximately three miles.

The 1880 census records for the Dakotas indicate that Clow was still in residence in an unincorporated town of South Dakota at that time. In fact, with his venture into cattle ranching, he apparently became quite a successful dairy farmer. Although the site of his ranch is not precisely known, according to McBee family legend, it lay somewhere along the upper reaches of Box Elder Creek to the southeast of Deadwood. It was close enough to Deadwood that Richard Clow did not lose contact with the families and friends he had made during those many years of mining the creeks above Deadwood, Dakota Territory.

Looking at the above records, it is easy to see that Clow saw how quickly many miners went broke due to their inability to manage their "gold" money. It also did not take him long to realize that money could be earned other ways than by breaking one's back over a pick and shovel. Additionally, he probably realized that in order to process large quantities of hard rock ore from his mine that a stamp mill would be necessary. Each stamp mill weighed on the order of 400,000 pounds and cost approximately $30,000 to deliver on site.[261] This amount of money would

---

[261] Parker, Watson, *Gold: In the Black Hills* (Pierre: South Dakota State Historical Press, 2003), 113.

have been well beyond the means of Richard Clow. Thus the sale of his mining shares to wealthy speculators once the mine had begun to prove itself was probably a smart idea.

In addition to his physical strength, which must have been of a very sturdy nature, Clow had a variety of other skills to fall back on to make a living when he eventually tired of mining. These included the abilities to read and write, keep books, farm, and also hunt and shoot.

Ultimately, he took his profits from the mining venture and put them into his ranch, which became a successful dairy business. The ranch was profitable enough to make the newspapers when it was finally sold in 1882 to a Mrs. Jos Kelly in 1882.[262]

Because Richard Clow was frugal, he very likely banked a good portion of any of his earnings, as he had done previously in the military. This is not to say that he did not know how to enjoy himself. If fact, the next section of his diary indicates that he may have frequented bars and taverns regularly for his own purposes. His diary shows that he was interested in writing down some of the songs he heard in the Deadwood area. This would suggest that he perhaps was interested in singing and in hearing others sing the ballads of the time. In the bars he would have had time to learn the melodies and to write down the words for later practice. It gives us another interesting insight into the life of this young man.

The first song in Clow's diary appears to be written in rudimentary Spanish. The words are misspelled and run-on in such a manner as to suggest that he probably wrote out the phrases of the song after listening to it a number of times or while sitting at a table with a Mexican friend who told him the ballad's words and phrases.

The complexity of the words means that he undoubtedly labored over this particular song for quite some time in order to get all the words written out for the eight verses.

It is unfortunate that I have only been able to decipher two of the eight verses due to the smeared pencil on the other pages. Hopefully, with better technology and the work of a more experienced linguist, the rest of his version of "Las Señas del Esposo" will be brought to light.

---

[262] *Black Hills Daily Times*, July 27, 1882, p. 3, col. 5.

"Las Señas del Esposo" or "The Characteristics of the Husband" is one of a large number of romantic songs or ballads having their origins in Spain. This particular ballad came to the New World with the Spanish Conquistadores in the mid-fifteenth century. Slightly different versions of the song were disseminated throughout the Caribbean, South and Central Americas, and into North America by these intrepid Spanish adventurers. Their ancestors continued to pass on the verses orally so that it is now a part of Hispanic oral tradition extending all the way from Chile to North America.[263] The versions of the "Las Señas del Esposo" song are numerous, with each area having local additions or twists to the verses. They sometimes go by other titles such as: "La Catalina" (Catalina's Song), "La Recién Casada" (The Newly Married Woman), "La Casada Fiel" (The Faithfull Wife), "La Mujer Abandonado" (The Abandoned Woman) and even a children's version from Nicaragua known as "Soldadito" (The Little Soldier). In Mexico alone, twenty one versions of this particular song have been described.[264] [265]

Below is Richard Clow's rudimentary phonetic version, which he wrote down in his diary somewhere between 1874 and 1876. The "Clow" version as he heard it and wrote it out is the first line of each stanza prefaced by "Diary." Beneath that is a line, "S," of possible Spanish that seems to fit it based on my review of other versions of the song that come from Mexico and Cuba.[266] [267] The original text and Spanish conversion are followed by a third line, "T," which is my translation into English. I have paired Clow's diary lines as they are generally written as pairs in

---

[263] Diaz-Roig, Mercedes, *"The Traditional Romancero in Mexico: Panorama,"* 2, no.2-3 (1987): 617-618, http://Journal.oraltradition.org.

[264] Ibid., 616-618, 629

[265] Alzu, Jose, L., and Fernando G. Cortes, *Musica Educacion Artistica: Serie 2000 Primeria* (Mexico, Santillana Press, 2000), 28.

[266] Diaz-Roig, Mercedes, *"The Traditional Romancero in Mexico: Panorama,"* 2, no.2-3 (1987): 616-632, http://Journal.oraltradition.org.

[267] Chacon y Cabo, Jose M., *Ensayos de Literatura Cubana* (Madrid, Saturnio Calleja, 1922), 103-116. http://openlibrary.org/books/ OL13510963M/Ensayos_de_literatura_cuba.

other versions to distinguish the dialogue that passes back and forth between the woman and the man to whom she is speaking. I have placed short notes under the translation where other words might be substituted depending on the translator's opinion of the original script. To see Clow's crossed out words see Appendix 1.

**Diary Page 24:**
Diary:            1. *Yoso way ladrasen casartha,   Conithen ma gosarah*
S.      1. Yo soy la recién casada, Conozco me gozara
T.      1. I am recently married, You know my enjoyment

Diary:          *Mea ah abdono me marathon, Por ahmar ha levertar*
S.      Me abandono mi marido, Por amar de libertad
T.      My husband abandoned me, For the love of liberty
Note:(Possibly 2nd stanza is, Por amar se levanter which would translate as: I advance myself by love.)
        <u>Cho[rus]</u>
Diary:          *Caviaro por me frigoloona,*
S.      Que sabíamos por me frigidez,
T.      What do you think of my coldness?

Diary *No me ah visto, Ah me maredo  S*
S.      ¿no me ha visto? ¿a mi marido?
T.      Haven't you seen?  My husband?

Diary:          *Señoría no lo conoscu, Demmi unna cennia ela digo*
S.      Señora no lo conozco,        Deme una seña y le digo
T.      Madam, I don't know him, Give me a characteristic, and she said.

Diary:          *Me marido es alto erotio, Tiñe poco dacortes*
S.      Mi marido es alto y erótico [y rubio?*], tiene poco de cortes
T.      My spouse is tall and erotic, He's not courteous

*Note: Although Clow's script seems clear here in his diary, the word *erotio* may be two words, *y rubio* meaning "and blond" which is found in many versions.

Diary:          *Enlacaba delioga tinie, Un latraro Francez.*
S.      En la chapa de lio ha tiene, Un letrero francés
T.      On the badge of his bundle is a French symbol

Diary:          2. *Polarsenos ca ustar ah dade, Su mariado muardo   louaz*
S.      2. Por las señas que usted ha dado, Su marido muerto
        lo vez
T.      2. From the signs you have given me, I saw your
        husband dead

Diary:          *Enlas garos davilencia lumato, un tradosa Francez*
S.      En las guerras de Valencia lo mato, Una traidor francés
T.      In the wars of Valencia he was killed, by a treacherous
        Frenchman

Diary:          *Cean Soldados locos disparartho, Donsavo noventah etras el acca*

S.      Cien soldados locos disparan, Dan nos noventa detrás el acá
T.      A hundred crazy soldiers shooting, With our ninety behind him
        there.

Diary: *Mas lo yoravva arrah eha, deon hanovas*
S.      Mas lo lloraba arras era, De un genovés
T.      But the most I could do was cry out, to the Genoan

---

It is unfortunate that use and handling of the diary for over one hundred years has smeared the pencil writing of the six remaining verses on the next pages. It is possible that in the future, a thorough handwriting analysis of pages 25 and 26 in the diary will yield some unique phrases and twists to this group of Hispanic ballads.

The common characteristics of all the versions of "Las Señas del Esposo" seem to lie in a conversation between a woman and a passing soldier who is returning from the wars. According to Chacon, 1922, there are four sections that are seen in the various versions: 1. The woman waiting for her husband, 2. The description of the husband, 3.

Notification of the husband's death, 4. The final revelation of the husband's identity.[268]

In Clow's version, the first three of these sections are present within the portions which have been studied in this text. The portion that follows is even more interesting and will hopefully be studied by a scholar of Spanish to reveal what the woman says after she knows that her husband is dead. Will she remain waiting faithfully for her husband as long as it takes for him to come back, or is this a version which characterizes the unfaithful wife who is now ready to marry the first person who comes along? What will the disguised husband who is standing there in front of her say after he has heard the end of her lament?

If the woman only laments the death of her husband, then she will be deemed to be faithful and the ending will be congratulatory as the husband reveals his identity. Conversely, he may have to chastise her verbally if she reveals herself to be thinking of unfaithfulness. It would be intriguing to know which type of an ending Clow's North American version has.

Because Clow's version contains run-on sections in the writing, caused by the phraseology of the song, it is probable that the singer could not read and correct the written errors. The singer may also have spoken a highly accented dialect of Mexican Spanish that gave Clow some of his strangely written words. He may have actually learned this song at his mother's knee years earlier, and being illiterate, had only the sounds as references from which to extract meaning.

Persons of Mexican origin were present on the Northern Plains long before the Black Hills gold rush. Charles Larpenteur's journal notes the presence of Mexican wood cutters at Ft. Buford on March 10, 1869, the same year that Richard Clow was posted to Fort Buford.[269] By 1875,

---

[268] Chacon y Cabo, Jose M., *Ensayos de Literatura Cubana* (Madrid, Saturnio Calleja, 1922), 107-108. http://openlibrary.org/books/ OL13510963M/Ensayos_de_literatura_cuba.

Mexicans could easily have made up a fair portion of the wood cutters, herdsmen, and cattlemen who were living in the territory between Laramie and the Missouri River some five hundred miles to the north. It is not unrealistic to believe that Mexican miners were also represented in the population of the city of Deadwood at that time. Mexican bounty hunters were certainly also present in the Black Hills during that exciting period of time.[270]

[269] Casler, Michael M., ed., *The Original Journal of Charles Larpenteur: My Travels to the Rocky Mountains between 1833 and 1872* (Lincoln: The Museum Association of the American Frontier, 2007), 210.

[270] McLaird, James C., "I Know… Because I Was There: Leander P. Richardson Reports the Black Hills Gold Rush," in *Gold Rush: The Black Hills Story*, ed. John D. McDermott (Pierre, SD: South Dakota State Historical Society Press, 2001), 78-79.

# Chapter 23—The Miner Sings and Falls in Love

Immediately following the Spanish song in Richard's diary is another tune, this time in English. It's a popular old-time favorite of the mining hills originating during or just after the California gold rush, entitled "In the Days of 49." Four of the six verses of this song have been well-enough preserved in the diary to be copied for comparison to more modern renditions seen in songbooks published even today. Again, the time slot for Richard Clow hearing this song and recording it appears to be after the death of his first wife and probably sometime after he arrived in Deadwood where a number of veteran miners congregated in the saloons.

Richard McBee Sr., told me that a song writer had looked at Clow's verses for "The Days of 49" in this diary in hopes of finding some new verses for the popular miner's song. Whether they found any new verses or not is not recorded. Several singers have popularized similar versions of these words.

As long as we have human imagination, bad hearing, and worse memories, there will be new verses for popular songs. As noted by John and Alan Lomax ". . . in a few years a great number of amusing '49er' songs were composed, enough to make possible the publication before 1858 of two pocket songbooks . . ."[271]

---

[271] Lomax, John and Lomax, Alan, eds., *Folk Song: USA: The 111 Best American Ballads* (New York: Duell, Sloan and Pearce, 1962), 162.

Richard Clow probably picked these words up in a similar manner to his Spanish song, most likely while sitting in a tavern or tent bar and listened intently to the verses as they were sung aloud. Then, at some later time, he may have sat with the singer and written down corrections or omissions to make the song as complete as possible. For all we know he may have even penned a couple of the verses which are transcribed below. Once again several verses of the song are unreadable due to smearing of the pencil, but pages 27 and 28 of the diary contain the following visible verses from "In the Days of 49."

1.  There is Kentucky Bill F[aro]w [d]im witts[sic]
    A fellow of many tricks
    At a poker game he was always ther[sic]
    And heavy [illeg.] as bricks
    He'd play you draw for only a slug
    Or go a hatful bliss et
    But in a game of death
    Bill lost his breath
    In the days of forty nine

2.  Theres[sic] Morito Pete, I new[sic] him well
    For the flask he always had
    Hed[sic] deal all day hed[sic] deal all night
    As long as you had a s[en]t
    One night a pistol laid him out
    Twas his last day try out in fame
    For it caught Pete over
    Right dead in the door
    In the days of forty nine.

3.  There is N.Y. Jake the Butcher Boy
    So fond of getting tight
    Whenever Jake went on a spree
    He was spiling[sic] for a fight
    On night he ran against a knif[sic]
    In the hands of Old Bob Cline
    So over Jake we held a wake
    In the days of forty nine

4.  Theres[sic] Rackensack Jim

> He could out roar a buffalo bull you bet
> He would roar all day, he would roar all night
> I expect he is roaring yet
> One night he fell in a prospect hole
> Twas a roaring bad design
> For in that hole Jim roared out his soul
> In the days of forty nine

5.    Theres[sic] old lame Jess a hard old cuss
> Who never would repent
> He was never known to miss a meal
> Or never J[ur]y a cent
> But poor old Jess like all the rest
> To death he did incline
> So in his bloom went up the flume
> In the days of forty nine

------------------------------------------------------------

The years that Richard Clow spent in the mining claim areas around Deadwood are not well documented in his diary and his name does not appear in the local newspapers telling us of any particular exploits. The final eleven pages of the diary, 34 through 44, have only a few notes of possible importance on them. These include the names of several persons with whom he was apparently acquainted: Henry Dieu, Theod Shenkenberg, Isadore Bartingette, and John McClellan. I have not yet been able to find any reference to these persons in Deadwood history.

Successful mining brought in money and as the mining business grew, so grew Deadwood. Town businesses, both legitimate and not-so-legitimate, found numerous ways to transfer that money out of the miner's hands as quickly as possible. The gambling halls, bath houses, brothels, and smoking rooms catered to every level of desire for the lonely, single miner. The tales of the West from California in 1849 to Alaska after the turn of the century are rich with stories of men and how they managed to burn up their hard earned loot, scratched from the bowels of the earth.

And burn it those miners did as they distributed their cash up and down the main streets of the new town. Their money dwindled quickly as it was spent on visiting local merchants, drinking in the saloons, or being swindled by professional gamblers and prostitutes. Before long, if a miner wasn't careful, he was dead broke with nothing to do but head back to the creeks and hope for more good luck. If lady luck didn't smile on him, he generally ended up working for one of those for whom she had.

The gold itself, now hidden away safely in the vaults of the assayers and bankers, eventually found its way into the safes and iron money boxes. These rode with the stage coaches on the roads out of town headed for the banks back east and eventually government coffers

Richard's early experiences in the military and his general temperance when it came to drinking probably helped him avoid much of this waste. He would have been one of the first men in the bank door with his cash, rationing himself carefully towards compiling a nest egg that would eventually buy him a piece of land for the farm of his dreams.

1876 was an exciting year to be in the vicinity of Deadwood. It was the year that saw: the arrival of Calamity Jane (who was to become a legend of the late frontier era), the Custer massacre in Montana, and increased Indian attacks in the Black Hills. It was also the year of the great Centennial Independence celebration of Deadwood, during which miners and frontiersmen fired off a hundred of rounds from cannons, which must have created a racket that echoed through the hills like a small war.[272] The crowning event of notoriety during that year was the death of a man who was perhaps Calamity Jane's beau and already a legend in his own time, Wild Bill Hickok.[273]

"'76" also saw the beginnings of the final great uprising by the Sioux Nation as the full extent of poverty on the reservations, and the white man's disregard for the sacred grounds of the Black Hills, became evident to these peoples. This was the last straw following years of treaty-breaking, buffalo-slaughtering, and land-grabbing by the whites. The beleaguered tribesmen and their families, who had not knuckled-under to reservation living, went on the war-path.[274]

---

[272] Parker, Watson, *Gold: In the Black Hills* (Pierre: South Dakota State Historical Press, 2003), 157-158.

[273] McLaird, James C., "I Know… Because I Was There: Leander P. Richardson Reports the Black Hills Gold Rush," in *Gold Rush: The Black Hills Story, ed. John D. McDermott* (Pierre, SD: South Dakota State Historical Society Press, 2001), 66, 76-77.

[274] Parker, Watson, *Gold: In the Black Hills* (Pierre: South Dakota State Historical Press, 2003), 130-131.

The uprising was a last-gasp attempt to break away from the reservation talismans of pork, bread, and blankets that had initially lured many Indians off the plains and to resist the continued intrusion of the railroad lines into the hunting grounds. It was too little and too late. Yet while it lasted, it brought renewed flames of terror to the hills and land snatched by settlers and miners. These innocents, the miners, settlers, and travelers, were generally the victims of the guerilla warfare-like strikes that made the headlines of newspapers. The politicians who wrote the rules in their cozy offices in Washington rarely had to face the "music."

Initially, the generals and soldiers sent to chastise the renegade Indians underestimated both their numbers and ability to resist a return to the reservations. This resulted in multiple defeats for the military by the combined Sioux and Cheyenne Nation forces under Crazy Horse, Gall, and Sitting Bull.[275] With the national outcry that followed the army's defeat, first on the Rosebud and later at the Little Big Horn, a new military strategy was approved to bring the Indians back to the reservations.

As a wave of hope for freedom from reservation life surged through the Cheyenne and Sioux Nations, a winter fighting strategy was devised by the Army to bring the rebellion to a close. Under General Miles, many running fights were fought through the winter of 1876 and into the spring of 1877. By the end of the winter, the Northern Cheyenne were exhausted and starving.[276]

It was early May 1977 when the end came and Crazy Horse led his winter-starved people into the Red Cloud reservation and surrendered.[277] This left only Sitting Bull and his loyal Hunkpapa Sioux as resisters. They fled to Canada where they managed to eke out a living for another five years while watching their numbers dwindle until only a few hundred were left. Ultimately Sitting Bull and his people were finally broken and on July 19, 1881, turned themselves in at Fort Buford, the fort they had once harassed daily. With this final surrender, peace returned to the plains.[278]

---

[275] Remele, Larry, ed., *Fort Buford and the Military Frontier on the Northern Plains: 1850-1900* (Bismarck: State Historical Society of North Dakota, 1987), 48.

[276] Ibid., 50-52.

[277] Ibid., 52.

[278] Ibid., 54.

By the late 1870s, Deadwood had also settled down to become a more sedate town. More businesses had opened up and Richard Clow was well along in his cattle business. Clow's Diary, Page 42, is noteworthy in that it has a brief description of Clow's horse, "Bay mare branded on left flank and figure 3 on left shoulder" (See Appendix 3 for drawing of the flying circle U brand). In addition to ranching, he had found other work that utilized some of his old military talents. He began riding shotgun on the stagecoach from Deadwood to Rapid City or Laramie and Cheyenne when he wasn't working the ranch.

Sam Hartman, or "Laughing Sam" as his partners called him, fit the description of a veteran stagecoach robber in the Black Hills. When he was finally captured, he was put on trial for highway robbery in Deadwood for his part in an October 1878 stagecoach hold-up. He was accused of being not only a member of the party that actually held up the stage, but also of being a member of the infamous "Hat Creek Gang," which had robbed numerous other stagecoaches in the area.[279] Richard Clow was listed as one of the members of the jury in that trial.[280] He would have known exactly what it was like to be in the sights of a man who was willing to kill in order to get what he wanted from others.

Riding a stagecoach was often a dangerous business. The Deadwood newspapers of 1877 and 1878 are full of repeated hold-ups on virtually every stagecoach route out of the town. In some cases it was the payroll or gold bullion that the robbers wanted. In other cases it was whatever the passengers had on their person in the way of valuables such as watches, cash, or jewelry.

A man who rode shotgun on a gold- or payroll-carrying stagecoach in the late 1870s and early 1880s had to know how to use his pistol or shotgun with deadly accuracy. The men who held up the stages were often military veterans themselves. They were not known for leaving the guard and driver in a condition fit for anything other than a pine box. Richard

---

[279] "Laughing Sam Trial," *Black Hills Daily Times*, October 5, 1878, p. 1, Col. 4.

[280] "Laughing Sam Jury," *Black Hills Daily Times*, October 6, 1878, p. 1, Col. 4.

Clow was lucky to not have ended up with a case of lead poisoning while carrying out his duties.

As we close our review of Richard Clow's diary we come across a brief note written by his daughter, Cora Cochrane (Clow) McBee on page 40. Written after Clow's death, it simply says, "Father was born May 25th 1847. He passed from this life Nov. 19, 1926. He was the last of the eight brothers and sisters to go. Aunt Bertha Cochrane preceeded [sic] him ten months, going on Jan 21st 1926."

Cora Clow was born in the hills of the Dakota Territory in 1881. Thus we can see that despite all of the adventure, action, moving, mining, and probably carousing, Richard Clow still yearned for a wife and family. He dreamed of having a place to settle down and call home. It was during the spring of 1880 that a new young lady came to live in Deadwood town.

# Chapter 24—Farming, Married Life, and On to Oregon

According to McBee family documents, it was the day before Christmas 1879, when Melinda (Linnie) Story and her sister, Arnetta (Nettie), departed from the little town of Tekamah, Nebraska for Deadwood, Dakota Territory.

Tekamah was no great shakes of a town in those days, with its one claim to fame being that it was the highest point on the map for miles around. Interestingly, the town was less than five miles away as the crow flies, from the town of Little Sioux, Iowa, where Richard Clow had once made his home with his wife, Mary.

Linnie and her sister had evidently been invited to stay with their older brother, William Story, who had been in Deadwood since at least June 7, 1876, when he and Alfred Mahler had staked their claim to the Esmeralda Mine.[281] As fate would have it, the Esmeralda lay on a ridge above Black Tail Creek, which placed it almost next to the Golden Seal Mine, which Richard Clow had sold off only a few years previously. The men were no doubt already well acquainted.

The Esmeralda had become quite a successful mine as Deadwood grew. William must have seen the growing commerce of the town and

---

[281] Story, William and Mahler, A., "Location Certificate: Survey & Plat, Esmeralda Lode," Book of Deeds, vol. 3, no. 2884, p. 365 (Deadwood, Lawrence County, SD., 1880), 365-367.

found it to be a place for his sisters to find meaningful work as seamstresses. The once rough-and-tumble mining town was developing a gentry-class culture where dresses and suits needed to be mended and sewn. Deadwood was becoming a place fit for ladies of a gentler nature. Thus, it was William Story who probably paid the passage and lodging for his sisters to come and live with him. In this way he unknowingly was settling the future fate of Richard Clow and his desire for a family.

The first stop for the women is documented in family records as being in Omaha, Nebraska. Their route after that could have been to travel to Cheyenne on the Union Pacific Railroad and then go overland to Deadwood. On this route they would have been retracing the old gold rush route via stagecoach. Their other possible route would have been to go directly north along the Missouri, passing through Sioux City, Yankton, Pierre, and Fort Sully before cutting west along the Cheyenne River into the Black Hills.

The first part of either route would have been possible in mid-winter due to the improved nature of travel in the ten years since Richard Clow left Fort Buford. But both routes had difficult portions of road for deep winter travel once the main railway line was left. Thus, it is likely that the women stayed with relatives somewhere along the route until spring broke. Because of this, the ladies finally arrived in Deadwood on May 15, 1880. They immediately took up residence in William's home on lower Main Street. From here they began to ply their trade as seamstresses, as documented in the census of 1880.

By 1880, Richard Clow had prospered sufficiently to have his dairy farm in full operation. The census of that year lists him as being a farmer in an unincorporated town just outside of Deadwood. The lush grass valleys along Box Elder Creek would have been ideal for dairy cattle and also would have provided ample hay for winter feed.

It is likely that Richard first met Linnie Story at a party orchestrated by her brother, William, to introduce his two sisters to friends in Deadwood. It must have been love at first sight. The opportunity for Richard to have an occasional shirt mended thereafter may have been an excuse for further meetings between the besotted couple.

In the space of only six months, Richard Clow had courted and proposed to Linnie. The two were formally married on November 25, 1880, by Rev. R. H. Dolliver at the home of Linnie's brother, William

Story, the wealthy Deadwood gold miner.[282] Linnie's sister, Nettie, followed her in matrimony on October 6, 1881, marrying a man named Frank Aikene.

An interesting twist to the Clow—Story wedding is that it was reported incorrectly in the *Black Hills Daily Times.* The actual newspaper announcement states: "The marriage of Mr. R. H. Cloid and Mis Linnie Story at the residence of the bride's brother on Lower Main Street, Deadwood, Nov. 25, 1880 by Rev. R. H. Dolliver of the Deadwood Methodist Episcopal Church." [283] The wedding certificate for the Methodist Episcopal Church is correctly filled out although Rev. Dolliver did not sign his name, but rather, just wrote in "M. E. Church" for the Methodist Episcopal Church of Deadwood on the signature line (See figures 32—34). A name correction was apparently never published by the newspaper for this error.

According to the family story of the wedding, Richard rode into town on that November day in a snowstorm with his best white shirt tied onto his saddle. Somehow it came loose, and by the time he noticed it missing, he was already in town. The wedding was still performed with him wearing his rough work clothing and shirt. Following the service they went down the street to a photographer's shop for pictures. At that point they both rented the formal attire for a posed picture of their wedding (fig. 33). Thus, the wedding day was a success despite the lack of the white shirt.

Following the ceremony, the newlyweds moved out to the small farm near Deadwood. They lived there while Richard farmed and perhaps continued his work as stage coach guard for the next few years. Their joy of marriage and Linnie's pregnancy lead to the birth of their daughter, Cora Cochran Clow, on November 4, 1881.

The decision by the family to leave the Deadwood area must have been made during the summer of 1882. At that point Richard and Linnie sold their ranchland and cows. This is documented in the *Black Hills Daily Times* which stated, "Mrs. Jos Kelly has bought Dick Clow's ranch and

---

[282] "Married," *Black Hills Daily Times*, Nov., 27, 1880, p. 4, col. 5, 1.

[283] Ibid., 1.

herd of cows. Henceforth she will furnish her custome(r)s with the pure carbonate of cow."[284]

The family continued living in the Deadwood area until April 15, 1883. At that time they uprooted completely, and after a long wagon trip west, settled in the Southeastern corner of Idaho near Montpelier on June 3, 1883, according to family records. Here they homesteaded, and this time ranched sheep, forming the CBR Sheep Company in 1896.

In 1898, after a long legal battle and the breakup of the CBR ranch, the family continued their journey westward. The next move took them to the gold fields of Granite, Oregon, for another spate of gold mining and then to the lush farming country of the Willamette Valley, Oregon.

They ultimately settled in the bustling Siuslaw River port of Mapleton, Oregon, just fifteen miles upriver from the ocean port of Florence, Oregon. With his ability to work with others and take command, Richard Clow became the manager of The Mapleton Hotel. He held this job for several years around 1910 and then ran a livery stable.

In the final years of his life, Richard and Melinda moved inland to Eugene, Oregon to be near their daughter Cora and their grandchildren. Richard Clow passed away on November 19, 1926 and was buried in the Eugene Cemetery.

---

[284] "Mrs. Jos Kelly," *Black Hills Daily Times,* July 27, 1882, p. 3, col. 5, 1.

# Chapter 25—Rough Enough

The human experiences in life are infinite. Many perspectives of the Civil War and the frontier have been lost because of the inability or unwillingness of the participants to write down and share what they saw or experienced. One thing that comes across very clearly about this historical era is that life was certainly extremely harsh. At times it seems as if it was something to be endured, rather than simply lived.

Richard Clow's letters help preserve some of those extraordinary experiences of endurance in the mid-nineteenth century. They show us how the experiences molded and changed a boy into a man. Through his vignettes of life in each letter we get a better understanding of the stressful life led by military men during times of war, or while stationed at an isolated frontier fort.

One of Clow's greatest deprivations may have been the isolation from family, friends, and a known way of life. A military tour of duty for three years truly meant complete separation from all of those things. There were no telephones or internet, and rarely even any letters to communicate with loved ones. There was certainly no system of rapid transport to allow a quick trip home to see family and friends on short notice. Having leave from the army for a week or two did not mean having a reunion with one's family or sweetheart, who might be half a continent or world away.

The records of military medical doctors often mention the depression of the men stationed at isolated posts. Suicide and desertion rates for men at Fort Buford were high because of their desperation to escape this post.

Richard Clow's own letters allude to this sense of "melancholy" and longing for family and friends.

The slow pace of much of the Indian Wars may have actually given hardened Civil War veterans too much time to think and reminisce about the past as well as ponder future possibilities of death at the hands of the Sioux. Time to contemplate one's fate is not necessarily conducive to good mental health, as all military units know. Death was a close companion for these men, often for years on end, and there was no place for "rest and recuperation." Thus Richard Clow's note in one letter that he has too much time to reflect is indicative of this condition.

The response by men to this isolation, reflection, and consequent depression is seen through a number of unhealthy outlets documented by others. These take the form of alcohol abuse, fighting, robbery, murder, and suicide.

An attempt was made during the Civil War to diagnose a condition which had been seen repeatedly in battlefield soldiers and was referred to by doctors of that time as "Nostalgia" or "Soldier's Heart." Dr. Jacob DaCosta described a number of symptoms which seemed to mimic heart disease in highly stressed Civil War soldiers. These symptoms included heart palpitations, pain in the chest, upset stomachs, anxiety, and depression. The general conclusion was that there was nothing "physically" wrong with the men, but rather that these symptoms were psychosomatic in origin the symptoms were related to stress, overexertion, lack of nutrition, and lack of rest. [285]

The name "DaCosta's Syndrome" is still a recognized psychosomatic disorder of soldiers today. We know now that soldiers can spend years recuperating from the mental injuries which are incurred through involvement in battle situations. What is now most commonly diagnosed as Post-traumatic Stress Disorder (PTSD) was probably a part of what Dr. DaCosta was seeing.

Since there was no real treatment of any war-related psychological traumas or the abuses suffered by soldiers other than giving them rest and

---

[285] *Da Costa's Syndrome*, (Bionity.com, 2012), http://
www.bionity.com/en/encyclopedia/ Da_Costa%27s_syndrome.html.

nourishment, it is likely that there were thousands of cases of PTSD among the veterans of the Civil and Indian Wars.

Because the soldiers or ex-soldiers were basically left to suffer and sort it out on their own, the end result produced men who may have been prone to outbursts of deadly rage against their families or innocent victims. A large number of outlaws appear in the West following the Civil War. These men, including such men as Jesse James and the Younger Brothers, may have been victims of untreated war syndromes. Other victims of the war were the men who found conditions to be so unbearable that they committed suicide to escape. Thus, Richard Clow was indeed fortunate to be able to return to civilian life and eventually succeed in raising two children and remaining married to his second wife for over forty years.

Outbursts of anger which resulted in the commission of a crime by soldiers on the frontier had harsh consequences. Deserters could be punished with death and even lesser crimes were punished heavily. The Record of Medical History for Fort Buford notes that four men from Fort Buford were sent down river after burglarizing the Durfee and Peck Trading Post. They were subsequently branded with a "T" on the left hip and then sentenced to ten years of labor at the penitentiary at Stillwater. One can well imagine the desperation of these men to avoid this type of punishment which resulted in them trying to escape on several occasions while being taken down-river to face justice.[286]

This particular burglary incident occurred just prior to the time when Richard Clow was transferred to Fort Buford. It is very likely that this burglary, which involved a sergeant, left an open slot for Richard Clow to be promoted to First Sergeant.[287] Clow's military experience, his ability to write, and probable temperance with alcohol were likely factors in his being promoted to higher rank in a fort where alcohol had been abused so severely at all levels. This temperance may have also influenced Charles Larpenteur in his giving permission for Clow to marry his step-daughter, as the trader was known for his own eschewing of alcohol.

As we consider the stresses for soldiers on the frontier, it is worth looking at the statistics of death for various periods of time at Fort

---

[286] Kane, L. M., ed. and transl., *Military Life in Dakota: The Journal of Philippe Regis de Trobriand* (Lincoln: University of Nebraska Press, 1982), 363.
[287] Ibid., 363.

Buford. During the four year period from 1866 through 1870, a total of eighteen civilians, scouts, or soldiers were killed in the vicinity of the fort by hostile Indians. Additionally, twenty-seven other deaths, due to a variety of other causes, occurred at the fort during this same period. These causes of death include: nineteen by disease, six by murder, and two from accidents. To some extent, life inside the fort was just as hazardous as life outside on the plains.[288]

Within two years the garrison had increased from the bare one hundred men in 1869—70 up to four hundred men by 1872. The expansion of Fort Buford meant stronger patrols to protect workers and travelers near the fort as well as better policing of the territory as a whole. Additionally, the non-reservation Indian villages moved farther to the West, away from the pressures of the invading settlements. Consequently, the demography of death at the fort changed substantially.

During the following fifteen years at Fort Buford, between 1871 and 1886, disease became the major killer, with a total of fifty-two deaths in that category. Other dangers over that same time period dropped off drastically with the exception of suicide. There were only six deaths by accidents, suicides increased to five in number, and finally there were only two actual deaths attributed to hostile Indians.[289]

The increased suicide rate may well be due to a different type of young soldier coming out onto the plains in those later years. The new men had not already been tested and weeded out by warfare, extreme hardship, or by their committing suicide due to harsh frontier conditions before arriving at Fort Buford. Thus the weak still had to be winnowed out through natural selection, which is not necessarily a positive thought.

Charles Larpenteur's writings also confirm that death was a close companion in his life. In his own immediate family, during the two year period from 1871—1872, Larpenteur lost his son Louis, his daughter Rebecca, his granddaughter Bertie Clow, his step-daughter Mary Bingham Clow, and finally passed away himself. All of these deaths were apparently due to a variety of diseases or infections of a sudden nature. Prior to this

---

[288] Innes, Ben, *Interments at Fort Buford 18996 to 1895* (Fort Buford: 6th Infantry Reg. Assn. Publ., 1996), 4-14.
[289] Ibid., 14-28.

time he had already lost one wife to hostile Indians and a daughter and son to disease.[290] [291]

From these descriptions, it is clear that life took its toll on even the toughest men and women of the frontier. Danger was everywhere; at times it was overt in nature such as fighting in the Civil War, opening up frontier forts, or traveling in hostile Indian territory. At other times danger was associated with apparently peaceful activities like running a trading post, raising a family, or visiting a sick friend.

During the next fifty years, great improvements took place in the living standards of all Americans. Those persons living to see the changes in transportation, health care, travel, food, and communication truly saw miraculous things happening. Life improved immensely to several notches above the barely tolerable level seen prior to that time. Indeed, these early folks saw frontier life when it was "Rough Enough."

---

[290] Coues, Elliott, ed., *Forty Years a Fur Trader on the Upper Missouri: The Personal Narrative of Charles Larpenteur, 1833-1872* (Minneapolis: Ross and Haines, Inc., 1962), 305, 394, 395.
[291] Casler, Michael M., ed., *The Original Journal of Charles Larpenteur: My Travels to the Rocky Mountains between 1833 and 1872* (Lincoln: The Museum Association of the American Frontier, 2007), 76, 230, 253.

# Epilogue—The Day After Cora, November 5, 1881

**Author's Note**: This final story is a brief fictional account written from notes left by Richard McBee (Senior) about the birth of his mother, Cora Cochrane Clow, who was born on November 4, 1881, as this story closes. His information came from his own memories and from stories told to him by his mother and grandmother, Melinda Story Clow, prior to Linnie's death in Eugene, Oregon, May 25, 1946. It shows that there was also a soft human side to life on the frontier.

-----------------------------------------------------------------

"The bay mare plodded wearily up the road, her hooves crunching on the rapidly freezing mud. The white trunks of the birches along Box Elder Creek made rows that flanked the gentle curves of the route. They shone with an ethereal brightness in the faded gray evening light of the overcast November sky.

The rider, Dick Clow, tugged his sheepskin coat tightly around his neck and shoulders to keep out the chill of the wind. He was just as weary as his horse, but hummed and sang snatches of a song he'd learned at Drewsy's horse ranch from some of the boys. The tune distracted his mind from the numbing cold and drag of having finished another long work day.

He'd been up before four in the morning three days ago, saddled up Belle, and ridden out to Deadwood on this same road. It had been before any hint of dawn had entered the eastern sky and sparkling frost glistened in crystals from the trees. The stars had that special twinkling cold look seen at the onset of winter.

He'd ridden out with some reluctance. Linnie was talking about having little twinges of contractions in her pregnancy-swollen belly. Now he pushed Belle forward again with a nudge of his blunt spurs praying that there would be a wonderful surprise for him at home.

Belle blew out her nose in a little snort at the touch of the metal on her flanks. She'd already pricked up her ears about half an hour ago, recognizing the smells of home that now was only three miles up the lonely wagon track that led to the cabin. She tried to get her pace up to a trot but it was just too much to ask. Dick reached down and patted the big horse's shoulder saying, "You tired too, Belle, or are you just thinking of hay?"

Dick had been doing a lot of thinking these past few days since he'd left Linnie standing in the cabin doorway. She'd been smiling and confident that if the baby came while he was gone, all would be well.

"Mrs. Sullivan will come over from Star Creek and help me out," she'd called as he rode off, leaving her silhouetted against the light of the lantern just inside the door.

"How will Mrs. Sullivan know what's going on here and that she'd be needed?" he'd thought as he made his way down through one of the narrow gorges that the creek had cut through the hills. "Did women have a sixth sense?"

He'd had plenty of time to think about Mary, his first wife and baby Bertie so many years ago. He'd not been worried then as he went off hunting with Don Driggs for deer on that particular day. Everything had worked out fine. It was only later that they were both taken away by that mysterious illness that seemed to come out of nowhere and pick innocent victims.

His eyes caught the flash of the white rumps of deer as he neared the final long bend in the road leading to the cabin. Only deer, his brain told him, as his head snapped up in alertness and his hand strayed to the butt of the carbine near his leg. There were lots of them in the hills. With any luck he'd have another three or four hanging in the barn soon. There would be plenty of meat to last out the winter.

His mind drifted back to when he and Linnie had first met in Deadwood over a year ago. He'd brought in the torn shirt to be mended. The picture of her with the dancing eyes and pixie face under reddish brown hair was still clear and fresh. She had smiled up at him from the sewing machine when he entered the small closet of a shop. It had been the jolt of those eyes locking onto his that had told him, "This is the woman."

He was glad that he'd sent a message from the ranch to Mrs. Sullivan about the baby being near to coming. She'd stop over to look in and help Linnie with the chores even if the baby didn't arrive the way he suspected it would. He could only pray that all had gone well.

Darkness had fallen completely by the time Belle reached the end of the curve and the black shape of the cabin showed ahead. A slight bit of white smoke stood out as it rose against the black sky. The yellow light passing through the oiled rawhide window covering showed that someone was up, awake and expecting him.

He didn't stop at the cabin despite the impulsive urge to jump off the horse and dash through the door. Dick could hear his father's voice as he reined up in front of the barn door and pulled it open. The voice came out of the past just like Pa was there. He remembered clearly that night some twenty years earlier as they returned exhausted from two days of hunting during a continuous wet snow storm.

"Better take them horses into the barn, Dick, and rub 'em down," Pa had said. "First time you forget to do that with a hot, wet and tired horse on a night like this may be last. If that horse is your lifeblood, then if he dies, you just kilt yourself."

He led Belle through the pitch blackness to the back wall. By feel he pulled off the bridle and slipped the halter over her nose, clipping the chin strap. Then his hands sought along the wall until the touched the old lantern. He struck a match and the yellow glow of the lantern flowed throughout the inside of the small barn. He pitched a couple of forks of hay under Belle's nose and then loosened the cinch, slipping the long oiled latigo out of its ring and pulling the saddle and sodden blanket off the sweat-blackened back of the horse.

In the corner were a couple of old blankets which he used to rub down the sweaty areas to partially dry them out. In the process his fingers briefly traced the Flying-Cirde-U brand on her left shoulder. He scooped half a bucket of rolled oats from the barrel and set it in front of Belle who immediately put her nose down into the whitish flakes, munching noisily. Then he blew out the lantern and headed for the cabin.

He had barely pulled the latch string on the door when it was pulled inwards and he was greeted by the smiling visage of his wife.

"Linnie . . . ?" the question barely began to escape his lips when his wife held up a finger.

"Dick, not so loud, you great lump," she whispered. "She's over there sleeping!" Her finger pointed to the small bundle on the bed in the corner of the one room cabin. "Come," she led him towards the bed.

He bent down to look and as his eyes focused on the pink wrinkled face. He vaguely heard her telling him about the experience.

"Mrs. Sullivan left with her man just about three hours ago. She had to get home for her children, you know the oldest is only eight and they have four now." She opened the baby blanket just enough so that he could see a small tightly clenched little fist. Then she stood up. "I think we'll call her Cora because she's so dear to the heart to look at."

"Yes, that's a good name," he said, feeling a swell of pride in his chest. He lifted up her chin with one finger and looked into those wonderful eyes. His arms folded about her in a bear hug. He could feel a couple of tears scouring trails down his cheeks. Turning her slightly he could see from across the room that the wood box, coal-oil lamp and water bucket were full.

"They did you right nicely," he said, releasing her from his grasp.

"Yes, even milked the cow and put the milk in the spring house. Why . . . Dick," she paused looking at his cheeks still glistening from those couple of tears, "I've never seen you cry before. Why?"

He brushed the last traces of moisture from his cheeks, shucking his jacket and reaching for the tobacco pouch and corncob pipe in his shirt pocket.

"No, Linnie, I reckon not," he replied with a wry smile. "I'm just a happy man. It's been a long road and it's been rough enough."

# Chronological Timeline for Richard Headley Clow's Life

**1847**—May 25, 1847: birth of Richard Clow in Nova Scotia, Canada. [The military records are incorrect in stating that Richard Clow was born in Boston, see below].

**1853**—Richard Clow, at six years of age, travels from Halifax, Nova Scotia, Canada, with his sisters, Agnes (22yr) and Alice (8yr) on the Brig "Belle" to Boston. [Note passenger list (fig. 39) gives the country of citizenship for the three as "Nova Scotia" and the country which they desire to become citizens as "U.S."]

**1853**—Approximate year of birth of Mary Bingham, first wife of Richard Clow, in Little Sioux, Iowa.

**1861**—June 6, 1861: Birth of Melinda Story, second wife of Richard Clow, in Tekamah, Nebraska.

**1864**—August 18, 1864 to November 2, 1864: Clow's first enlistment in Civil War (100 days) in 22$^{nd}$ Massachusetts Volunteers. He was not assigned to a unit from this enlistment.

**1865**—January 1865: Clow's second enlistment in Civil War (a 3-year enlistment which only lasts 7 months) in 56$^{th}$ Massachusetts Infantry, serving at Petersburg through July 1865 when he mustered out at the end of the war.

**1865—1967**: Clow moves west to live with his brother and family in Minnesota and Wisconsin and farms with them.

**1867—1870**: On April 26, 1867, Clow signs his third enlistment, a 3 year period in the 13$^{th}$ Infantry, Company C. He joins in Minneapolis,

Minnesota, enlisting from his home in Wisconsin. Known postings are: Ft. Shaw, Camp Cooke and Ft. Buford. Clow's possible other posting is Ft. Ellis. On April 26, 1870, Clow musters out of the 13[th] Infantry, Company C, as a First Sergeant in Dakota Territory and goes to work as a clerk for Charles Larpenteur at the Ft. Buford trading post. During the year of 1870, Clow marries his first wife, Mary Bingham (Charles Larpenteur's stepdaughter).

**1871**—May 15, 1871: Clow, his wife, and the Larpenteur family close the trading post at Ft. Buford and travel together from Ft. Buford down the Missouri to farm outside of Little Sioux, Iowa. Clow buys land for a farm and also works for Charles Larpenteur.

**1872**—Baby Bertie Clow is born January 19, 1872, and dies on March 4 of that same year. She is buried on March 9 according to her tombstone. Clow's first wife, Mary Bingham Clow, dies on April 6, 1872. Following Charles Larpenteur's death on November 15, 1872, Clow moves in with the Driggs family after selling off his land.

**1873—1875**: Clow stays in the Little Sioux, Iowa area and works the farm for himself and his mother-in-law, Rebecca.

**1875**—Richard Clow leaves the Little Sioux area and passes through Laramie and Cheyenne, Wyoming Territory en route to the Black Hills.

**1876—1879**: During the next three years he stakes a claim and mines the Golden Seal Mine outside of Deadwood.

**1879—1882**: Clow buys and works a small dairy farm in the Black Hills near Deadwood. He rides a guard on the Deadwood to Rapid City stagecoach.

**1879**—December 24, 1879: Melinda (Linnie) Story, the future wife of Richard Clow, leaves Tekamah, Nebraska, arriving in Deadwood, Dakota Territory on May 15, 1880.

**1880**—The census of 1880 documents Clow as owning a small farm in an unincorporated town outside of Deadwood, Dakota Territory. It documents Melinda Story as a seamstress in the town of Deadwood.

On November 25, 1880, Richard Clow marries his second wife Melinda Story. The Methodist/Episcopal Pastor, Rev. R. H. Dolliver, presides at the wedding in the town of Deadwood, Dakota Territory.

**1881**—November 4, 1881: Daughter Cora Cochran Clow is born to Richard and Melinda Clow in Deadwood, Dakota Territory.

**1883**—April 15, 1883: The Clows leave Deadwood and travel by wagon to Bear Lake County, Idaho, arriving on June 3, 1883.

**1888**—April 16, 1888: Son Robert Denton Clow is born to Richard and Melinda Clow in Montpelier, Idaho. The birth is documented in the log of births kept by the county midwife Mrs. Francis E. Bridges.

**1891**—February 13, 1891: Richard Clow applies for and receives a homestead, Certificate #1096 for lots 3 & 4 of Sec35Twn13SR46E and lots 1 & 2 of Sec2Twn14R46E. This is 158 acres with a contiguous four mile stretch of land that runs along the Idaho/Wyoming border near Raymond Canyon and Raymond Mountain, Wyoming. The Clows begin sheep farming.

**1895**—Richard Clow incorporates his ranch with two other men, Beckman and James Redman, to form the 320-acre "CBR Sheep Company" outside of Montpelier, Idaho.

**1896**—The ranch dissolves and settlement goes to court. Richard Clow assigns his stock to his wife Melinda. The final ruling of the Supreme Court of the State of Idaho, March 24, 1897, rules against the Clows.

**1898**—March 2, 1898: The Clows sell out and leave Bear Lake County, Idaho, traveling by wagon to Granite, Oregon. They arrived on May 5, 1898. Richard Clow takes out several mining claims and tries mining for gold a second time.

**1899**—July 31, 1899: The Clows leave Granite, Oregon and travel by wagon to Eugene, Oregon at urging from their daughter Cora Clow who was teaching in Eugene. They arrive August 18, 1899. They remain in Lane County, Oregon for five years.

**1905**—December 26, 1905: The Clows depart Eugene for Mapleton, Oregon, arriving on December 29, 1905. In Mapleton they run a livery stable and a small farm. They then begin managing the Mapleton Hotel about 1907. They do this up until about 1909, after which time they go back to running the horse stable and small farm. Their son, Robert Denton Clow, runs the mail boat between Florence and Mapleton for a period of time.

**1907—1913**: The Siuslaw River freezes over during the winter of 1907. During this period Richard and Robert Clow are documented in a photograph swimming in the Siuslaw River during the summer of 1907. In 1913, new construction in Mapleton includes Joe's Warehouse, New Hotel, Bigelow's Pool Hall, and Noffzinger's Boat Shop. On April 11, 1913 the ship, Anvil, runs aground on North Beach near Florence,

Oregon. The Clow family goes down river by boat to see the stranded ship on the beach and take photos.

**1915**—July 3: Richard Clow returns to Granite County, Oregon to mine for gold with his son, Robert Clow. A relative, Oma McBee, cousin by marriage of Clow's daughter Cora to Elmer McBee, travels through Mapleton on her way to teach in the tiny town of Earl.

**1921**—October 28, 1921: Richard and Melinda Clow move from Mapleton to Eugene, Oregon and buy four acres of land on River Road where they live until August 11, 1925.

**1926**—March 1, 1926: The Clows buy land from their daughter and son-in-law, Elmer and Cora (Clow) McBee.

**1926**—November 19, 1926: Death of Richard H. Clow in Eugene, Oregon.

**1946**—May 25, 1946: Death of Melinda (Story) Clow in Eugene, Oregon.

# Appendix 1: Richard Clow's Diary

**<u>Diary Page 1</u>:**
Mark for Frost
Feb. 14th Friday (Remainder of page illegible (illeg.) with the exception
of numbers)

**<u>Page 2:</u>** (illeg.) Mary Clow
(Fort) Buford, D.T.
(Numbers added together)
Dan Moore Onowa Iowa D [Onawa, IA] (ec?) 22
Commissioned Mr Cassiday Oct 27, 1873

**<u>Page 3</u>:** Due Chas Driggs Dec 17" $17.25 Paid on team $130.14 Paid
Driggs $7.70 for board Board for team $5.00 ~~Total Due Driggs $7.80~~
Total Due Driggs $3.30

**<u>Page 4:</u>** May the 14th (1871) making packs of robes & peltries. The
steamer Ackly [Ackley] arrived at ten AM. Made arrangement to go on
board of it and started up work.
Firm Don
Bumber & Sqim                    3.15
Nails                              .54
Friday night and meals (followed by numbers 2, 3, 6 and several illeg.)

**Page 5:** May the 15th (1871) Left Buford at 12 and stop at the [illeg.] White earth (illeg.) The day was quite warm and L [illeg.]

**Page 6:** May the 16th (1871) St [orm] y wind is gust [illeg.] day and making [illeg.]. Reach Berth [old] at 2 PM Stevenson at 3 PM Reach [illeg.] Curry [Carie] & Koontz about 12 [illeg.]  The Far West 25 miles below Stevenson. Stop for the night [illeg.]
May the 17th (1871) Wed. Strong headwinds all day Took in 25 cords of wood at George Ba [kers] wood yard at painted [illeg.]

**Page 7:** May the 17th Wednesday Remained at Rice the balance of the night waiting on the Bay [liff]
May the 18 (1871) Thursday Still strong headwinds met the Nellie [P]eck at about nine AM Reached Grand River Agency at eleven AM left at 3 PM Stoped for the night about ½ hour befor [sic] Sun Set on account of a heavy Storm

**Page 8:** May the 19 (1871) Friday the day was beautiful[,] reached shienne [sic] at quarter after nine AM [.] left at one reached Sully at 2 [illeg.] and left at five [.] Stop for the night about 25 miles below Sully in Company with the Steamer May Lowery who left Sully about 2 hours before us

**Page 9:** May th[e] 20th (1871) Saturday Left very early reached the Brule Agency at 9[illeg.] Left the agency at half past 10 May Lowry passed us at the Agency. Passed the May Lowry again stuck on a bar near White River. Reached Whet Stone at half past six when we fell in with the Miner She left about 1 hour before us an we lef[t] at dusk and stoped at P Martin Near Randall
**Page 10:** May the 21 (1871) Sunday Passed Panca [Pancaw] Agency at 7 A.M [,] Running Water at ½ [?] Seven where we D [illeg. possibly Docked][,] met the [illeg. possibly boats] K[o]ontz and the Mollie Maser[.] reached Yankton at ¼ after 11[.] Landed to put out one passenger & Wife [.] Miner left at the same time.

**Page 11:**              Father to cash      5.00
                        "    "    "                 7.00
                     Harvey Driggs cash 5.00

Feb 3" Paid Emeline for Pork 5.00
Mr John Kellogg  Laramie City W.T.
Acct with Crouts
    18 meals          $6.00
    13 days lodging
$13 paid by Castiday

**Page 12:** Mary Clow   1871
Comensed taking Dr Garmalds medisen on the 18th of September
[Richard Clow's receipe for tanning hides.]
Fur Tanning One Table Spoon full of Sulphuric Acid to one pail full
warm water soak over night. [Rest of page filled with random addition
numbers]

**Page 13:**
Causo Testia    Horse
Buanis                  Good
Somberero           Hat
See                      Yes
Sea                      Saddle
Frano                   Bridle
Comesa                Shirt
Pantaloonas         Pants
Botas                   Boots
Sapatoes              Shoes
Mideas                 Socks
Guiena                 Chicken
Guio                    Rooster
Plato                   Plate
Cucheo                Knife
Ducks killed by Clow and Don [followed by a column of numbers
down the right hand side of the page 50, 6, 35, 8, 19, 11, 10, 6, 5, 6, 5,
1, 27, 9, 6, 10, 13, 5, 10, 13, 2, 3, 23, 4, 4
[The numbers of ducks continue onto the next page, #14.]

**Page 14:**
[Numbers of ducks killed by Clow and Don continued from page 13]
9, 4, 8, 28, 9, 8, 2.

**Page 14 (Continued)**: [A poem or song, of anonymous origin, possibly an original by Richard Clow.(See Appendix 2 for handwritten version)]

Waiting for Thee

[Verse 1] I've been waiting for more than a year love

Yes waiting and watching for thee

Hopeing [sic] and praying youd [sic] come love

To Keep your true promise to me

Cho [rus]

By the lilies that float down the river

And the cowslips that grow by the lee

By the roses that bloom in the forest

Im watching and waiting for thee

[2] I've waited for more than a year love

For that promise from you to receive

So surely you'll not break your word love

And leave me your absence to grieve

Cho [rus]

[3] So Ill wait another year love

In hopes of your coming this way

When the daintyist [sic] shades of th[e] twilight

Will shut out the dawn of the day

Cho [rus]

**Diary Page 15:** ///////// [Nine hash marks at the top of the page perhaps indicating nine work days.]

I commenced work for Hutton Yesterday July 10 at noon and worked 8 ½ days. Commmced[sic] for Sprague Sunday July 19" in the morning [1874]

Due me from Hutton $17.00

| Posts 48 | Rails | 58 |
|---|---|---|
| 11 | | 53 |
| 9 | | 121 |
| 8 | | |
| 13 | | |
| 21 | | |
| 12 | | |

22
44
188
Total 185[sic]

**Page 16:** / / / / / / / / [Hash marks again for apparently eight more work days.]

Comminced [sic] work for Keller on May 18" Monday [1874]
From Sheyenne [sic]
½ lbs Powder
2 Box caps
2 lead Pencils
Powder Flask
Envelops Stamped
1 Paper Tacks
1 Bottle Ink                                                        15
6 little Envelopes stamped
6 sheets paper                                                     30
1 Pair large Shears                                               150
1 lead Pencil with rubber                                         20

[These following numbers may have to do with calculations of Richard Clow's net worth prior to settling up accounts with the Larpenteurs as seen on the next pages]

| 15 | 365 | 75 | 86.32 |
|----|-----|----|-------|
|    | 40  | 25 | 63.50 |
|    | 405 |    | 149.82 |

640, 235, 405, 15, 30, 150, 20, 20, 235

**Page 17:** [*Omitted as it appears to have been erased and recopied on page 18.*]

**Page 18:** Acct with Chas Larpenteur [1871 and 1872]

| Dec 22" | paid Bassett | 6.00 |
|---------|--------------|------|
| " " | " Haynes | 2.00 |
| " " | " Doctor | 6.00 |
| " " | " Freight Bill | 1.72 |
| " " | " Corn | 2.00 |
| " " | 4 lbs Candles | 1.00 |
| " " | one lead Pencil | .10 |

| Jan | 10" | Shoeing Horses | .75 |
|---|---|---|---|
| Jan | 3" | 25 Bush Corn | 5.00 |
| " | 18" | 12 " " | 2.40 |
| " | 18" | Paid to Bassett | 23.20 |
| " | 22" | Horse Shoeing | 1.25 |
| " | " | Soap | .50 |
| " | " | Salt | .20 |
| " | 25" | 20 Bush Corn | 4.00 |
| " | 30" | 4 lbs Candles | 1.00 |
| " | " | Dried Apples | 1.00 |
| Feb 2" | | 25 Bush Corn | 5.00 |
| " | 4" | Paid Chas Driggs | 15.00 |
| " | 4" | Paid for Pork | 3.20 |
| " | 5" | Paid for Horse Medisine | 2.65 |
| " | 22" | 20 Bush Corn(Morde) | 4.00 |
| " | 29" | Candles 100 Dried Apples100) | 2.00 |
| " | 29" | Wiseman for Hay | 2.00 |

**Page 19**: Acct with Chas Larpenteur

| | | Paid Lewis | 2.00 |
|---|---|---|---|
| | | Harness Complete | 40.00 |
| April 25 | | 8 lbs Nails | .60 |
| " | " | Gardin Seeds | 1.20 |
| May | 11" | 50 lbs Nails | 4.00 |
| " | " | Seed Potatoes | 1.00 |
| " | " | Cash to Jack | .95 |
| July 23" | | Cash to Stewart | 15.00 |

Received Payt Dec. 12" 1872
    Richard Clow

**Page 19 (Continued):** [The following section, because of the 1874 date, appears to be a settling up of accounts with the Driggs family after the winter of 1875 when Richard Clow finally departs the farm on Soldier Creek, Iowa and heads to the Dakota Territory.]

Dec 10" 1874

Erb

38 = 14

 3 = 12

```
 7 = 16                    347
March  29"      335        335
                          682
```

**Page 20:**
39, 7, 7, 65, 273, 18, 56, 347

**Page 21:** [A repeat of the numbers found on page 20 with the bottom of page cut out]

**Page 22:** Acct With McGreavy

| | |
|---|---|
| 1 Pair Blankets | 5.50 |
| 1 Axe | 2.00 |
| 1 Handle | .75 |
| 1 Plug tobacco | .75 |
| 1 Bale Smoking | .30 |
| 40 lbs Beef | 4.00 |
| 5 " Sugar | 1.00 |
| 2 Boxes Yeast Powder | .75 |
| 1 Whet Stone | .30 |
| 1 lbs Tea | 2.50 |
| 1$ Tobacco | 1.00 |
| Pork | |
| 1 lb Tea | 2.50 |
| Peaches | 1.00 |
| Pork | |
| 1 lb Tea | 2.50 |
| Peaches | 1.00 |
| Pork | |
| Matches | .20 |
| Soap | .15 |
| 1 Bale Tobacco | .30 |
| 1 Sack Flour | 6.00 |
| 1 Broad Axe | 3.00 |
| 5 lbs Sugar | 1.12 |
| 1 ¼ Butter | 2.12 |
| 1 Axe handle | .65 |

**Page 23:** McGreavy

| | | |
|---|---|---|
| 11 lbs | Beef | 1.10 |
| 5 | Butter | 2.50 |
| 3 lbs | Currants | .90 |
| | Tobacco | 1.00 |
| 1 | Pipe | .75 |
| 1 | Pocket Knife | 1.25 |
| Beans | | 7.00 |
| | Peaches | 36.07 |
| 1 | Box Yeast Powders | 3.20 |
| 1 | Sack Flour | 2.75 |
| | Butter | 31.29 |
| | Sugar | 3.00 |
| | Beef | |

**Page 24:** [Richard Clow phonetic rendition of an old Spanish song or poem apparently as he heard it spoken or sung.]

1. *Yoso way ladrasen casartha*
*Conithen ma gosarah*
*Mea ah abdono me marethon*
*Por ahmar ha levertar*

Cho[rus]
*Cavi aro por me frigoloona*
*No me ah* ~~mi marido~~ *visto*
~~Senora no loconosco~~
*Ah me mare do  S*

Señoría no lo conoscu
*Demmi unna cennia_ela digo*
*Me marido es alto erotio(erubio)*
*Tinie poco dacortes*
*Enlacaba delioga tinie*
*Un latraro Francez.*

**2.**

*Polarsenos ca ustar ah dade*
*Su mariado muardo louaz*
*Enlas garos davilencia lumato*
*un tradosa Francez*

*Cean Soldados locos disparartho*
*Donsavo noventah etras el acca*
*Mas lo yoravva arrah eha*
*deon hanovas*

**Pages 25 and 26**: [Six more verses of the above phonetic Spanish poem/song follow on these next two diary pages which are unfortunately almost completely obliterated by smearing of the pencil.]

**Page 26 (Continued): [**Two pencil smeared unreadable verses of a variation of "In the Days of 49".]

**Pages 27 and 28**: [Verses from "In the Days of 49".]

1. There is Kentucky Bill F[aro]w [d]im witts[sic]
   A fellow of many tricks
   At a poker game he was always ther[sic]
   And heavy [illeg.] as bricks
   He'd play you draw for only a slug
   Or go a hatful blisset
   But in a game of death
   Bill lost his breath
   In the days of forty nine.
2. Theres[sic] Morito Pete, I new him well
   For the flask he always had
   Hed[sic] deal all day hed[sic] deal all night
   As long as you had a s[en]t
   One night a pistol laid him out
   Twas his last day try out in fame
   For it caught Pete over
   Right dead in the door
   In the days of forty nine.

3. There is N.Y. Jake the Butcher Boy
    So fond of getting tight
    Whenever Jake went on a spree
    He was spiling[sic] for a fight
    On night he ran against a knif[sic]
    In the hands of Old Bob Cline
    So over Jake we held a wake
    In the days of forty nine

4. Theres[sic] Rackensack Jim
    He could out roar a buffalo bull you bet
    He would roar all day, he would roar all night
    I expect he is roaring yet
    One night he fell in a prospect hole
    Twas a roaring bad design
    For in that hole Jim roared out his soul
    In the days of forty nine

5. Theres[sic] old lame Jess a hard old cuss
    Who never would repent
    He was never known to miss a meal
    Or never J[ur]y a cent
    But poor old Jess like all the rest
    To death he did indine
    So in his bloom went up the flume
    In the days of forty nine

**Diary Page 29**: Account with F. Stevens
Commenced work Jan 1"

| | |
|---|---|
| Tobacco | .50 |
| Smok Tobacco | .50 |
| Tobacco | .65 |
| Socks | .65 |
| Stamps | .25 |
| Drawers | 1.00 |
| March 8  lost four days | |
| Kerwin | |
| Gumy Boots | 8.00 |
| Stamps | .12 |
| Tobaco | .35 |

| | |
|---|---|
| Axe halve | .65 |
| Tobaco | .35 |
| To Woods | 2.54 |
| | 11.97 |
| **Page 30**: Kerwin | 11.97 |
| Shirts and Drawers | 7.55 |
| | 19.52 |
| | 18.00 |
| | 37.52 |

[Other miscellaneous arithmetic with no notes]

**Page 31**:  Comminced boarding at Driggses Oct 10"/74
From Driggs
~~Due me 60 Bush Corn~~
Cash                          .40
"    Hotel Bill   1.75
One day shipping hogs
½  "   butchering
Posts
Left Home April 28
Laramie Thursday night 29 [1875]
**Page 32:**  Dons Work
On Celler 2 half days
On logs   2 days
Lumber from Driggs
2 boards 14 ft 10 inch wide
4 "     10   8 "    "
1 "      8   8 "    "
23 ½
30
6
59 ½
[Bottom half of page cut off]

**Page 33:** [Blank]

**Page 34:** [4 neatly spelled names of possible friends.]
Henry Dicu

Theod Shenkenberg
Isadore Bartingette
John McClellan

**Page 36:** 333 3/3 five threes

**Page 37:** [Blank]

**Page 38:** [Probable initial mining claim site notes from Richard Clow's first Deadwood mining claims.]
No 8 below J S Collins
No 41 below P J Grounds

**Page 40:**
"Father was born May 25th 1847. He passed from this life Nov. 19, 1926. He was the last of the eight brothers and sisters to go. Aunt Bertha Cochrane preceeded [sic] him ten months, going on Jan 21st 1926." [This notation was written in the journal by Cora Cochrane (Clow) McBee, daughter of Richard H. Clow. She was married at that time to Elmer Francis McBee and lived in Eugene, Oregon.]

**Page 42:** Bay mare branded on left flank and figure 3 on left shoulder. [The drawing of a flying circle U and text is scanned and in Appendix 3.]

**Page 43:** Blank

**Page 44:** A monkey in every fork nigger spurs. [This cryptic phrase is written above a drawing of two brick pillars which come together to hold a pointed arch with perhaps a lintel above as in a mining shaft entry-way. The figure is scanned in Appendix 3.]

**Diary Page 45:**[These pages appear to date from the period of time in 1874 and early 1875 when Clow was still living at the Driggs family residence in Iowa and may have to do with Richard Clow selling out and settling up on his cattle, land, split fence posts and other items prior to departing for Deadwood, D.T.]
Due me
22.00

4.95
1.75
 .40
29.10
17.45
11.65
Braid
15.85
 .70
 .90
17.45
May 1" 1875 Due me 11.65
Driggs

**Page 46:** Lumber received   [numerous additions]
216 ft Don
360

| | | |
|---|---|---|
| Cattle | 84 | |
| | 55 | |
| Harness | 25 | |
| Board | 40 | |
| | 199 | increase on old cattle 28 |

**Page 47:** [A lot of scratched arithmetic beneath the following.]
Number of posts made 480

| | |
|---|---|
| 400 yds long | 73 |
| 160 " lower esid | 29 |
| 200 " Long lower side 36 ½ | |

**Page 48:** [Miscellaneous arithmetic on page in addition to text.]
Ties made for Kerwin

| March 18" | Friday [1874] | 11 |
|---|---|---|
| | Saturday | 15 |
| | Monday | 14 |
| | Wednesday | 13 |
| | Friday | 11 |
| | Tuesday | 9 |
| | Wednesday | 17 |

| | |
|---|---|
| Thursday | 14 |
| Friday | 10 |
| Saturday | 4 |
| Tuesday | 13 |
| Wednesday | 11 |
| Friday cut poles | 1.50 |
| Saturday | 8 |
| Tuesday | 12 |
| Wednesday | 15 |
| Thursday | 11 |
| Friday | 12 |
| Monday | 15 |
| Tuesday | 1.50 |
| Wednesday | .75 |
| Saturday | 1.50 |

April 19 Total Due $1.73

**Pages 49, 50 and 51** [unintelligible arithmetic]
[All remaining journal pages are blank]

# Appendix 2

A sample of Richard Clow's writing.
The poem "Waiting for Thee" from Diary p. 14.

# Appendix 3

The Clow brand (Diary p.42).

Mine shoring diagram (Diary p.44).

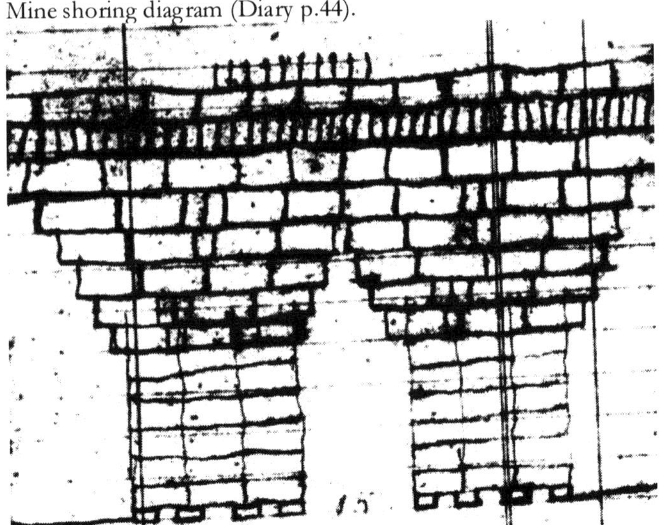

# Photos and Figures for *Rough Enough*

Fig. 1: Federal Soldiers in the Trenches before battle at Petersburg 1865  (Photo – Gov. Archives 11-B-157)

Fig. 2: Federal soldiers on picket duty opposite Fort Mahone Petersburg, Virginia (Photo: National Archives)

Fig. 3: Confederate Maj. Gen. Mahone who commanded
Ft. Mahone at Petersburg (Photo: Natl. Archives 11-B-5123)

**Fig. 4: Confederate Bunkers in Ft. Mahone at Petersburg, Virginia (Photo - National Archives)**

**Fig. 5: John Sherwin (Sher)  Clow older brother to Richard Clow about 1860 (photo – McBee)**

**Fig. 6, 7, 8: Agnes Clow, Alice Anne Clow and Jessie Clow, older sisters to Richard Clow about 1865    (photo – McBee)**

Fig. 9: John Stevenet Clow, father of Richard Clow  about 1865 (Photo – McBee)

Fig. 10: Richard Clow (R) and friend pretend to be medical students about 1867 (Photo – McBee)

Fig. 11: Richard Clow about 1867 just prior to third enlistment in the military. (Photo – McBee)

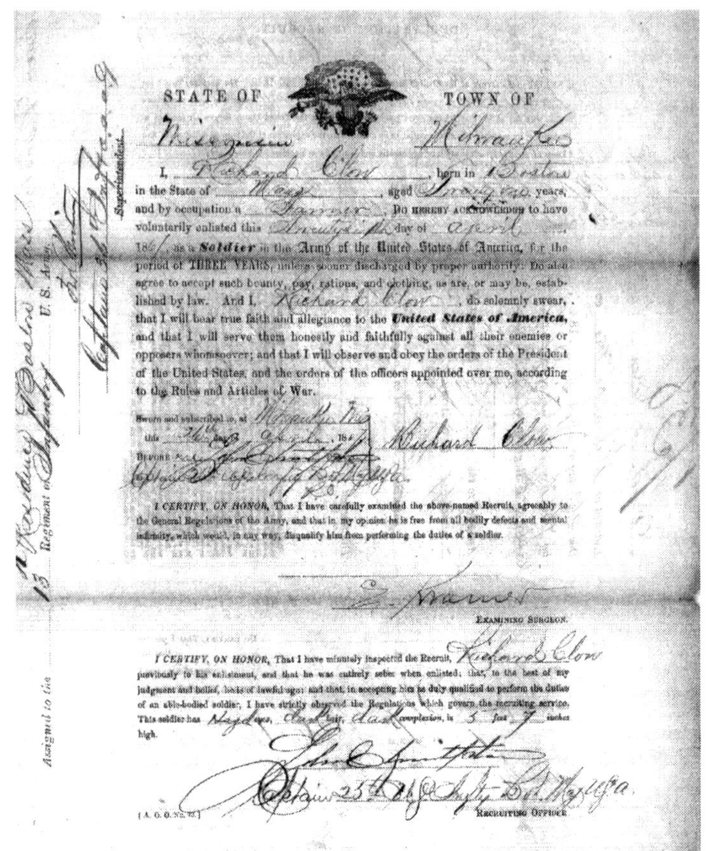

**Fig. 12: Third Enlistment of Richard Clow in 13th Infantry Reg. on 26 April, 1867 (Photo – McBee)**

Fig. 13: Old Fort Union reconstruction, Montana. Dismantled to construct parts of Fort Buford , D.T. in 1867 (photo – McBee)

Fig. 14: Inside of Fort Union reconstruction, Montana (photo – McBee)

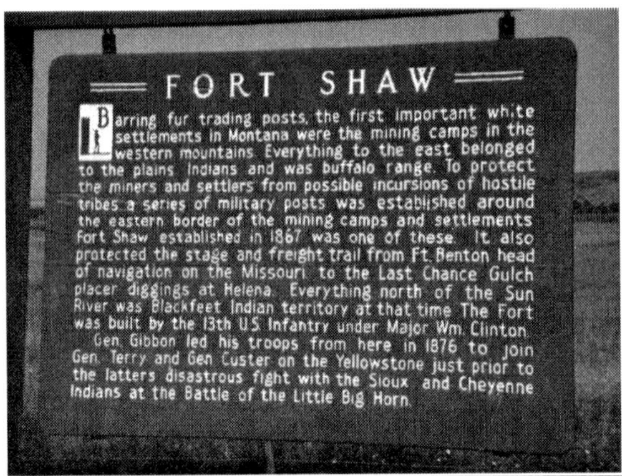



Fig. 15: Montana Historical Sign at sight of old Fort Shaw (photo – McBee)

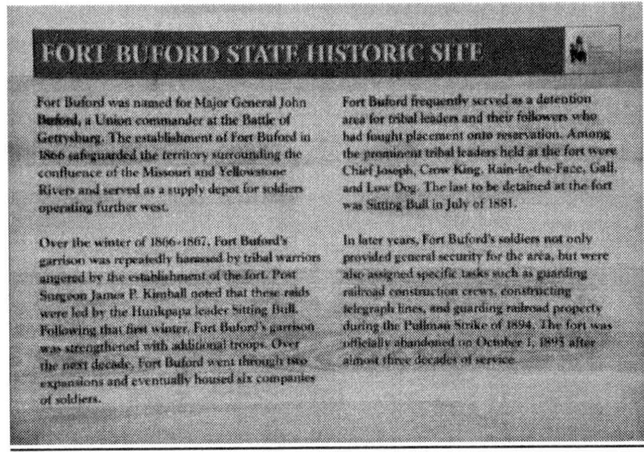

FORT BUFORD STATE HISTORIC SITE

Fort Buford was named for Major General John Buford, a Union commander at the Battle of Gettysburg. The establishment of Fort Buford in 1866 safeguarded the territory surrounding the confluence of the Missouri and Yellowstone Rivers and served as a supply depot for soldiers operating further west.

Over the winter of 1866-1867, Fort Buford's garrison was repeatedly harassed by tribal warriors angered by the establishment of the fort. Post Surgeon James P. Kimball noted that these raids were led by the Hunkpapa leader Sitting Bull. Following that first winter, Fort Buford's garrison was strengthened with additional troops. Over the next decade, Fort Buford went through two expansions and eventually housed six companies of soldiers.

Fort Buford frequently served as a detention area for tribal leaders and their followers who had fought placement onto reservation. Among the prominent tribal leaders held at the fort were Chief Joseph, Crow King, Rain-in-the-Face, Gall, and Low Dog. The last to be detained at the fort was Sitting Bull in July of 1881.

In later years, Fort Buford's soldiers not only provided general security for the area, but were also assigned specific tasks such as guarding railroad construction crews, constructing telegraph lines, and guarding railroad property during the Pullman Strike of 1894. The fort was officially abandoned on October 1, 1895 after almost three decades of service.

Fig. 16: Fort Buford Historical Site (photo of display - Richard McBee)

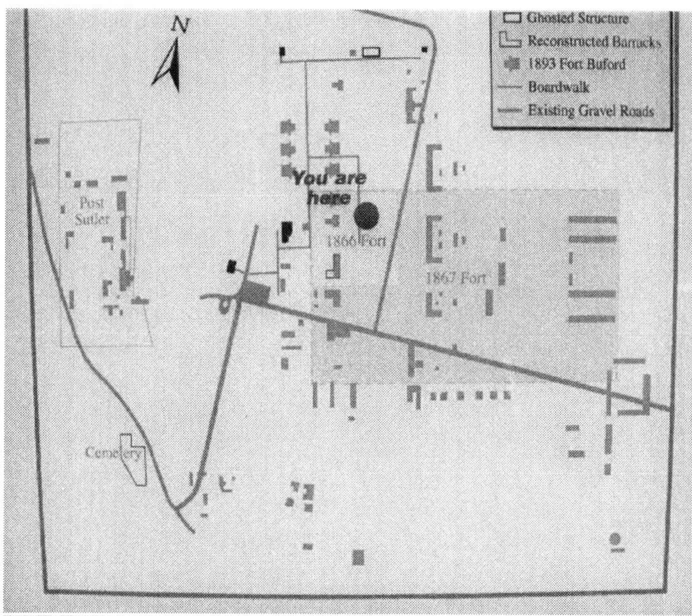


Fig. 17: Relative positions of Fort Buford and the Fort Sutler (Larpenteur) circa 1867 (photo of display - McBee)

Fig. 18: The landscape around present day Fort Buford, North Dakota (photo – McBee)

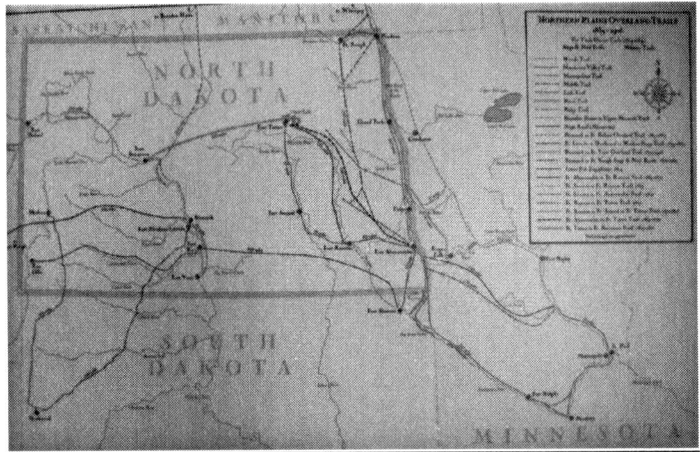

Fig. 19: Dakota Territory Trails circa 1870 - Fort Buford display (photo – McBee)

Fig. 20, 21, 22, 23: Fort Buford tombstones of the four men described in Richard Clow's letter who were killed in ambush August 10, 1869 (photos – McBee)

**Fig. 24: Model of Steamboat used on the Missouri in 1970's - Fort Buford, ND display (photo – McBee)**

Fig. 25: First Sergeant uniform and buffalo robe - Fort Buford 1870 period display (Photos – McBee)

Fig. 26: First Sergeant quarters 1870 period display at Fort Buford (photos – McBee)

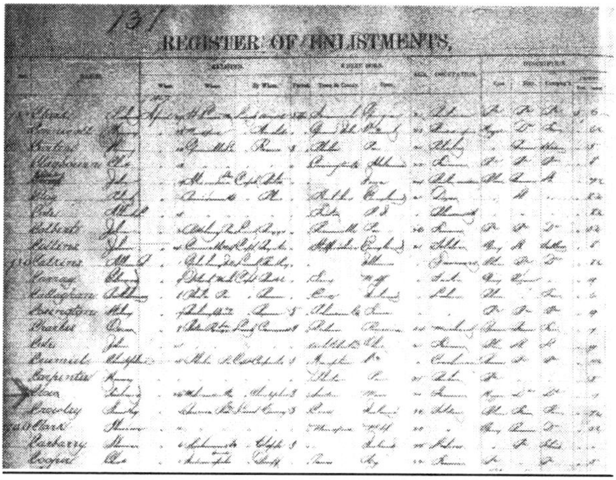

Fig. 27: Richard Clow Military Discharge p. 1 at Fort Buford from US Military Document (photo – McBee)

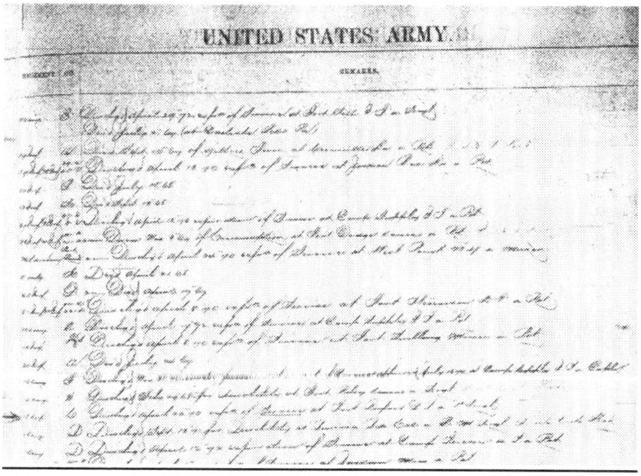

Fig. 28: Richard Clow Discharge at Fort Buford, D.T. from Military Records p. 2 (photo – McBee)

**Fig. 29: Mary Bingham Clow about the time of her wedding to Richard Clow in 1870 (Photo – McBee)**

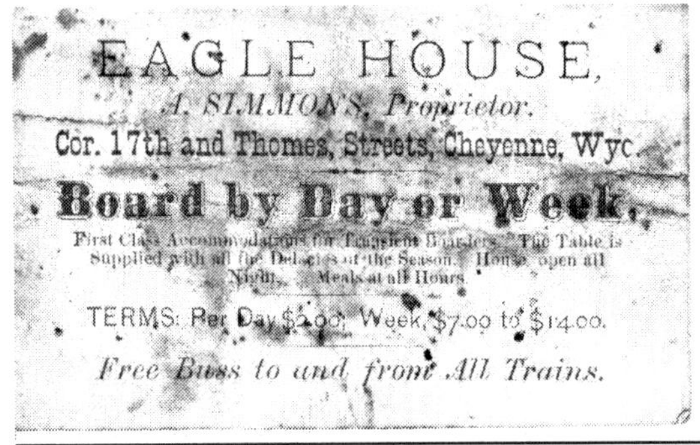


**Fig. 30: Eagle House Card in Cheyenne, Wyoming about 1875 (photo McBee)**

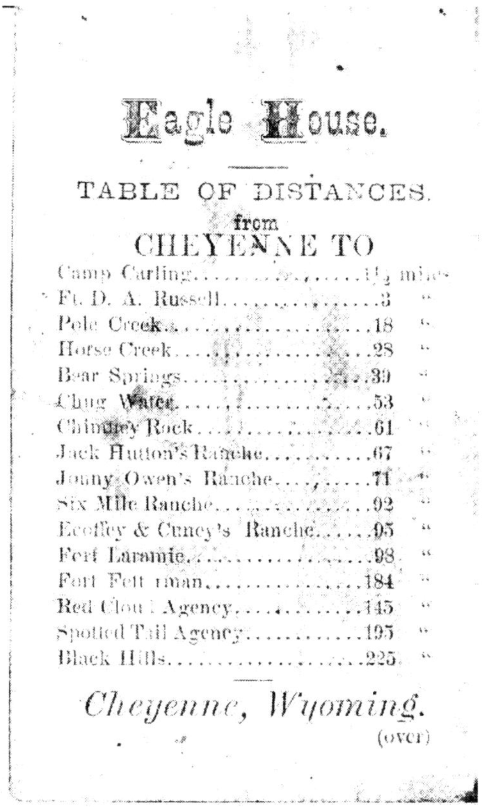

**Eagle House.**

TABLE OF DISTANCES.
from
CHEYENNE TO

| | | |
|---|---|---|
| Camp Carling | 1½ | miles |
| Ft. D. A. Russell | 3 | " |
| Pole Creek | 18 | " |
| Horse Creek | 28 | " |
| Bear Springs | 39 | " |
| Chug Water | 53 | " |
| Chimney Rock | 61 | " |
| Jack Hutton's Ranche | 67 | " |
| Jonny Owen's Ranche | 71 | " |
| Six Mile Ranche | 92 | " |
| Ecoffey & Cuney's Ranche | 95 | " |
| Fort Laramie | 98 | " |
| Fort Fetterman | 184 | " |
| Red Cloud Agency | 145 | " |
| Spotted Tail Agency | 195 | " |
| Black Hills | 225 | " |

*Cheyenne, Wyoming.*

(over)

**Fig. 31: Obverse of Eagle House Card (Photo – McBee)**

**Fig. 32: Wedding Photo of Linnie Story (center front) with her family - 1880 (photo - McBee)**

**Fig. 33: Wedding Photo of Richard Clow and second wife,
Melinda (Linnie) Story (Photo – McBee)
Nov. 25, 1880, Deadwood, D.T.**

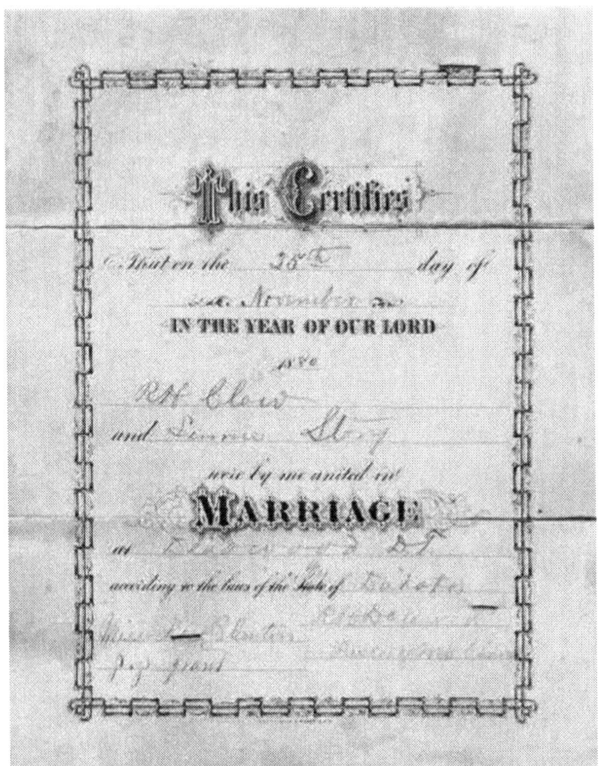

**Fig. 34: Wedding Certificate Richard Clow and Linnie Story – 1880 (photo – McBee)**

Fig. 35: Richard and Linnie Clow with Daughter, Cora Cochran Clow, 1885, Montpelier, Idaho (photo – McBee)

**Fig. 36: Richard, Linnie, Cora and son Robert Denton Clow, 1890 in Montpelier, Idaho (photo – McBee)**

Fig. 37: Clow family with grandchildren Elma (lf) and Chloe (rf)about 1915 in Mapleton, Oregon

Back row L to R - Cora, Robert, Linnie and Richard Clow (photo-McBee)

Fig. 38: Richard Clow with Cora's son, Richard McBee about 1920 in Mapleton, Oregon

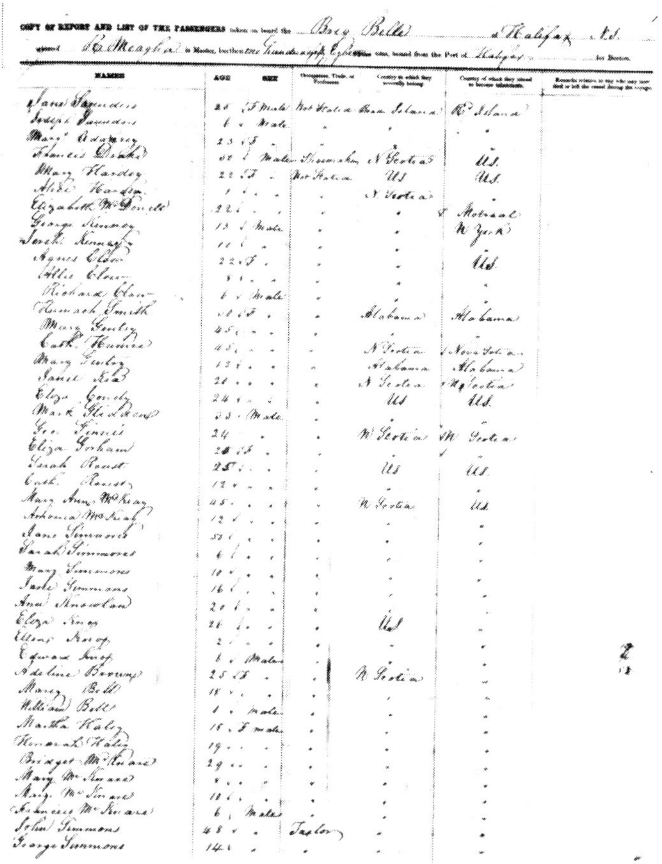

Fig: 39: Passenger list for the Brig. Belle in 1853 carrying three of John Stevenet Clow's children to US. Note citizenship is Canadian. They became U.S. citizens by parental naturalization. (photo – McBee)

# Index


**"**

"Dutch" Adams ·
124

**1**

115th NY Regiment·
34
13th Infantry · 80,
83, 84, 86, 89,
91, 92, 95, 97,
100, 102, 103,
105, 106, 114,
117, 152, 154,
215, 244

**2**

22nd Infantry · 105,
106
22nd Massachusetts ·
22, 23, 24
Volunteer · 215
Infantry · 22
26th Infantry · 80

**3**

31st Infantry · 105,
106

**4**

4th Minnesota · 43,
61, 67

**5**

54th Colored
Regiment of
Infantry · 33
56th Massachusetts
· 28, 38, 39, 50,
57, 58, 62
Volunteer
Infantry ·40, 215

**7**

76th Pennsylvania ·
34

**A**

Adam Jones · 124

Adams Press
Company · 43
Adjutant General
Greene · 104
adobe · 85, 95, 98,
99, 105, 106,
108, 130, 135,
159
Agnes, Clow · i, ii,
15, 19, 24, 28,
72, 215
ague · 160
Aikene, Frank · 203
alcohol · 136, 137,
142, 206, 207
Alex. · 15
Alexander
Cruikshank · 20
Alexander Dunbar ·
185
Alexandria, VA · 60,
63, 67, 68, 70
Alfred Mahler · 186,
201
Alice Clow · 215
Alvin C. Leighton ·
142
American Fur
Company · 135
Andrew Ackley,
Steamboat · 143,
149
Appomattox · 58,
59, 64, 71
armored warship ·
37

Army of Georgia ·
65
Arnetta (Nettie)
Story · 201
Assiniboine · 111,
135, 167
Auman, Capt. · 101

**B**

barracks · 23, 32
Bassett · 223, 224
Bear Lake, ID. · 216
Belknap · 142
Bertha Clow · 79,
95, 121, 122
Bertie Clow · 162,
163, 208, 212
Black and Whites ·
59
Black Hills · 153,
155, 156, 169,
170, 173, 174,
175, 176, 179,
180, 181, 183,
192, 196, 198,
202, 216
Black Tail Creek ·
201
Blacktail Gulch ·
182
Boston, MA · 15,
17, 23, 25, 29,
32, 34, 35, 37,
41, 46, 60, 64,

70, 72, 77, 79,
167, 215
bounty · 27, 29, 31,
32, 43, 77, 121,
192
Bowman, Colonel ·
103, 126, 136
Box Elder Creek ·
186, 202, 211
Bozeman Pass, · 87
Bozeman Trail, · 87,
89, 92
Bridger Mountains ·
89, 92, 94
Bridges, Francis E. ·
217
Brig. Belle · 215
Brule Agency · 154,
220
Buffalo fish · 159
Bureau of Indian
Affairs · 95

**C**

Calamity Jane · 196
Camp Cooke · 80,
89, 91, 94, 97,
98, 99, 100, 101,
105, 106, 216
Camp Meigs · 21,
22, 23
Canada · 15, 97,
117, 118, 148,
197, 215

Captain Auman · 101

Captain Clift · 93, 94

Captain Dickey · 104

Captain James McArdle · 39

Captain Moffit · 124

Captain Rankin · 112

Carolina Campaign · 54

Carrie Bertha Clow, · 67

Cassiday, Mr. · 219

CBR Sheep Company · 204, 217

Celinda Warren Burnap Clow · 67

Centennial · 196

Central City, SD. · 186

Charles Collins · 170

Charles Driggs · 159

Charles Van Alstyne · 182

Charleston, MA · 25, 42, 46

Chelsea, MA · 25, 36, 42, 46

Cheyenne Nation · 197

Cheyenne River · 153, 176, 202

Cheyenne, WY · 175, 198, 202, 216

Clift, Captain · 93, 94

Cloid, R. H. · 203

Clow, Agnes · i, ii, 15, 19, 24, 28, 72, 215

Clow, Alice · 215

Clow, Bertha · 79, 95, 121, 122

Clow, Bertie · 216

Clow, Cora Cochrane · 145, 199, 203, 204, 211, 216, 218, 230

Clow, Frederick Redman · 67

Clow, George Wyman · 21, 23, 24, 25, 36, 42, 46

Clow, John Sherwin (Sher) · 15, 43, 60, 61, 65, 66, 67, 79

Clow, John Stevenet · 242

Clow, Mary Bingham · 139, 140, 141, 156, 157, 158, 161, 162, 163, 167,

208, 215, 216, 219, 222

Clow, Melinda (Linnie) Story · 201, 202, 203, 211, 215, 216

Clow, Robert Denton · 217

Col. Bowman · 104

Collins · 230

Colonel Sackett · 155

Columbia Fur Company · 149

Columbia, · 44

Congress, U.S.S · 36, 37

consumption · 141

Council Bluffs · 173

Crazy Horse, Chief · 117, 147, 197

Crazy Mountains · 92, 93

Crook, General · 118

Cumberland, U.S.S · 36, 37

Custer, General · 117, 174, 175

Custer City, S.D. 176, 180

Custer Expedition · 170

Custer Massacre · 111, 176, 196

## D

DaCosta, Jacob, Dr. · 206
DaCosta's Syndrome ·80, 206
Dakota · i, 102, 103, 104, 105, 112, 117, 119, 129, 131, 151, 154, 156, 170, 199, 224
Dakota Territory · 83, 182
Deer Lodge, Steamboat · 103
De Molay · 31, 33, 34, 37
Deadwood, S.D. · 156, 175, 176, 177, 180, 181, 182, 183, 184, 186, 187, 192, 193, 195, 196, 198, 199, 201, 202, 203, 204, 211, 212, 216, 230
Deer Lodge · 99, 154
del Esposo · 188, 191
depression · 62, 78, 80, 126, 163, 205, 206

deserters · 40, 44
Dolliver, R. H., Rev. · 203, 216
Dr. Garmalds · 161
Driggs, Don · 77, 156, 157, 158, 163, 166, 170, 173, 212, 216, 219, 220, 221, 224, 229, 230, 231
drinking · 132, 133, 136, 137, 195, 196
Drowned Man's Rapids · 98
ducks · 36, 37, 141, 145, 159, 161, 221
Dugdale · 183
Durfee and Peck Trading Post · 135, 207

## E

Earl, OR. · 218
Early, General · 19, 49
Elizabeth Larpenteur · 140, 141
Elmer McBee · 218
Emeline · 220

enlistment · 17, 20, 22, 23, 24, 28, 29, 30, 32, 33, 43, 46, 67, 80
epidemic · 162
Esmeralda Lode · 185
Esmeralda Mine · 182, 185, 201
Eugene, OR. · 145, 204, 211, 217, 218, 230

## F

F. Stevens · 228
Farmville, VA · 59
Flathead Pass · 94
Fletcher · 19, 29, 30
Florence, OR. · 204, 217
Fort Abercrombie, · 83
Fort Abraham Lincoln · 152
Fort Alexander Hayes · 34, 35, 38
Fort Benton · 80, 84, 85, 86, 88, 89, 97, 155
Fort Berthold · 84, 150
Fort Buford · 80, 84, 94, 99, 101,

103, 105, 106,
107, 108, 111,
112, 114, 115,
117, 118, 119,
121, 122, 123,
124, 129, 130,
131, 134, 135,
136, 137, 139,
140, 141, 142,
143, 147, 151,
154, 166, 167,
184, 192, 197,
202, 205, 207,
208, 216
Fort Ellis · 89, 91,
92, 94, 106, 216
Fort Hayes · 35, 38,
41, 50
Fort Laramie · 87,
89, 112, 173,
174, 175, 176
Fort Mahone · 38,
50, 52, 53, 57,
58, 63, 68
Fort McKenzie ·
150
Fort Meigs, · 30
Fort Monroe · 34,
40
Fort Peck · 124
Fort Randall · 154,
155, 220
Fort Rice · 84, 89,
151, 152
Fort Ripley · 83
Fort Sedgwick. · 38

Fort Shaw · 80, 86,
91, 94, 95, 97,
98, 100, 105,
122, 151, 216
Fort Stedman · 40,
50
Fort Stevenson · 84,
100, 104, 105,
114, 129, 151
Fort Sully · 153, 202
Fort Totten · 83,
151
Fort Union · 85,
105, 135, 150
fortifications · 38,
45, 52
Fred Brown · 36
Fredrick Redman
Clow · 67

## G

Gall, Chief · 117,
197
Gallatin Valley · 87,
89, 91, 92, 117,
197
Garmalds, Dr. · 221
General Crook ·
118
General Grant · 49
General Hazen ·
118
General Johnston ·
61

General Lee · 49
General McClellan
·19, 24
General Meade · 65
General Miles · 197
General Parke · 53,
57, 58
General Sheridan ·
24, 49, 50, 53,
54, 59, 61
General Sherman ·
16, 24, 42, 43,
51, 53, 54, 61,
65, 66, 67, 68,
104
General Trobriand ·
100, 103, 104,
114, 129, 131,
137, 148, 150,
151, 154, 156
Generals Miles ·
118
General Warren ·
50, 54
George Baker · 151,
220
George Wyman
Clow · 21, 23,
24, 25, 36, 42, 46
Gibson, Mrs. · 63,
66, 68
gold · 80, 83, 86, 87,
88, 91, 98, 113,
155, 169, 170,
173, 174, 175,
176, 180, 181,
183, 184, 185,

187, 192, 193,
196, 198, 202,
203, 204, 217,
218
Golden Seal Mine ·
181, 182, 183,
185, 186, 201,
216
Grand Army of the
Potomac · 65
Grand Review · 61,
65, 66, 67
Grand River · 153
Grand River Agency
· 152, 220
Granite, OR, · 204,
217
Grant, General · 18,
24, 49, 50, 54,
60, 61, 65
Gros Ventre · 150

**H**

Hancock, Maj.
Genl. · 100
Harvey Driggs · 220
Hat Creek Gang ·
198
Haynes · 223
Helena · 80, 86, 87,
89
Henry Dicu · 195,
229
Henry Mott · 42, 46

Hickok, Wild Bill ·
184, 196
Hill City, SD · 180
Hispanic · 188, 191
Hutton · 170, 222

**I**

Ictiobus sp · 159
In the Days of 49 ·
193, 194, 227
Indian · 98, 153,
176, 207
Indian Territory ·
87, 88, 89, 107,
111, 112, 116,
118, 148, 153,
154, 155, 170,
174, 179
Infantry · 103
Isaac N. Kierstead ·
60
Isadore Bartingette ·
195, 229
Italian · 124, 125
IX Army Corps ·
53, 57, 58, 60, 67

**J**

J. B. Gerard · 136
J. S. Collins · 182,
183
Jabez Chase · 185

Jack McCall · 184
James Collins · 182
James Kipp · 149
James MacLane ·
124
James River · 34,
35, 37, 38
Jarves, Lt. Col. · 36,
39, 67, 69
Jefferson Davis · 54
Jefferson River · 87
Jesse James · 207
Jim Bridger · 91
John Bozeman, · 91
John Christopher,
Cpt. · 80
John Kellogg · 166,
220
John Sherwin (Sher)
Clow · 43, 60,
61, 65, 66, 67, 79
Johneys · 36, 39
Jos Kelly, Mrs, ·
187, 203
Joseph Araldo ·
124, 125
Joseph Henry
Taylor · 127
Judith River, · 80,
85, 97

**K**

Keller · 170, 223

Kelly, Luther
"Yellowstone" ·
22, 123, 184
Kerwin · 228, 229,
231
Kimball, Dr. · 130
Knott, Alf · 141
Koontz, Steamboat
· 155

**L**

Lame Bull · 111
Lane County, OR. ·
217
Laramie, WY · 91,
166, 167, 169,
175, 176, 192,
198, 216, 220,
229
Larpenteur, Charles
· 85, 123, 126,
133, 135, 136,
139, 140, 141,
142, 143, 147,
148, 149, 155,
156, 157, 158,
159, 160, 161,
163, 165, 166,
167, 192, 207,
208, 216 223,
224

Larpenteur,
Elizabeth · 140,
141
Larpenteur, Rebecca
· 139, 140, 156,
157, 165, 166,
170, 208, 216
Latin · 167
latrines · 131
Laughing Sam · 198
Lawrence County,
SD. · 182, 186
Lead, SD. · 185, 186
Leander P.
Richardson · 176
Lee, Robert E.,
General · 50, 52,
54, 57, 58, 59,
60, 62
Leighton, Alvin C. ·
142
Lewella Mine · 182
Lewis, Mr. · 224
Lewis and Clark ·
91, 98
Lincoln, President
Abraham · 19,
24, 28, 61, 62,
63, 64, 65
Linnie Story · 202,
203
liquor · 136
Little Big Horn ·
117, 197
Little Sioux, IA. ·
139, 143, 148,
156, 157, 158,

160, 161, 162,
163, 166, 167,
168, 173, 201,
215, 216
Livingston, MT · 92
Longhair Smith ·
123
looting · 71
Louis Larpenteur ·
162, 208
Lt. Col. Horatio D.
Jarves · 39, 67,
69
Lt. Col. Morrow ·
106
Lt. Cusick · 116
Lt. James B. Goe ·
80
Lt. Leonard · 104
Lt. Wann · 93
Lucius Bingham ·
139
Lynchburg, VA · 44

**M**

mackinaw · 86, 89,
134
Major General
Hancock · 100
Major Little, · 104
malaria · 160
Mandan Indians ·
84, 148, 150, 152

Mapleton Hotel · 204

Mapleton, OR. · 204, 217, 218

Marias River · 150

Martin E. Posh · 185

Mary Bingham Clow · 139, 140, 141, 156, 157, 158, 161, 162, 163, 167, 208, 215, 216, 219, 221

May Lowery, Steamboat · 153, 154, 220

McArdle, Cpt. · 42

McClellan, John · 195, 230

McGreavy · 225

Meade, General · 65

Melinda (Linnie) Story · 201, 211, 215, 216

Methodist Episcopal Church · 203

Metz Massacre · 176

Mexican · 166, 188, 191, 192

Milk River · 97

Milwaukee, WI · 79, 80, 83

Miner, Steamboat · 154, 155, 220

Minnesota · 67, 79, 83, 151, 159, 215

Miss Adams · 42

Mississippi River · 83, 160

Missouri River · 80, 84, 85, 86, 87, 89, 91, 97, 98, 101, 105, 106, 107, 112, 113, 116, 129, 134, 143, 147, 148, 150, 151, 152, 153, 154, 155, 184, 192, 202

Model 1861 Springfield Rifle · 38

Moffit, Captain · 125

Mollie Maser, Steamboat · 155, 220

Montana · 69, 81, 83, 84, 85, 86, 87, 89, 91, 92, 95, 97, 99, 100, 103, 105, 106, 117, 137, 145, 150, 151, 155, 159, 169, 181, 184, 196

Montpelier, ID. · 204, 217

Moore, Dan · 219

Morrow, Lt. Col. · 107

muskets · 38

Musselshell River · 102

**N**

Nellie Peck, Steamboat · 152

Nelson Story · 92

Nevada · 80, 86

Nez Perce Indians · 93

Niobrara River · 155

North Carolina · 44, 61

North West Trading Company · 135

Northern Cheyenne · 197

nostalgia · 46

**O**

Ocean Wave Mine · 182

Oma McBee · 218

Omaha, NB. · 173, 202

Onawa, IA · 158, 219

**P**

P J Grounds · 230
Packrat Gulch · 182, 184
Paha Sapa · 175
Painted Creek · 126
Pancaw Agency · 155, 220
Parke, General · 53, 57, 58
Pawnee Indians · 140, 156
Peter Dugan · 124
Petersburg, VA · i, 16, 18, 24, 34, 38, 39, 40, 41, 44, 45, 49, 50, 53, 54, 57, 58, 59, 60, 62 64, 71, 181, 215
Piatt, Captain · 104
picket · 38, 40, 42, 44, 49, 51, 53
plague · 32
Post-traumatic Stress Disorder (PTSD) · 80, 206, 207
Powder River · 155
Private Conry · 94

**R**

Ranaldo · 124, 125

Randall, Fort · 154, 155, 220
Rankin, Col. · 104, 113
Rapid City, SD. · 175, 176, 198, 216
rats · 71, 98, 99, 100, 155
Raymond Canyon, WY. · 217
Readville, MA · 21
Rebecca Larpenteur · 139, 140, 156, 157, 165, 166, 170, 208, 216
rebel yell · 54
Red Cloud, Chief · 116
Red Cloud Reservation · 197
Red River · 83, 151
Rees Indians · 152
Reina · 25, 27, 28, 30, 46, 77
Rev. R. H. Dolliver · 202
Richard McBee (Senior)  211
Richmond, VA · 18, 49, 54, 58, 61, 63
Robert Denton Clow · 217
Robert Gould Shaw · 33
Running Bear · 126

Running Water · 155

**S**

Sam Hartman · 198
Secretary of War, William W. Belknap · 142
Señas del Esposo · 188
Shenandoah Valley · 18, 19, 24, 61
Shenkenberg, Theod. · 195, 229
Sheridan, General · 24, 49, 50, 53, 54, 59, 61
Sherman, General · 16, 24, 42, 43, 51, 53, 54, 61, 65, 66, 67, 68, 104
Sheyenne · 223
Shields River · 92, 93
Ship Anvil · 217
Sioux Indians · 83, 85, 93, 107, 111, 112, 113, 117, 135, 140, 150, 151, 153, 154, 156, 175, 176,

181, 196, 197, 206
Sioux City, IA · 89, 157, 170
Sitting Bull, Chief · 107, 111, 112, 113, 114, 116, 117, 118, 119, 147, 153, 197
Siuslaw River · 204, 217
Sixteen Mile Creek · 94
Soldier Creek · 158, 173, 224
Soldier River · 157
Soldier's Heart · 80, 206
Spanish · 166, 167, 187, 188, 191, 193, 194, 226, 227
Spanish Conquistadores · 188
Sprague · 170, 222
sternwheeler · 84, 89, 143, 148
Stevens, F ·228
Story, Arnetta (Nettie) · 201
Story, Melinda (Linnie) · 201, 202, 203, 211, 215, 216
Story, Nelson · 92

Story, William · 185, 202, 203, 210
Sublette and Campbell · 135
suicide · 126, 206, 207, 208
Sun River · 80, 86, 89, 105


**T**

Tekamah, NB · 201, 215, 216
temperance · 137, 142, 196, 207
Tongue River · 184
trading post · 105, 107, 130, 135, 139, 140, 141, 142, 143, 147, 166
Treaty of Laramie, 1868 · 181
trenches · 39, 45, 49, 53
Trobriand, General · 100, 103, 104, 114, 129, 131, 137, 148, 150, 151, 154, 156
typhoid · 39


**U**

Union Pacific Railroad ·169, 173, 202


**V**

Virginia · 34, 35, 37, 44, 45, 57, 61, 62
Virginia City, MT · 80, 86, 87


**W**

W. H. Hibbard · 185
Wainwright, Captain · 104
Waiting for Thee · 167, 168, 222, 233
Warren, General · 50, 54
Waterhouse, Private · 122, 126
Whet Stone · 154, 220, 225
White Earth River · 149
White River · 154, 220

Whitewood Quartz Mining District · 182

Wild Bill Hickok · 184, 196

Willamette Valley, OR. · 204

William Story · 185, 201, 202, 203

William Woodruff · 185

Wlm. W. Foster · 183

wood cutters · 148, 151, 152, 153, 166, 192

Wyoming · 87, 89, 166, 167, 169, 173, 175, 216


##  Y


Yankton, SD · 155, 156, 202, 220

Yellowstone Kelly · 97, 124, 184

Yellowstone River · 87, 91, 155, 184

Yellowstone Valley · 91

Younger Brothers · 207

# Bibliography

Adams, Virginia M. *On the Altar of Freedom*. Cambridge: Univ. of Massachusetts Press, 1995.

Athearn, Robert G. *Forts of the Upper Missouri*. Lincoln: University of Nebraska Press, 1967.

Batty, Peter and Parish, Peter, *The Divided Union: The Story of the Great American Civil War, 1861-65*. Topsfield: Salem House Publishers, 1987.

Bonekemper, III, Edward H. *How Robert E. Lee Lost the Civil War*. Fredericksburg: Sergeant Kirkland's Press, 1998.

Brown, Mark H. *The Plainsmen of the Yellowstone: A History of the Yellowstone Basin*. Lincoln: University of Nebraska Press, 1961.

Casler, Michael M., ed. *The Original Journal of Charles Larpenteur: My Travels to the Rocky Mountains between 1833 and 1872, by Charles Larpenteur*. Lincoln: The Museum Association of the American Frontier, 2007.

Catton, Bruce. *A Silence at Appomattox*. Garden City: Country Life Press, 1953.

Catton, Bruce. *Never Call Retreat: The Centennial History of the Civil War (Vol. 3)*. Garden City: Doubleday and Co., 1965.

*Compiled Military Service Records for Richard Clow*. Form 86: US National Archives and Records Request. March, 2008.

Convis, Charles L. *Soldiers: True Tales of the Old West (Vol. 2)*. Carson City: Pioneer Press, 1996.

Coues, Elliott, ed. *Forty Years a Fur Trader on the Upper Missouri: The Personal Narrative of Charles Larpenteur, 1833-1872.* Minneapolis: Ross and Haines, Inc, 1962.

Diaz-Roig, Mercedes. *"The Traditional Romancero in Mexico: Panorama",* vol.2:2. March 1987, pp. 616-32, http://Journal.oraltradition.org.

Dingle, Susan, ed. *At the Confluence: Now and Then: Papers Presented at the Symposium Held in Williston, N.D., June 29, 2002,* Bismarck, North Dakota: State Historical Society of North Dakota, 2003.

Goe, James B., Lt. "The Thirteenth Regiment of Infantry" In *The Army of the United States: Historical Sketches of Staff and Line with Portraits of Generals-in-Chief,* edited by T. Rodenbough and F. Hasking, 575-585. Maynard, Merrill & Company, 1896. http://www.history.army.mil/books.

Hafen, LeRoy R., ed. *Mountain Men & Fur Traders of the Far West.* Lincoln: Univ. of Nebraska Press, 1982.

Hesser, Genia. *Letter by author.* Ft. Buford State Historical Site, North Dakota, April 21, 2006.

Idaho Daily Statesman, *Legal Notice,* Boise, Idaho: May 30, 1899.

Innis, Ben. *Interments at Fort Buford 1866 to 1895:* Revised Edition. North Dakota: Ft. Buford 6th Infantry Reg. Assn. Publishers, 1996.

Johnson, W. Fletcher. *Life of Sitting Bull and History of the Indian War of 1890-91: The Red Record of the Sioux,* Edgewood Publishing, 1891

Kane, L. M., ed. and transl. *Military Life in Dakota: The Journal of Philippe Regis de Trobriand.* Lincoln: University of Nebraska Press, 1982.

Keenan, Jerry. *The Life of Yellowstone Kelly.* Albuquerque: University of New Mexico Press, 2006.

Kennedy, Frances H., ed. *The Civil War Battlefield Guide: 2nd Ed.,* Boston: Houghton Mifflin, 1998.

Lee, Bob. *It Started With a Mining Boom."* In *Gold Rush: The Black Hills Story,* edited by John D. McDermott, 85 – 104. Pierre, SD: South Dakota State Historical Society Press, 2001.

Lomax, John and Lomax Alan, eds. *Folk Song: USA: The 111 Best American Ballads.* New York: Duell, Sloan and

Pearce, 1962.

Marine Intelligence, New York Times, August 20, 1863.

McBee, Oma Belle Emmons. *I Carry the Torch*. Florence, Oregon: The
    Siuslaw Pioneer, 1957

McLaird, James C. *"I Know…Because I Was There: Leander P.
    Richardson Reports the Black Hills Gold Rush"*. In *Gold
    Rush: The Black Hills Story*, edited by John D. McDermott, 55–
    84. Pierre: South Dakota State Historical Society Press, 2001.

McPherson, James M., ed. *The Atlas of the Civil War*. New        York:
MacMillan Inc, 1994.

*Passenger List of the Brig Belle*. From: *Archives of Ancestry
    .com: New York Passenger Lists, 1820-1957.*, Utah:
    http://www.Ancestry.com, 2008.

Quaife, M. M., ed. *Yellowstone Kelly*. Lincoln: University of Nebraska
    Press, 1973.

Remele, Larry, ed. *Fort Buford and the Military Frontier on the
    Northern Plains 1850-1900*. Bismarck :State Historical Society of
    North Dakota, 1987.

Richards, Sarah, ed. *Civil War Sites: Official Guide to
    Battlefields, Monuments and More*. Guilford: Globe Pequot Press,
    2003.

Shaw, Robert Gould. *Letters to his family and other papers*,
    Robert Gould Shaw, 1837-1863. in Houghton Library, Online
    section, Harvard College Library.

Stiles, T. J., ed. *In Their Own Words: Warriors and Pioneers*.
    New York: Berkley Publications, 1996.

The Siuslaw Pilot, "Anvil Taken off with Little Damage," May 21,
    1913.

The West, "Anvil Pulled off Sand", May 23, 1913.

Waldo, Edna LaMoore. *Dakota*. Caldwell: The Caxton
    Printers Ltd., 1936.

# Acknowledgments

I want to thank my wife, Jill, for her patience, comments, and proofreading through the five years of work on this manuscript. It would not have been completed without her input.

I am also especially grateful for correspondence from historian Genia Hesser, Site Supervisor for the North Dakota Fort Buford State Historic Site, containing information about the 13th Infantry in Fort Buford during 1869.

Additionally, the recent publication of *The Original Journal of Charles Larpentuer*, 2007, Michael Casler, editor, has been an invaluable work for gathering details of Richard Clow's life. Mr. Casler, Park Ranger and Historian at the Fort Union National Historic Site, also corresponded with me on several occasions and I am grateful for his fine work which has assisted me immensely in completing this book.

Finally, my work on the Spanish language poem/song, "The Husbands Characteristics," would not have progressed without guidance to several references by Kathy McGregor, PhD. Her initial reviewing of some of the original enlarged copies of the diary pages helped sort out Richard Clow's phonetic and run-on Spanish.

# About the Author

**Richard McBee** has been a secondary school principal and teacher for over thirty years in the international and local schools of South America, Africa, Europe and the U.S. His keen interest in following the life of his great grandfather, Richard H. Clow began some twelve years ago upon reading Clow's letters from the Civil War and his letter and short diary from the Indian Wars in Montana and the Dakotas. He has written another book, *Kalahari*, a work of fiction about the struggle for Black African rule in southern Africa, based on his life in Botswana during the 1970's. He currently lives with his wife and does his writing in Hood River, Oregon.

# Feedback Request

Thank you for purchasing my book. I hope you have enjoyed it as much as I enjoyed writing it. Please take a few minutes to leave a review for my book on Amazon.com.

Simply visit Amazon.com and insert ISBN 978-1-58982-713-4 in the search box and my book will come right up.

Feel free to express your thoughts and feelings both positive and otherwise. Your feedback is deeply appreciated. While you are there, you may notice what others thought of my book as well; perhaps your insights are shared with other commenters.